SALMAN RUSHDIE
NEW CRITICAL INSIGHTS

Volume - I

Edited by
Rajeshwar Mittapalli
Joel Kuortti

ATLANTIC
PUBLISHERS & DISTRIBUTORS (P) LTD

Published by

ATLANTIC

PUBLISHERS & DISTRIBUTORS (P) LTD

7/22, Ansari Road, Darya Ganj,
New Delhi-110002
Phones : +91-11-40775252, 23273880, 23275880, 23280451
Fax : +91-11-23285873
Web : www.atlanticbooks.com
E-mail : orders@atlanticbooks.com

Branch Office
5, Nallathambi Street, Wallajah Road,
Chennai-600002
Phones : +91-44-64611085, 32413319
E-mail : chennai@atlanticbooks.com

Printed in India at Nice Printing Press, A-33/3A, Site-IV, Industrial Area, Sahibabad, Ghaziabad, U.P.

PREFACE

For well over a quarter century Salman Rushdie has been an impressive presence on the world literary scene. Starting with *Grimus* (1975) he has published eight novels, the latest being *Fury* (2001). Despite their relatively small number, the impact Rushdie's novels have had on common readers and critics alike is profound by any reckoning. His *Midnight's Children* (1981) gave a new direction and orientation to fiction all over the world. The intellectual, intercultural and intertextual richness of this novel, and indeed of every other novel of Rushdie's, teases the readers and challenges them to comprehend and come to grips with them. His books create tension, induce anticipation, and evoke conflicting emotions between (and within) the readers. With each new novel Rushdie initiates fresh discussion and debate. All this attests to a creative genius which compels us to re-evaluate every so often.

Rushdie has been a much discussed author, and a great number of critical studies have already appeared, the earliest being the essays in 1982 by Maria Couto in *Encounter*, Uma Parameswaran in *Toronto South Asian Review*, and Tariq Ali in *New Left Review*. But what happened in 1988-89 was something unprecedented in the history of literature. With the publication of *The Satanic Verses* in 1988 the discussion of Rushdie went beyond the realms of literary criticism. This book inaugurated what has come to be known as the "Rushdie Affair," and highly polemical views began to be expressed, sometimes to the complete exclusion of any mention of his novels. The intercultural conflict which ensued, with its deep interest, is now a part of history, but it is not a point of discussion in these two volumes. Still, they acknowledge the implications of this 'affair' for the image of Rushdie the novelist. An important consequence of the 'affair' which merits special mention is that to read

Rushdie without reference to his (auto)biography has been rendered impossible, even in the current postmodern, post-structuralist literary context.

However, Rushdie has since emerged from the political and religious quagmire and re-embraced the literary world. It is therefore important to continue the 'literary-critical' study of his works, a task which these volumes set out to accomplish by bringing together some of the very best critical essays written in the post-'*Verses* controversy' period. We believe that these seventeen articles (eight in this volume and rest in Volume II) present fresh insights into Rushdie's works, not necessarily overshadowed by the controversy that surrounded him at one time. They represent varied critical and theoretical approaches and attempt an honest assessment of Rushdie's novels by creatively engaging with the issues each of them raises.

The articles have been organized in the order of appearance of Rushdie's novels so that discussion proceeds from *Grimus*, through *Midnight's Children*, *Shame*, *East, West*, *The Moor's Last Sigh*, and *The Ground Beneath Her Feet*. Towards the end of Volume II there are three articles that discuss Rushdie's novels from general and comparative perspectives. A useful bibliography of Rushdie's works and another of recent Rushdie criticism have been appended to Volume I and Volume II respectively.

We would like to thank the contributors for their cooperation and for permitting us to include previously published (although often revised) material.

—Rajeshwar Mittapalli
—Joel Kuortti

Contents

Contents

1

Grimus and the Alchemical Tradition

MARGARETA PETERSSON

Grimus was Rushdie's entry for a literary competition in the genre of fantasy and science fiction. He did not win, but the novel was published. It was coldly received by the critics and has been viewed by scholars as difficult to understand or even incomprehensible, a chaotic fantasy without a discernible purpose (Cundy 131, Brennan 70). There seems to be a great need for a probable context in which to find a pattern in its mimetic multiplicity.

The novel contains a patchwork of myths collected from different parts of the world. Several scholars suggest that the myths lack inner coherence. I, on the contrary, see them as subordinated to one myth or one symbolic language, the language of alchemy, which also plays a part in Rushdie's later works. The alchemical tradition is essential in the interpretation of Rushdie's works because it contests the accusation against him for taking part in western orientalism. It also shows his universal ambitions over and above his more local political and satirical ambitions.

The alchemical pattern has not been observed before in Rushdie's works and is of varying importance in his novels, most obviously in his début, *Grimus.* A hermaphrodite and the phoenix that dies and is reborn play an important part here. The hermaphrodite drinks an elixir of life, which makes him immortal, and he undertakes a migration where the elements are transmuted and merge into one another. A mystical rose is waiting at the end of his path. All these motifs are highly representative of alchemy. *Grimus* is in fact so context-bound that the totality built up by the motifs is incomprehensible if the alchemical structure is not understood, as the reception of the novel shows.

The novel consists of three parts, "Times Present," "Times Past" and "Grimus." In the first part, the main character Flapping Eagle arrives miraculously through a *hole* in the sea at Calf Island, where two older people, Virgil Jones and his wife, are sitting on the beach. Rushdie presents Flapping Eagle's background and his upbringing as a North American Indian on a plateau isolated from the surroundings. From the very beginning, he is a deviant. His mother died when he was born; that is why he is called "Born-From-Dead." His sister Bird-Dog disappears after having given him an elixir of life, and during his continued life on earth he searches for her. Like a wandering Ahasuerus, he lives for more than 700 years before he at last arrives at Calf Island where an almost legendary man, Grimus, is master.

Virgil Jones becomes his guide. Together they start ascending the mountain Calf, overcoming horrifying obstacles. Halfway to the top they stop in the city of K, which is populated by immortals. Life here is described in the second part of the novel.

In the third part, Flapping Eagle acquires the explanation for the existence of Calf Island. He reaches his goal-the mystical Grimus, his own sister Bird-Dog and the object which has made existence on Calf Island possible, the Stone Rose. The novel ends with the slow annihilation of the island.

The alchemical tradition

Alchemy is one of the oldest eclectic traditions. It was prevalent in Europe and Egypt, among the Arabs, in China and India, and the different traditions have influenced each other. Its origin is veiled in obscurity, but it is often placed in Alexandria and the first centuries AD. Many cultures converged here: Greek, Jewish, Egyptian, Persian, Syrian and Christian, and out of this cosmopolitan environment thronging with immigrants grew syncretistic rites, cults and a conception of the unitary character of nature or matter.

The Arabs controlled the alchemical tradition starting in the eighth century. The Arab or Persian alchemist Ibn Sina, mentioned in *Midnight's Children,* developed an elixir as a universal remedy. The alchemical elixir was regarded as having the same therapeutic role in sixteenth-century Europe. From this conception, the idea of an elixir of life arose.

Alchemy has been called the art of transmutation. The adepts tried to force substances to transmute into each other in the alchemical laboratories. Above all, they wanted to transform lead into gold. The basis for the idea of transformation was the monistic conception that everything that existed consisted ultimately of the same substances-everything corresponded. The idea has a parallel in early Greek philosophy where it was assumed that all things, even metals, consisted of different combinations of the four elements, earth, water, fire and air. This concept became a philosophical basis for the idea of transmutation and it exists in the multiple tradition of alchemy side by side with the conception of monism (DiBernard 1).

The mapping of the process and the ambiguous and secret language that developed out of this originate in the world of the laboratory. The point of departure is that base metals cannot be directly transmuted into noble ones, but must first be brought back to their origin, to *prima materia.* Prima materia may be manifested in a multiplicity of ways. It contains all oppositions or polarities, for example, male and female. At its most basic philosophical level, alchemy embodies the union of opposites (DiBernard 3). Prima materia must be crushed in order for something new to emerge. *Solve et coagula, dissolve and reunite,* is a recurring formula in alchemy. It expresses the cyclical nature of the process.

The first phase of the process-the black condition, "death" or "putrefaction"—is necessary for continued development. Thus, "death" means dissolution, or in a figurative sense, the laying aside of the past, sometimes understood as a regression to the amorphous, prenatal stage, a reunion with chaos (Eliade 153). After the dissolution of the substrate, chemicals must be added to bring about a new joining (coagulation). The alchemists try to make the black preparation white through purification-the phase is often called "The Small Work"-and after that, yellow and red (pure gold), "The Great Work." This may be symbolised by the red bird Phoenix and is often preceded by a multiplicity of colours.

Since the work is cyclical, the ultimate goal and the beginning are often considered identical. The symbol of this is the worm Ouroboros, which bites its own tail thus slowly consuming itself, which is the precondition for new life. When the goal is attained and coagulation has occurred, a new dissolution is necessary and the process continues. A symbol of transmutation is the homunculus to which Rushdie alludes in his latest novels. The goal is secret, but also well known. It can be found everywhere, but few people notice it; it is the highest but incarnated in the lowest, "although it is everywhere, it is also the most elusive of things" (Eliade 165). The state of affairs may be symbolised by the fact that dung or fertilizer, "the lowest," can acquire a prominent place in alchemical descriptions.

Alchemy as a concrete metallurgical process was important in Egypt, but could also be understood in a figurative sense. Eliade points out that the Alexandrian alchemists seem to have projected the initiation of the mystery cults, that is, symbolical death and rebirth, on to matter. They could thereby participate themselves in the different phases of the alchemical Work (Eliade 160). The Work of the alchemists might thus mean concrete gold or metaphorical gold, which in turn might be charged with different meanings, for example, the ennoblement of the soul, the improvement of the world or a work of a spiritual kind, music, art or literature.

Jung makes a connection between alchemy and creation. The alchemical operation, he writes, seems to be the equivalent of the psychological process of active imagination (Jung, *Mysterium* 526). The writers to whom Rushdie often calls attention have often used alchemy as motifs or as fundamental themes. Christina Degli-Esposti even maintains that there is an alchemical trend in postmodern literature. She has analysed texts by Eco and Calvino from this perspective (Degli-Esposti 1990 & 1991). Rushdie alludes to the latter in *The Satanic Verses.* Nabokov's *Pale Fire* and Pynchon's *The Crying of Lot 49* have been analysed in the same way. In *The Satanic Verses*, there are explicit references to *Pale Fire*. More important for Rushdie however, is Joyce, whose *Finnegans Wake* has been convincingly interpreted from the premises of alchemy by Barbara DiBernard. This novel contains a multiplicity of explicit references to traditional alchemical texts and processes. DiBernard asserts that Joyce turned to alchemy because it deals with basic concepts and cycles in human life, such as death and rebirth, body and soul, change and unity. In addition, Rushdie's novels are often compared to *One Hundred Years of Solitude*. This novel has a distinctly alchemical frame and the alchemical gold acquires a metaphorical significance; it thus corresponds, as in *Finnegans Wake*, to the completed novel (Halka).

Initiation and alchemy

Even if the alchemical symbols are revealed in *Grimus*, as I will soon show in detail, the meaning of the novel is far from clear. Several of the novel's myths overlap and almost seem to merge. They create a vast room that embraces creation and destruction, search and insight, hell and paradise. The myths have several common components, above all, the way through great difficulties, a kind of death and after that a rebirth. This is a classical theme in what is usually called an initiation quest or rite, which Joseph Campbell names monomyth in *The Hero With a Thousand Faces*. The same theme recurs in the alchemical process. Campbell refers to Jung's interpretation of alchemy and uses a similar syncretistic method, which involves ahistorical comparisons between myths.

Campbell bases his description of the monomyth on religious myths from many sources and on literary texts. At heart, he means that all myths express a psychological process of maturing. This can be construed as a quest into the unknown, which is an expression of the unconscious. The hero might travel to Aladdin's unknown caves where not only jewellery, but also djinns are waiting. Maturity, a rebirth, requires some kind of death. This is why texts and myths speak of a "night journey." One of Campbell's most important examples is Dante's *Divine Comedy* and the journey down to

Inferno. On the road to hell Dante meets unknown and superseded parts of himself that are materialised as monsters, according to Campbell-in that way it is also possible to understand Flapping Eagle's encounters with odd figures. If the hero does not halt on the threshold of the unknown, he ends up in a dreamy world of strangely fluid and ambiguous shapes. This description is in accordance with the difficulties during Eagle's journey.

Two scholars have particularly stressed the similarities between *Grimus* and Dante's *The Divine Comedy*. In their relatively short analyses, Ib Johansen and Catherine Cundy compare the guide Virgil to the same figure in Dante's divine comedy. As in *The Divine Comedy*, Eagle's wanderings on Calf Island have a tripartite structure. He first meets multiple difficulties, which could correspond to Dante's wanderings in Inferno. Then follows purification in Purgatory, and the last section has at least some similarities to Paradise. The comparison with Dante seems to be relevant also with regards to the topography of the novel. The mountain Calf on the island of the same name resembles with its concentric circles the mountain of Purgatory in Dante (Johansen 24, Cundy 131). Cundy declares that the goal of the pursuit is the same in both texts. The Stone Rose in *Grimus* corresponds to Dante's celestial rose (Cundy 131).

The most central myth in the novel deals with the pilgrimage of the birds to Simurg. The classical shaping of this myth is found in Farid-ud-din Attar's poem from the twelfth century, *The Conference of the Birds,* which is also represented among the epigraphs of the novel. The name Grimus is an anagram of Simurg, as is explained in the text. The myth is described in the following way in the novel:

> The Simurg [...] is the Great Bird. It is vast, all-powerful and singular. It is the sum of all other birds. There is a Sufi poem in which thirty birds set out to find the Simurg on the mountain where he lives. When they reach the peak, they find that they themselves are, or rather have become, the Simurg. The name, you see, means Thirty Birds. Si, thirty. Murg, birds [...] The myth of the Mountain of Kâf. (261)

Farid-ud-din Attar describes the pilgrimage of the Sufis through seven different stations that the soul must pass before it can be merged into God. The journey is dangerous, filled with difficulties and adventures. It takes place on both an external and an internal level.

Kâf (simplified to Calf in the novel) is the name of the mountain that Flapping Eagle ascends and on which Grimus lives. The mountain recurs in Islamic mythology, where God is said to have created it to support the world. Men and animals would not be able to exist on earth if the mountain was not there. The earth would incessantly shake—Calf is affected by trembling in the novel. The mountain is remote to men. It marks the border of the earth and the name Kâf is sometimes used metonymically for this border, that is, for death. A theme connected to death and renewal is stressed in the novel and acquires a contextual charge here. Simurg has his abode on this mountain (Streck 400).

The fundamental pattern of initiation and alchemy-death and rebirth-structures the course of events in *Grimus* and is stressed by a multiplicity of motifs. One of the oldest symbols for the myth of death and rebirth, especially in the alchemical tradition, is the phoenix. This mythical bird has the faculty of being born anew after every death. The phoenix is found at important places in the novel. We meet it as early as the beginning of the novel. Flapping Eagle was born on a plateau near the city of Phoenix, a city, it is said, that had risen from the ashes of an earlier city destroyed by fire. It appears again at the end. Grimus identifies himself here with the bird and wants to devise its death and resurrection, now in the figure of Eagle.

The concept of past and coming golden ages is strong in the alchemical tradition. The fate of the phoenix thus corresponds to that of societies. Grimus has created Calf Island as an island for the immortals. The island is represented as a paradise; it is green and fertile, happiness and joy reign. In the beginning, the men live as if in a materialised utopia, in a golden age. There is no money and everything is distributed according to need. Twice, Calf and Grimus are connected with ether, which is the fifth element of alchemy, the quintessence, synonymous with gold. The utopia turns out to be false, however; everything goes astray after just a couple of months. Some men commit suicide and the inhabitants turn against the ruling trio, Deggle, Virgil and Grimus. These three are then separated from each other. Deggle breaks off a bit of the Stone Rose and an Effect arises which Grimus cannot control, an Effect which creates a hint of non-existence, death.

Deggle's effect frightens people, who in the city of K cling firmly to fixed ideas, to monomania. They live a frozen life; they constantly repeat the same biological day. A woman who was pregnant when she drank the elixir of life is forever pregnant without ever giving birth. People continue living following exactly the same customs and lifestyles from which they have moved away. For this reason, their lives correspond to the title of this part of the novel: "Times Past." The revolutionary of the island has become stuck in his world of slogans, never noticing that his paradise, at least in a way, has been achieved. Life as a process has come to an end on Calf.

The description of life in K functions as a criticism of religious and political utopias, of conceptions of golden ages and of an ultimate goal-immortality, a stagnant utopia. Within the idea of process is the insight that a goal can be nothing but a starting point for a new process. This seems to be the meaning of the myth of the phoenix. The theme acquires a formal shape since the novel is constructed in a circular manner. Eagle sees similarities between Axona at Phoenix, which is described at the beginning of the novel, and the city of K, which is the scene of action in the second half and whose inhabitants play important parts at the end of the plot. A shared trait is the narrow outlook that has ritual, religious overtones in Axona, while in K it is instead secular.

One aspect of the cyclical theme functions as a leitmotif in the novel. The connection between completion or perfection and destruction recurs several times. When Eagle experiences his two women Elfrida and Irina as one, "Elfrina," the narrator comments that the moment of perfection carries destruction (216).

It is possible to read the novel as a description of an alchemical process of which the longest part constitutes dissolution. Not until the end does union arise (*solve et coagula*). In the concluding lines, a new dissolution occurs as Eagle appears to the peculiar gorfs as the last piece of a puzzle before Calf reaches perfection. It is therefore consistent that the island is annihilated when he has reached his goal.

The alchemical process

The novel opens with Eagle's arrival on the island, however, the course of events has a long prehistory that is gradually disclosed. An important aspect of his quest is that, little by little, he becomes aware of the presence of several levels of existence. At the bottom, there is an ordinary world where Flapping Eagle and all the other characters in the novel have their origin. A number of individuals, however, are relocated to Calf Island. They have all drunk the elixir of life and become immortal. The elixir comes from the third level, the world of the gorfs. The gorfs are stones and thus not really alive. They need neither food nor atmosphere. They are the most intelligent forms of life in their galaxy.

One gorf, Koax, looked into the past for contact with other civilizations. He realised that everything one could imagine could become concrete reality and he consistently imagined other "Dimensions" with different forms of life, and in that way, the previously isolated life of the gorfs ended. Koax dispelled the hesitance of the other gorfs concerning the change by imagining an "Object" which would exist in every imaginable Dimension. Only by contact with these objects could movements between the Dimensions be possible. In this way, the gorfs would be able to control their new idea.

Through such an object, a Stone Rose, the gorf come into contact with Virgil, Deggle and Grimus. It is also through the gorfs that Grimus gets hold of the elixir of life. The Stone Rose makes travel between the dimensions possible and, at the beginning, both Grimus and Virgil Jones find such travels enormously valuable: the world seems filled with fantastic possibilities-until Virgil goes on a destructive journey into the inner dimensions. Unknown and menacing as well as promising dimensions of reality therefore exist on the external as well as internal level. It is a question of perspective-a central theme in Rushdie's subsequent works.

The gorf Koax abandons his own world for Calf Island, inquisitively following the events and also trying to interfere. The gorfs can thus move in spite of their stone nature, not in the ordinary way, but in a manner which reminds one of the *solve et coagula* of alchemy: "by a process of physical disintegration and reintegration" (247).

Calf Island then, in the novel, exists on a fictional level of its own; it is a materialised imagination created by Grimus. It is possible to perceive it as a world of projections or as a dream.

Three men-Mercury

Eagle derives his origin from Axona. The name reminds one of Ascona in Switzerland, where Jung gave two lectures that were published, entitled "The Spirit Mercurius" (Jung, *Alchemical* 191). The novel contains many motifs pointing at an alchemical Mercury context.

Grimus belongs to the trio of men who find the Stone Rose as well as the elixir of life. His character suggests associations with a god. The second man, Deggle, is connected to the devil in different ways, while the third, gravedigger Virgil Jones, seems the wisest of the three. As singular figures, these three men appear thin and caricature-like, while read together they seem to form the mythical Mercury. This is the Latin name for the so-called father of Western alchemy, Hermes Trismegistos, the threefold powerful Hermes. He is a coalescence of the Greek Hermes, the gods' messenger and psychopomp and the ancient Egyptian bird-god Thot, father of the art of writing. Thus Mercury is often represented as winged and as a guide.

Virgil becomes Eagle's guide on Calf Island, a degraded version of the guide in *The Divine Comedy*. He is perceived as a village idiot in K, but significantly enough, has a chain of gold.-Virgil Jones has several traits that recur in other figures in Rushdie's work. The most important is that he is, or once wanted to become a historian, and he realises that a historian is not a neutral, Olympian chronicler, but takes part in the events he is describing; his presence influences the image of the past. The relation between image and perspective becomes a significant theme in later novels.

Nicholas Deggle, the second man in the trio, has acquired many seemingly disparate qualities that are extremely difficult to explain without links to alchemy. He earns his living as a magician and is interested in spheres that are close to alchemy: tarot, cabbala and the art of divination. He is more ambivalent and critical of the blessings of the Rose than Virgil is. Some of his very specific attributes are Saturn lips, dark clothes and associations with Ethiopia. Jung points out, however, that Mercury's masculine, dark or devilish Saturnic side, is sometimes called "Ethiopian" (Jung, *Mysterium* 38). Deggle functions as a Lucifer.

Grimus obtains power over the Rose; he is a magician and a master of disguise. He is associated with birds in various ways. At the very first encounter with gravedigger Virgil he carries a bird which is to be buried, a strongly coloured bird of paradise. Later in the novel, this bird is associated with the Simurg. The process of death and rebirth is thus underlined. In his house in the ordinary world, he has a great number of ornithological attributes, stressed especially at the end. These bird attributes arouse associations with Hermes and are well known in alchemical tradition. The alchemist Melquíades, in *One Hundred Years of Solitude*, has a large-brimmed black hat for the same reason-it is compared to the widespread wings of a raven; Buck Mulligan has a Mercury hat, utters bird cries and waves with wing-like hands in *Ulysses*. Both of the poet Shade's parents in *Pale Fire* are ornithologists. Birds and ornithological interests recur in Rushdie's works.

Furthermore, Grimus has a monk-like character; thus, he has no interest in women. As a basis for this lack of interest, Rushdie stresses his repudiation of the world, his distrust of man. He seems to repress his emotional life. Ideas and intellect are the only things which give man a right to exist, he thinks. In this way, he is depicted as an extremely one-sided person.

His Puritan character creates associations with representatives of several religions, particularly the Semitic religions. He even plays God, Deggle points out, when he tramps around under the name of Sispy and chooses the men who will collect the elixir and come to Calf Island. In many respects, Grimus appears as a God figure. He has created the world where events take place, but he has withdrawn and made it impossible for men to get in touch with him. The distance to him is so great that men in K completely deny his existence. An interesting trait in Grimus in this respect-and in the light of Rushdie's later criticism of religion-is his despotism. He might be understood as a secular Imam (Grant 37). Brennan maintains that Rushdie, here as in his later works, associates inverted or jumbled order with divine or supreme powers (Brennan 77). Syed sees the novel as written with iconoclastic intention (Syed 146). On the other hand, the narrow-minded rationalist Gribb, who denies Grimus's existence, is ridiculed. Here, then, the "disbelievers" are represented as blind.

Virgil, Deggle and Grimus play central roles in Flapping Eagle's life. Deggle turns up during Eagle's wanderings in the ordinary world and shows him the way to Calf Island. Virgil is his guide during the first stage on Calf and views him as his son, as Grimus does as well.

The figure of Mercury is evasive in alchemy. It is defined in a variety of ways and seen as the beginning of the process, prima materia or chaos, as well as the end of it. Mercury contains all conceivable opposites. This is expressed in the novel by connecting God and the devil; both become aspects of Mercury. The novel, as a whole, is structured so that the opposites face each other on all levels. Within man, there is the opposition between static atoms and dynamic ions. At the level of plot, Eagle searches for "stasis" in K but is forced to "kinesis" (235). In K, the revolutionary shares a house with the count. Eagle is drawn between two pale witches he says, identical twins, "opposite and the same" (165).

Opposites and their union are central motifs in the novel, as in the monomyth and in alchemy. Campbell refers to Joyce's words in *Finnegans Wake* "equals of opposites [...]

polarised for reunion" (Campbell 108, Joyce 92). Phrases like "equal and opposite" are frequent in Rushdie's novels.

The fact that opposites depend on each other, "the mutual need of opposites" (227), means that theories of purity and originality and the existence of something absolutely good or evil are questioned-as Rushdie depicts with intensity in his later books.

The uniting of opposites is often expressed as sexual intercourse in alchemical tracts and images, since the masculine and the feminine are examples of ultimate opposites. Intercourse is strikingly found a couple of times in the novel, in the form of incest. Incest between sister and brother is a common motif in alchemy, an image of the merging of the central ingredient of sulphur and mercury or for the restoration of a divided hermaphrodite. Jung interprets Mercury as a personification and materialisation of the collective unconscious (Jung, *Mysterium* 462). Incest with mother or sister then designates a confrontation with chaos, a descent into the unconscious (Sandqvist, 255).

Sandqvist stresses that the *mandala* in Jung is a symbol for the uniting of the opposites, that is, a union of conscious and unconscious. A mandala always has a centre, the psychological centre of personality, and can be combined with a circle (for example, flower or wheel) or a square (Sandqvist 264). Jung sees the rose as a mandala figure (Jung, *Alchemical* 295). In *Grimus*, a Stone Rose plays a decisive part. It makes the whole supernatural world possible. The Rose has the ability to heal as well as harm, and several of the important persons in the novel agree on the necessity of the destruction of the rose. Flapping Eagle is not allowed to see the Rose until the end of the novel:

> Around the top of a central shaft, or stem, were a series of thin, star-shaped slabs of stone. Flapping Eagle counted seven such slabs. The top two had four points each, the next eight, the next sixteen and so forth. Each slab rotated independently around the central stem. (304)

Geometrical symbols and numerical symbolism are prominent in the description. Associations with circles as well as squares are evoked. A square inscribed in a circle is a symbol of totality-of cosmos or, as in Jung, of the self. Two prominent numbers in the description are four and seven. Jung maintained the importance of these numbers in alchemy. The number four is central in the mandala and corresponds to the four elements. The number seven refers to the alchemists' seven metals or seven planets.

The movement of the slabs, the rotation around the centre of the Stone Rose, suggests concentration on the most important, the Self, according to Jung. The novel has many rotations and circling movements at crucial moments. These are common in texts influenced by alchemy. Virgil, like Grimus, engages in dances that explicitly imply dissolution and union. Jung calls them Ouroboros motifs (Jung, *Alchemical* 90).

Flapping Eagle's wanderings

The main character Flapping Eagle has acquired many qualities that have alchemical overtones, as he is at the same time a hermaphrodite and the *Philosopher's Stone*. The hermaphrodite, with his/her combined attributes, designates the beginning as well as the end of the process. This duality makes the hermaphrodite synonymous with the Philosopher's Stone. Eagle is born an American Indian and, because of his hermaphroditic character, acquires the name Joe-Sue. Rushdie directly alludes to the Philosopher's Stone when he lets Eagle see himself as this stone (156). Moreover, he escapes out of the city of K clothed in the figure Stone's rags. Eagle is then the substance that will be transformed. In order for the Stone to be transformed in alchemy, however, it must first be "slain "(Jung, *Mysterium* 18).

The quest in the novel is not only Eagle's however. The gorf Koax wants to stabilise or definitively fix Calf Island. His goal is abstract and above all seems to give the satisfaction that a well-constructed play can give. Flapping Eagle has a part in this final fixation of Calf Island as he appears to be the last piece of the puzzle, and the gorf interferes in different ways to guide the course of events in the right direction. He is seeking perfection. For Grimus, the quest is analogically egocentric or aesthetic. His great interest in Eagle is based on the fact that the latter resembles him. He wants to realise the Phoenix myth in his own person. Rushdie concentrates the (not very strong) emotional charge on Eagle's goal, which is both of an internal and of an external kind. He wants to find Bird-Dog and Grimus and to get the efficacy of the elixir of life withdrawn. He reclaims his humanity.

Virgil stresses that just as there are several different outer dimensions, there might also be unknown inner ones. These are lonely and frightening places. Each man is his own universe (87). Virgil's emphasis on a psychic dimension acquires a vital importance for the interpretation of the novel. Eagle moves in an external world; he is sailing on a sea, wandering in a forest and climbing a mountain. Early on, he understands that he is also on an internal journey, that he is searching his own face. On one occasion he experiences that the world is turned upside down: "I was climbing a mountain into the depths of an inferno, plunging deep into myself" (84). Grimus' interpretation at the end of Eagle's hardship during the wandering is explicitly psychological. Eagle has moved from a state of self-consciousness to a state of "Grimus-consciousness" (279), that is, from a limited to an extended consciousness.

The section which describes Eagle's wandering is the most difficult to understand. It is significant that scholars have hardly considered this section, which is the longest in the novel.

Eagle finds out that his sister Bird-Dog is living with Grimus at the top of the mountain and therefore, with Virgil's help, he starts on his quest to get there. Virgil thus becomes guide and psychopomp; he becomes the Old Wise Man like in alchemy or the monomyth. The trek acquires a ritual character since Eagle indicates ceremonial dress by putting a feather in his hair. It begins in a forest "dark as the tomb" (81). The motif might suggest that Eagle is in the nigredo state. He is tormented in different ways and at last, the quest becomes impossible. Exhausted and filled with dread, he falls to the earth. He now has an experience of a "myriad transmutations in which colours altered, the trees became moving creatures, the ground became liquid and the sky solid, grass spoke and flowers played music [...] It was a baptism of fire" (84). The merging of the elements into each other as well as "a baptism of fire" are typical alchemical motifs. The latter is an example of a process of purification.

The novel thus contains a multiplicity of motifs that seem to stress the state of nigredo or the night journey of the monomyth: incest, chaos, dissolution, encounters with monsters, associations with the river Styx of the nether regions. Virgil comes to the rescue since he is afraid that Eagle's mind will overheat and burn out (perhaps an echo of the heating in the alchemical vessel). He dances a dance for Eagle's life, a spiral dance where matter and energy move like fluids. This stresses, then, the circle, the spiral, the concentration on a centre, and the narrator makes an explicit association with an appropriate alchemical motif: "The worm biting its own tail" (74). When matter and energy come together and create a union, they are dancing "the Strongdance. When they fell back into the Primal, they were dancing the Weakdance" (92). The Strongdance suggests the *coagula* of the alchemists, the Weakdance suggests the *solve* and the connection to *prima materia* is obvious. Virgil now formulates an idea of monistic unity. Everything consists of energy; everything that exists is made of the same primal matter. The dance leads to communication with this primal matter, with "the Oneness" totally surrounding them.

New experiences of the same kind follow; the elements are transmuted again. They then arrive at the plateau and the city of K. The first part is over and so is the long night. The moon shines and sheds a white light. In alchemy, the moon and the white colour usually indicate that The Small Work has been achieved. One of Eagle's first acts in K is to have a bath. He has to change the water three times before he becomes clean. The emphasis on the bath has no significance on a realistic level, but acquires its meaning only if the behaviour is placed in an alchemical context.

A brothel occupies a central position in K, where the pursued Virgil (and later Eagle) is offered a refuge. Eagle starts the last stage from here. Jung points out that the whore is a well-known figure in alchemy. She is the secret substance in its first chaotic, maternal phase (Jung, *Mysterium* 302). Several of the women in the novel are or have been prostitutes. Together with Virgil, Eagle departs for the house of the former brothel madam, Liv. Unseen behind them, Media the whore follows them from the brothel. She has fallen in love with Eagle.

Eagle's stay at Liv's house has a ritual character: candles are lit, a litany is formulated and Liv recites from Virgil's diary, which gives Eagle all the knowledge he needs about Virgil, Grimus and Calf. She offers her body as an altar to Eagle (who resembles her former lover Grimus in a remarkable way). The four elements are joined in her figure, which strengthens her importance in foreboding the ultimate goal. Liv thus acquires significance at several levels. In addition to the level of plot, she plays a mythical and a cosmic role.

Her beauty is glaringly, overwhelmingly perfect. She interrupts the sexual intercourse with Eagle just before the climax to take revenge on Grimus's image; she stands like a Valkyrie, another psychopomp, over him. The interruption, Grimus later says, was decisive, because it robbed Eagle of his last obstacle, that is, of his masculinity, before he was prepared to meet Grimus (279). She thus dissolves the mask he has taken after his original hermaphroditic condition. In this respect, Liv is the Gate that leads to the last stage of the wandering. Eagle spends the night outside the house in foetus position-which might hint at a possible rebirth.

Only Media follows the last distance up to Grimus. Grimus' house is a low building of stone, a miniature fortress. It is in the shade of a big ash tree. Birds fly around them. The house even has a bird room with a multiplicity of living or stuffed birds and mythological birds, above all a huge multicoloured Phoenix that is said to be the Simurg himself, painted on the walls. The many colours are stressed once more in the description of a peacock. In the heart of the house is the room of the Rose.

Grimus takes Eagle into this room. Here he picks up a spherical object (a very common shape in alchemy) with two handles. A peculiar course of events takes place. Grimus's and Flapping Eagle's identities unite in something Eagle experiences as a glowing bowl or globe. *"You swallow me, I swallow you. Mingle, commingle. Come mingle. Grow together, come. You into me into you* [...]. We were one there in the glowing bowl, two here in the flesh" (306). Campbell describes the ultimate encounter, that is, the merging of opposites, which is one of the late stages in the monomyth, but Rushdie's images if anything remind one of the alchemical process in a vessel, which also leads to a merging of opposites. Eagle and Grimus are of the same appearance and background as victims of expulsion, an Indian and a Jew. However, they are opposites in other ways: Grimus represents cold, Eagle heat. Grimus is a vegetarian, Eagle a meat eater. Grimus as Simurg is king of the heavenly birds, Eagle as eagle is king of the earthly birds. These opposites are now merged. Eagle afterwards sees in a mirror that his hair has become white and that his face is exactly like Grimus's. Their consciousnesses have almost completely fused.

In the conclusion of the novel, Grimus is maltreated by the men from K, fastened to the big ash tree outside the house, and he dies when the ash burns. Eagle destroys the Rose by imagining an island without Object, without Rose. The effect is that the whole island slowly disintegrates, "its molecules and atoms breaking, dissolving, quietly vanishing into primal, unmade energy. The raw material of being was claiming its own." Meanwhile Eagle and Media are making love. She has very few attributes and plays no part in the plot; her role seems to be the very act of love, the melting together, that is, completion and dissolution.

Alchemical and Jungian conceptions thus seem to structure Eagle's wanderings. He was born a hermaphrodite but undergoes a disintegration of his character so that the feminine side is subdued and he appears as a man. On Calf Island, he encounters his sister. Their incest is a sign of the state of nigredo, or in Jung's words, of the meeting between conscious and unconscious. The elements merge into each other a couple of times, chaos reigns and he gets out of this with the help of concentration on circles (or mandalas), Virgil's dance and at last through the journey to the circular temple in the middle of the lake. Eagle undergoes baths and purifications. The moon shines and white colours are stressed. This might designate the Small Work.

He starts his wandering anew and at first ends up in a new state of nigredo, which implies that his masculine identity is shattered. Then he is prepared for a new union that takes place in two stages. The multiplicity of colours in the bird room is striking. They can forebode the Great Work in alchemy. First he is united in the vessel with Grimus (the masculine) and then in the intercourse with Media (the feminine). The union is followed by dissolution. Thus, the cyclical process can begin again.

The significance of the novel

Model is put on model in the novel: Dante's pilgrimage, the birds' journey to Simurg, the alchemical process, the initiation journey, the Jungian individuation process. The surface of the novel thus displays a confusing multiplicity. The models partly cover each other, it is true, but it is still difficult to read the motifs together to form a thematic wholeness. The writer's performatives appear diffuse. I will now discuss two possible interpretations.

There are many thematic ways to interpret the novel. To read it based on a Jungian model would mean that it should be possible to interpret Flapping Eagle's development in such a way that he at last reconciles the conflicting elements within himself and reaches a balance. He is explicitly searching for his own voice, and it may seem that he finds it in the end. Understanding Calf Island as a projection from Eagle's unconscious makes it natural that this projection dissolves when he has reached the goal. Using Campbell's more religiously and psychologically oriented monomyth, it seems possible to maintain that the myth of Simurg here acquires meaning, because in a monomyth the goal can be expressed in such a way that the hero encounters and assimilates his opposite (his own unknown self) by swallowing this or by being swallowed himself (Campbell 108). The hero and the god he is searching for must therefore be understood as being the inside and outside of one single mystery. What Eagle so intensely seeks is not a separate divinity or sister, but himself.

Speaking against these interpretations is the fact that Eagle is not represented as a psychological character. He does not experience any noticeable development. His inner life is not elucidated. The novel, therefore, cannot be said to express either a psychological or a religious quest.

The motifs might instead be given a metafictional meaning. The significance of the novel could be sought in the focus on narrative methods and on Rushdie's way of applying the myths. The most striking thing is that the myths have been degraded, as in Menippean satire (Johansen 27). Instead of God, Grimus is waiting at the end of the road. The guide Virgil lacks dignity. Many other motifs have a similar meaning, for example, the wanderer Eagle's experience of moving around as in a fictional story, not in an elevated epic but in a bad western (232). The whole body of myths to which Rushdie alludes are parodied, also the alchemical ones, which might be an explanation for the fact that when Eagle has reached his goal it seems empty, since it seems impossible to understand the significance. The goal, too, is parodied. The very degrading, the transformation of myth to our time, is a central device in Rushdie's works.

The novel then could be said to deal with a writer searching for his voice. Rushdie himself has suggested such an interpretation: "I feel very distant from [*Grimus*], mainly because I don't like the language it is written in. It's a question of hearing your own voice, and I don't hear it because I hadn't found it then"(Rushdie, "Interview" 125).

The search for a writer's identity, however, cannot be said to be clearly developed. The motifs where such a pursuit is displayed are too few and not sufficiently pronounced. The activities of the gorfs, however, perhaps can be understood as motifs in this direction. Their work might be compared to a writer's. By imagining something, they make it real. Virgil and Grimus learn the art, which is double-edged, at the same time filled with pleasure and responsibility. Grimus created the island with a consciousness of its ending. Who would write a story without knowing the end, he asks. Every beginning carries its end. That is why Grimus planned the island with his death in sight. In the same way, the ending of the novel might be understood as a dissolution that makes a new coagulation possible, that is, new novels. The Stone Rose might thus be perceived as a symbol of creative activity. Brennan sees it as a materialised dream for a writer. It constitutes a connecting link between alchemy and artistic creation, as in Joyce. It makes it possible for Grimus to enter a boundless number of possible lives.

Grimus might be seen as writer's play with a symbolic world, a puzzle where several pieces are lacking and where the point never becomes evident. Rushdie, as we have seen, has worked with a couple of fictional levels and built up complicated worlds. The characters in the novel tend to perceive their level of reality as the real one. The reader, however, like Eagle, soon becomes aware of the existence of several levels and several perspectives. On a very general level, Rushdie can be said to anticipate what will become fundamental factors in his following works, structurally as well as thematically: the nature of reality and different ways of portraying it, the role of perspectives for what one sees. When Rushdie turns from abstract symbolic language to concrete historical application, the questions become politically charged as well.

The novel might thus be said to configure a writer's process of individuation, in an allegorical but incomplete way. Read in this way, Rushdie transforms a myth about religious insight, the myth of Simurg, into a myth where art has taken a place equivalent to, or perhaps superior to the religious one. The theme recurs in *The Satanic Verses*. Cundy's interpretation of the novel leans in this direction. In the myth of Simurg, the unity behind the multiplicity is stressed and here, Rushdie tries to fuse the cultural multiplicity into an aesthetic unity (Cundy, 133).

The multicultural has become one of Rushdie's characteristics. This is visible above all on the intertextual level in *Grimus*. Cultural encounters in his later books are often expressed by the motif of exile. Scholars have above all focused on this motif in analyses of *Grimus* as well. Cundy sees the novel as the writer's first tentative investigation of postcoloniality. She is then irritated by his lack of postcolonial awareness (Cundy 129 and 134). *The Satanic Verses* is the obvious context.

The motifs taken into account are Eagle, who is from the beginning viewed as different since he is a white Indian. This is one of the reasons for his being expelled from his birthplace among the Axona Indians and becoming a chameleon turncoat, who recurs in the Toady Saladin Chamcha in *The Satanic Verses.* In K, he tries to find a home. "The Way of K" is the name of the philosophy of life-a way of living which preserves the men in the cocoon of the past and in the minutiae of the present (228). "It is the natural condition of the exile-putting down roots in memories" (132).

Syed Amanuddin, like several other scholars, maintains that here Rushdie initiates the exploration of the heritage of colonialism. He sees Grimus as a European, "discovering" the native Eagle and exploiting him for his own purposes (Amanuddin 143). Cundy also emphasises the oppressive white power. Tending towards the same direction is Johansen's opinion of Grimus as a Prospero figure and Eagle as a Caliban (Johansen 22).

Another fact seems more important. Rushdie repeatedly describes in his works the situation of the migrant. Important here is a recurring difference between gravity and lightness, where gravity is usually connected to a settled condition and lightness to migration. The migrant, says the narrator in *Shame,* has overcome the law of gravity and learned to fly. In *Grimus,* too, this difference exists. It is materialised here in the life of gorfs and birds. The gorfs represent gravity, immobility, sterility and intellect. They are contrasts to those men who are connected to birds, Eagle and Grimus, both migrants.

The men in K seem to be created in analogy with the gorfs because the first man that Eagle meets in K is Stone, a man who seems to be deeply engaged in an act of worship. He is down on all fours, crawling the length of the only street in the city. The street is said to be his microcosm (130). Everybody in K gradually appears petrified-in striking contrast to the birds. Migrants, who in a similar way petrify in reiteration of the manners and customs of their native place, recur in Rushdie's later novels.

We can find still other interpretative possibilities. The word "gorf" is an anagram of *frog*. The name of their master is Dota, which could be another anagram, *toad*. They live on Thera, which could be an anagram of *earth*. Making and deciphering anagrams is one of the most important occupations of the gorfs.

The gorfs' explicit role in the plot is small. However, they constitute the condition for the created world and seem to have a hidden significance. The toad (Dota) is a fairly common symbol for primal matter, prima materia, in alchemy. It is then possible to see the gorfs as the basis for the construction of the novel, the primal matter out of which the novel grows. They have the Rose and the elixir of life, which the alchemists extracted from primal matter. This important but concealed part of the gorfs is strengthened by the significance of the gorf Koax. Koax, who lives on Calf, has a name that seems to be based partly on "chaos" (*CAOS*) and maybe partly on "croaks." Chaos is synonymous with prima materia. This primal matter must incessantly be transformed in alchemy. In the end Koax, like Calf and Eagle, is dissolved, entering as a component of another primal element.

The opposition between toad and bird might have still another meaning. In *Mysterium Coniunctionis*, Jung writes about the toad as representing the element earth (terra), in contrast to the eagle, representing air. The analogy to the names Dota, Thera and Eagle seems obvious. The two elements, air and earth, are necessary for the Opus and examples of opposites uniting in fusion. Michael Maier, one of the most influential Western alchemists in Prague during the seventeenth century, provided the great predecessors in the alchemical tradition with emblems. His tracts and pictures have been spread all over Europe (Jung, *Mysterium* 4). On Avicenna's emblem, he has reproduced an eagle and a toad. Avicenna is the

Western name for Ibn Sina, the Persian alchemist whose name occurs in *Midnight's Children*. Maier's emblem shows Ibn Sina on a height outside a city. Beside him on the earth, a toad is lying down with a long chain around its body. The other end of the chain is attached to an eagle still hovering with unfolded wings.

Allusions to this opposition reappear in Rushdie's novels. In *The Ground Beneath Her Feet*, the tensions between space and earth recur. The different perspectives these positions offer are characterised by the eccentric myth scholar Darius and the godlike Ormus on the one hand, and on the other, the digging amateur historic scholar V.V. Merchant and Umeed Rai, the narrator who cannot stand the beauty of the unforgettable awe-inspiring heights where one sees only pinnacles, and who instead wants to get down to the city streets and the details of its life.

It seems possible to charge the relationship between toad and eagle with an immense significance. Here, finally, it could represent Rushdie's specific narrative strategy. He is mixing dross and gold. Slang, filth and everyday motifs contrast with the most exalted dreams: art, religion and love. Both poles stand out as equally important in the subsequent works, where the allusions to alchemy are more veiled.

Alchemy thus constantly turns up in the analysis of *Grimus,* but not alchemical doctrines, whether chemical, psychological or religious. It seems to be the ambiguous language and the charged symbols for death and rebirth, transformation and encounter between opposites that Rushdie has found productive. The diversified, suggestive language is probably one important factor in explaining the power of the attraction of alchemy. The language is ambiguous, full of contradictions and intentionally deceptive, thus completely the opposite of monological language which Rushdie often satirises in political and religious leaders.

It should be stressed that an alchemical context does not exclude other ways of understanding the novel. On the contrary. One could argue that migration is a basic experience of many characters in Rushdie's texts, and migration is seen as a wholly revolutionary process. It leads cultures to mix and change, and for humans to be transformed. Migration means that old certainties are questioned, which in turn leads to doubt and the necessity of compromise—this is one of the themes of *The Satanic Verses.* All these themes are comprehensible without reference to alchemy. However, this tradition elucidates the themes and clothes them in a powerful symbolic language while at the same time also dressing them in existential and political dimensions.

Notes

1. This is a rewritten version of a chapter in my book *Unending Metamorphoses: Myth, Satire and Religion in Salman Rushdie's Novels.* References to *Grimus* are interpolated in the text.
2. Joel Kuortti has collected many of the intertextual sources (Kuortti 34-36).
3. Compare: "An iceberg is water striving to be land; a mountain, especially a Himalaya, especially Everest, is land's attempt to metamorphose into sky; it is grounded flight, the earth mutated-nearly-into air, and become, in the true sense, exalted" (*The Satanic Verses* 303).
4. Rushdie mentions Ouroboros when talking about *Moby Dick:* "The ocean always was our Other, manifesting itself to us in the form of beasts-the worm Ouroboros, Kraken, Leviathan" (*Imaginary Homelands* 422). The worm is also mentioned in *The Moor's Last Sigh* (433).
5. *Pale Fire* has much in common with Rushdie's work, especially with *Haroun and the Sea of Stories,* where the motto alludes to Nabokov's Zembla, the country with the shadow figures.
6. The very designation, monomyth, is taken from Joyce's *Finnegans Wake* (Joyce 581, Campbell 30). I do not treat the monomyth in all its complexity but have chosen certain traits.
7. The myth of the Simurg recurs in Rushdie's books. In *Midnight's Children* 30 birds assemble outside the window of Aadam Aziz's father. In *Shame,* there is a carved screen with the circle round mountain Qaf and its 30 birds (*Shame* 33). In *The Satanic Verses* men appear in "simurgh-effigies," during the carnival of Jahilia (120).
8. That Vina Apsara in *The Ground Beneath Her Feet* is also connected to "crystals and ether" is a clear sign of Rushdie's continuous use of the alchemical symbolism (337).
9. The development is suggested in the very name of the island. "Calf" is a bastardizing of "Kâf," writes Virgil in his diary, and wonders if it is a question of the golden calf-which in alchemical traditions functions as a symbol for the greedy man's false gold (265).

10. Webb stresses that Ascona was the place for the most important of several colonies for theosophists and occultists during the first half of the twentieth century. Jung was one of many lecturers here (Webb 57).
11. Mercury is Saturn's child (Jung, *Alchemical* 227).
12. Further attributes link Grimus with Mercury. He uses a crystal to detect key moments, crossroads in time. Hermes-Mercury has been represented specifically as the god of crossroads (Jung et al. 156). Also in *The Moor's Last Sigh*, there is a Virgil figure, Lambajan Chandiwala, who has a parrot with clipped-wings (126).
13. The novel contains a thrice repeated detail about the lapsed Catholic Dolores, who satisfies her sexual urges with church candles (12). Eroticism and religion encounter one another here as in *The Satanic Verses*—but here clearly directed against religion.
14. Three of the names for Mercury are Mediator, Servator and Salvator. Grimus could be seen as Servator; he has to continuously preserve Calf by re-imagining it. Deggles thinks of himself as a Salvator (Jung, *Alchemical* 235).
15. Irina is said to be a *femme fatale,* with great experience of men. She married a man who was the opposite of her first lover (212). A distinguishing quality is her icy chilliness. Elfrida seems to be her opposite, beautiful as an Elfin, innocent, faithful to her husband, ethereal. But she is called Miss Snowflake and has glacial control over her life, in diametrical contrast to her mother's life. (Her father incidentally killed himself in a way which echoes in Rushdie's following novels. He jumped off a roof like several characters in *The Satanic Verses* and like uncle Hanif in *Midnight's Children*). When Elfrida at last relaxes the control, she throws herself into a new opposite and gets a job at the brothel.
16. The union is an expression of an ultimate peak. This is obvious in the description of Eagle's merging with Irina: "He lay in Irina's bed, balanced between love of innocence and lust for experience, between denial and consummation, standing at the peak, from which the only direction was down" (216). The last phrase recurs exactly in Allie Cone's reflection in *The Satanic Verses,* when she stands on the peak of her mountain.
17. Jung writes that Mercury as hermaphrodite was split and become brother and sister, who were later joined in coniunctio (Jung, *Psychology* 295).
18. Halka discusses the motif of incest, which has a similar meaning in *One Hundred Years of Solitude* (51).
19. In *Pale Fire,* too, there is a "rose-stone palace," functioning at last as a prison with three guards at one place and four at another (Nabokov 119).
20. Cundy, who has not seen the alchemical symbolism, perceives Eagle's androgynous nature only as a stigma (130).

21. The narrator in *The Moor's Last Sigh* acquires many alchemical attributes too. He is called "precious stone" (113), and "peacock" (224), has broken wings (146), and is said to be "a union of opposites" (259).
22. Jung maintains that the spherical shape is a prototype of the Hermetic vessel (*Alchemical* 72).
23. In *Grimus*, Gandhi (Mr Gandy) is mentioned in a degrading context (138). Florence Nightingale is a prostitute and—as in *The Satanic Verses*—black (141).
24. Quoted after Cundy (137).
25. The Stone Rose reminds one of Rosa Diamond in *The Satanic Verses*. In alchemy, the diamond has a specific significance, depending on its prismatic character. It contains all the colours of the rainbow (Jung, *Psychology* 187). The story about Rosa Diamond in the same way occupies a prismatic position in the novel. *Rosa* Diamond and Martin de la *Cruz* further point to the Rosicrucians, which is the most well known of the secret societies during the seventheenth century that took up alchemcial conceptions and symbols. A characteristic trait in this movement was the apocalyptic view of history, a line of thought that the narrative of Rosa Diamond highlights
26. Brennan has a similar idea. He notes the "transcendent vision of heterogeneity" in the novel (77).
27. Jung uses the very word "cocoon" about the condition which the man who spoils his life ends up in, not consciously, because it is an unconscious factor which spins the illusions concealing the world. In the end, the cocoon will totally enclose this man (*Essential* 93). The word recurs in *The Satanic Verses* a couple of times. The cocoon can point towards a coming transformation when the case will burst.
28. In "Septem Sermones ad Mortuos" Jung writes about the god Abraxas, the "hermaphrodite" who later turns up in *Midnight's Children:* "He is the lord of toads and frogs [...]" The text ends with an anagram that no one so far has been able to decipher (Hoeller 51).

Works Cited

Amanuddin, Syed. "The Novels of Salman Rushdie: Mediated Reality as Fantasy." *World Literature Today* 63.1 (1989): 42-5.

Brennan, Timothy. *Salman Rushdie and the Third World: Myths of the Nation.* London: Macmillan, 1989.

Campbell, Joseph. *The Hero With a Thousand Faces.* Princeton: Princeton UP, 1973.

Cundy, Catherine. "'Rehearsing Voices': Salman Rushdie's *Grimus." The Journal of Commonwealth Literature* 27.1 (1992): 128-38.

Degli-Esposti, Christina. "The Alchemical Language of Italo Calvino's *Six Memos for the Next Millennium* and *Invisible Cities." Rivista di Studi Italiani* 8.1-2 (1990).

____. "The Poetics of Hermeticism in Umberto Eco's *Il Pendolo di Foucault.*" *Forum Italicum: A Journal of Italian Studies* 25.2 (1991).

DiBernard, Barbara. *Alchemy and Finnegans Wake.* Albany: State U of New York P, 1980.

Eliade, Mircea. *The Forge and the Crucible: The Origins and Structures of Alchemy.* Trans. Stephen Corrin. Chicago and London: U of Chicago P, 1978.

Grant, Damian. *Salman Rushdie.* Plymouth: Northcote House Publishers, 1999.

Halka, Chester S. *Melquíades, Alchemy and Narrative Theory: The Quest for Gold in* Cien Años de Soledad. Michigan: International Book Publishers, 1981.

Hoeller, A. *The Gnostic Jung and the Seven Sermons to the Dead.* Wheaton, Madras, London: The Theosophical Publishing House, 1982.

Johansen, Ib. "The Flight from the Enchanter: Reflections on Salman Rushdie's *Grimus.*" *Kunapipi* 7.1 (1985): 20-32.

Joyce, James. *Finnegans Wake.* New York: The Viking Press, 1947.

Jung, C.G. *Alchemical Studies.* 2nd ed. Trans. R.F.C. Hull. *The Collected Works of C.G. Jung.* Vol. 13. Princeton: Princeton UP, 1983.

____. *The Essential Jung: Selected Writings.* Princeton: Princeton UP, 1999.

____. *Mysterium Coniunctionis: An Inquiry into the Separation and Synthesis of Psychic Opposites in Alchemy.* 2nd ed. Trans. R.F.C. Hull, *The Collected Works of C.G. Jung.* Vol. 14. Princeton: Princeton UP, 1989.

____. *Psychology and Alchemy.* 2nd ed. Trans. R.F.C. Hull. *The Collected Works of C.G. Jung.* Vol. 12. Princeton: Princeton UP, 1980.

____. et al. *Man and His Symbols.* New York: Garden City, 1979.

Kuortti, Joel. *Fictions to Live In: Narration as an Argument for Fiction in Salman Rushdie's Novels.* Frankfurt am Main: Peter Lang, 1998.

Nabokov, Vladimir. *Pale Fire.* New York: Vintage International, 1989.

Petersson, Margareta. *Unending Metamorphoses: Myth, Satire and Religion in Salman Rushdie's Novels.* Lund: Lund UP, 1996.

Rushdie, Salman. *Grimus.* London: Victor Gollancz, 1975.

____. *The Ground Beneath Her Feet.* London: Jonathan Cape, 1999.

____. *Imaginary Homelands: Essays and Criticism 1981-1991.* London: Granta Books, 1991.

____. "Interview with Salman Rushdie." *Scripsi* 3.2-3 (1985): 107-26.

____. *Midnight's Children.* London: Jonathan Cape, 1981.

____. *The Satanic Verses.* New York: Viking, 1988.

Sandqvist, Mona. *Alkemins tecken i Göran Sonnevis* Det omöjliga. Lund: Lund UP, 1989.

Streck, M. *The Encyclopaedia of Islam,* IV. Ed. H.A.R. Gibb et al. Leiden and London: E.J. Brill, 1960.

Syed, Mujeebuddin. "Warped Mythologies: Salman Rushdie's *Grimus." ARIEL* 25.4 (1994): 135-52.

Webb, James. *The Occult Establishment.* Vol. II: *The Age of the Irrational.* Glasgow: Richard Drew Publishing, 1976.

2

Allegories of Fiction: *Grimus* and *Haroun and the Sea of Stories*

JOEL KUORTTI

Allegory has lost much of its charm as a literary form during the past decades and much of this has undeniably to do with the growth of postmodernist literature, in which one can perceive a tendency to emphasise a more open-ended alternative instead of the allegorical mode. In fact, however, its trivialised status may be traced back even for two centuries, as the English and German Romantics were ill-disposed towards this form. This has not meant the end for allegories, however, and most certainly it has not put an end to allegorical readings. Furthermore, Carolynn Van Dyke notes that allegory "has also become a positive term for many poststructuralists," perhaps for the linguistic aspect of Quintilianian *aliud verbis aliud sensu*: to say one thing and mean the other. Fables, parables and allegories have for centuries been important genres for morality stories and there is still a large reading public who are willing to look for such morals in a tale, despite the fact that many others are more than willing to deny the validity of such a reading practice.

As with all literary classification and categorisation, it is not a simple matter to define allegory. With its additional burden of having been regarded as a minor mode or genre, it is even more difficult to reach a neutral (if not positive) definition. J.A. Cuddon defines it satisfactorily as follows:

> As a rule, allegory is a story in verse or prose with a double meaning: a primary or surface meaning; and a secondary or under-the-surface meaning. It is a story, therefore, that can be read, understood and interpreted at two levels (and in some cases at three or four levels). It is thus closely related to the fable and the parable.

What is central in this definition, and in definitions of allegory in general, is the pervasiveness of interpretative layers. At its crudest, then, allegory means substituting one thing with another. It is often connected with that frame of mind which considers implications as conveyors of truth and the explicit as illusion.

Two of Rushdie's novels can most easily be classified as allegorical (or postallegorical): *Grimus* and *Haroun and the Sea of Stories*; *Grimus* for its overt allegorical intertextual reference and *Haroun and the Sea of Stories* for its fable-like narrative together with the alleged proximity with its author's situation. They are also both non-topological, utopian, situated in no place specifically, rendering them susceptible to speculation and interpretation. While they indisputably evoke these allegorical readings, in their complexities they also tend to elude the neat one-to-one associations common to many traditional allegories. However, since these two books do work in an allegorical way, they will be read here as such, *Haroun and the Sea of Stories* as more like a fable about the power of story-telling and *Grimus* as more like an allegory proper.

1. *Haroun and the Sea of Stories*: "Where do Stories Come From?"

Rushdie's own fiction on the significance of fiction is most pronouncedly found in *Haroun and the Sea of Stories*. Haroun's story is also at least seemingly Rushdie's simplest. On closer scrutiny it does, however, reveal several complex and multilayered interpretations and intertexts. In his astute article, Aron Aji (himself another Haroun) tracks down various possible readings of several details in the book. He also acknowledges the possible, even probable, biographical overtones and undertones in the book, but nevertheless opts for a wider contextual setting than the simple biographical one. In the present approach, again, it is certainly fitting to adhere to an even more formal aspect of the story.

To begin with, the book can be taken as a quite straightforward narrative, telling the tale of Haroun Khalifa and his father Rashid and their adventures in Gup and Chup in search of Rashid's lost talent of storytelling. Haroun's story begins with a proper fairy tale line: "There was once, in the country of Alifbay, a sad city, the saddest of cities, a city so ruinously sad that it had forgotten its name" (*HSS* 15). One could cut the story short by commenting that in the end the city turns happy when it remembers its name, "Kahani [...]. Isn't it a beautiful name for a city? It means 'story,' you know" (*HSS* 209). In this way, one would get to the conclusion of the story, but at the same time one would lose all the thematic tendrils in the middle. And it is the tendrils that matter, after all. It is there that the fable lies, with a possible moral to be learned. What the narrator tells as Haroun's story is actually Rashid's story as well, a fact we are later made aware of (*HSS* 206), thus increasing the narrative complexity.

Rashid, known to his rivals by the irreverent name of the Shah of Blah and to his admirers by the even more ironic title of the Ocean of Notions, prefers detours whenever he can. Only once does he come up with something like an almost straight answer to Haroun, who had been pondering: "Where did all these stories come from?" (*HSS* 16). But the truth he tells him so bluntly that he gets them through a Water Genie's Tap from the Story Sea-is so fantastic that it is impossible for Haroun to believe him. And so Rashid can only give the advice suitable for all theorists of fiction: "So now kindly desist from this Iffing and Butting and be happy with the stories you enjoy" (*HSS* 18).

However, one cannot desist from Iffing and Butting, kindly or otherwise; that would be quite unlike human behaviour after all. So it happens that "one day Haroun asked one question too many, and then all hell broke loose" (*HSS* 18). And from such disrespect for one's elders the plot is really set in motion. If we consider also Rushdie's other novels in this way it can be claimed that the emerging function of fiction, as a part of its ethics, is to interrogate, to "ask one question too many," not to let the world rest. The question Haroun asks his father is momentous. It is the same question that the scornful Mr. Sengupta, the neighbour with whom Haroun's mother Soraya had just eloped, keeps asking her: "What's the use of stories that aren't even true?" (*HSS* 20).

"What's the use of stories that aren't even true?" This is the critical question everyday reality puts to fiction. And it is indeed the critical question the novel itself puts forward. Mr. Sengupta in his utilitarian imagination-free mind has no use for such a thing as fiction. However, the narrator also provides us with an answer, and from the point of view of fiction it is a proper utilitarian answer, to this question:

> Nobody ever believed anything a politico said, even though they pretended as hard as they could that they were telling the truth. (In fact, this was how everyone knew they were lying.) But everyone had complete faith in Rashid, because he always admitted that everything he told them was completely untrue and made up out of his own head. (*HSS* 20)

What we have here is perhaps as straight a statement as we are likely to find in fiction about the meaning of fiction-that it tells the truth by way of a lie-and as is the case with politics, claiming to be in truth would only result in the reverse. If the conclusion were that simple we could discontinue this investigation and rest assured that it is the moral of the fable. But there is more to the picture.

It is clear that Rashid's interests do not rest in the practical side of things, because for him the stories mean everything, for them he lives. What ensues from this obsession is one of the structuring storylines in the novel. One day Soraya, Rashid's wife and Haroun's mother, stops her characteristic singing for one reason or the other. And Rashid's utter preoccupation with stories is what prevents him from even noticing: "Rashid Khalifa was so busy making up and telling stories that he didn't notice that Soraya no longer sang" (*HSS* 16). This rupture in family relations leads to trouble and Soraya begins to detest Rashid's storytelling impracticality so much that she ends up running off with Mr. Sengupta.

This episode is vital for the plot as it provides Haroun with an additional reason for his quest, as he tries to get back his lost mother. What it brings to the thematic plane is perhaps a caution against the dangers of obsession, even being obsessed by stories. In the aftermath of Soraya's departure Rashid, in the manner of the Untime of Imam in Salman Rushdie, *The Satanic Verses,* breaks every clock in the house and time ceases to run. Furthermore, he experiences even greater loss, as Haroun in his anxiety for the lost mother asks the critical question: "What's the use of stories that aren't even true?" It is exactly this question which causes Rashid to lose his talent for tales.

Rashid is noted for his availability to appear in political (as well as in other) contexts. In fact his storytelling capacities are so famous and in demand that he is able to choose whom he would be willing to represent, whose invitations he really wants to accept. He is, in a way, in control of things, for through his performances a politician's success could be ensured. But when to his utter shock he finds that he has run out of stories, he realises that he is losing this controlling power as well. He is no longer in charge. He therefore decides to visit the Valley of K and sort out his problem, because he believes that this ancient locale with its magical, fairylandish properties will revive his storytelling abilities. In order to be able to accomplish this, he decides to accept the invitation of the local politician Mr Buttoo, whose politics he in fact dislikes intensely.

While Saroya finds Rashid's impractical storytelling impossible to stand, Haroun on the other hand finds his father's skill fascinating. Despite the innate dangers inherent even in the practice of storytelling, the talent of the storyteller is celebrated:

> Haroun often thought of his father as a Juggler, because his stories were really lots of different tales juggled together, and Rashid kept them going in a sort of dizzy whirl, and never made a mistake. (*HSS* 16)

The nonlinear mode of storytelling alluded to here in the figure of story-juggling, the intertwining of multiple simultaneous storylines, is the oral one which is traditional especially in India and the Middle East, found also in literary form for example in *Mahabharata*, Ramayana and *The Thousand and One Nights*. It is also a technique Rushdie has often used in his novels. Here, in *Haroun and the Sea of Stories*, it is also a major theme.

In response to such narrative layering of story-juggling, on one narrative plane Haroun and Rashid embark on their trip to the Valley of K in order to recover their respective losses (of a mother and stories) before they end up in the palimpsest story-world of Kahani. On their way they come to remember one of Rashid's old stories, the story about Khattam-Shud who

> is the Arch-Enemy of all Stories, even of Language itself. He is the Prince of Silence and the Foe of Speech. And because everything ends, because dreams end, stories end, life ends, at the finish of everything we use his name. 'It's finished,' we tell one another, 'it's over. Khattam-Shud: The End.' (*HSS* 39; see also *HSS* 79)

This Khattam-Shud of Rashid's story also turns out to be the Arch-Enemy within the story in the novel (along with Mr Sengupta and Mr Buttoo); the various layers are thus interrelated in many ways. Khattam-Shud's world is the one from Ray Bradbury's *Fahrenheit 451*, or the Imam's from *The Satanic Verses*, where books are dangerous and they are burned: "Burn the books and trust the Book" (*SV* 211). What is envisaged in the image of Khattam-Shud is the Apocalypse, the End, "the finish of everything." It is thus no trifling matter, from the human point of view, to save the talent for tales; only that the real world, or Buttoo and his company, do not seem to be of any help in Haroun's and Rashid's search.

Then, in one passage between sleeping and waking, Haroun bumps into the Water Genie Iff and there is a meeting of the two worlds, real and magical: "Are you trying to claim you're really one of those Genies my father told me about?" (*HSS* 56) Haroun wonders. He has already come to realise that his father's stories, quite contrary to what Rashid once in his despair has claimed (*HSS* 48), are *not only stories* (*HSS* 50 and 57), so it is not entirely impossible for him to accept this contact with the fantastic, the world of genies. To convince himself, he argues that because "the real world was full of magic, so magical worlds could easily be real" (sic; *HSS* 50). Once he has acquiesced in this fact, Haroun manages to blackmail Iff to help him in sorting out the problem with his father's storytelling, and they go to Kahani.

The Ocean of the Streams of Story, where Haroun is first taken by his fabulous (mechanical, vegetal, or simply magical) companions in the palimpsest Kahani, is a truly fantastic place, as it combines all of the stories in the world, those already told, those in the telling, as well as those yet untold. This motif grows in the course of the story, producing in the end an exemplary picture of a polyphonic postmodern text. We are told that

> because the stories were held here in fluid form, they retained the ability to change, to become new versions of themselves, to join up with other stories; so that unlike a library of books, the Ocean of the Streams of Story was much more than a storeroom of yarns. It was not dead but alive. (*HSS* 72)

This character of stories is something which is theoretically perhaps most frequently covered with the label 'intertextuality.' Many studies have been made of various texts, trying to find 'influences' and 'sources' for certain passages, ideas and so forth in them. This has certainly been the case with Rushdie's texts; they have been subject to repeated attempts to track down these influences, but Butt the Hoopoe in *Haroun and the Sea of Stories* assures us: "Any story worth its salt can handle a little shaking up" (*HSS* 79). While it is a truism in much of postmodern theory that all modes of writing, unavoidably, bear this element of intertextuality, some texts play with the notion on a metatextual level. And it is precisely this play which is indeed a major feature in Rushdie's writing.

As an indication of this metatextual/intertextual

connection we may consider another text. In by far the most substantial contribution to date by Rushdie to film criticism, *The Wizard of Oz: A Short Text about Magic* Rushdie pays tribute to the film's significance for his career as a writer: "When I first saw *The Wizard of Oz* it made a writer of me. [...] [O]f all movies, the one that helped me most as I tried to find the right voice for *Haroun* was *The Wizard of Oz*" (*WO* 18). Ascribing this status to a single film is saying a lot if one considers the extent to which cinematic influences play a part in Rushdie's works. And indeed, among other things, as a children's story with profound adult dimensions, *Haroun and the Sea of Stories* really does have remarkable intimacy with *The Wizard of Oz*.

What is even more to the point, Rushdie considers the various versions of the story of Oz and comes to the following conclusion: "If *The Wizard of Oz* is art," which Rushdie readily admits it is, "it's extremely difficult to say who the artist was" (*WO* 13). While Rushdie is clearly familiar with many of the concepts of modern literary theory, he nevertheless maintains a certain distance from them. Thus he comments on *The Wizard of Oz* that "this great movie [...] is as near as dammit to that will-o'-the-wisp of modern critical theory: the authorless text" (*WO* 16). There is a problematic relation with a notion such as the Barthsian "death of the author." This issue of authorship can be said to be an important one in many of Rushdie's texts. It is linked up with views about the significance of the storyteller as well as that of fiction.

Following from this, it is not only the importance of fiction which is foregrounded in *Haroun and the Sea of Stories*. There is also the aspect of the importance of the storyteller, the artist. While there is the need for equality of fiction ("Story Water facilities must be provided across the entire planet with an even hand" [*HSS* 67]), there is also the demand for great storytellers, as we know from the grandeur of Rashid's reputation. "Anybody can tell stories," we are told by Iff. "Liars, and cheats, and crooks, for example. But for stories with that Extra Ingredient, ah, for those, even the best storytellers need the Story Waters" (*HSS* 58).

It is remarkable that it is Haroun the child, someone without any authorised status in society, who is finally able to rescue the Story Waters. But then again, in *Midnight's Children* Saleem describes childhood as the third principle which is capable of negotiating between a dilemma like the one between the Guppees and the Chupwalas. At first he is not capable of concentrating on wishing back for his father the storytelling powers, because the picture of his lost mother intervenes constantly (*HSS* 70-71). Later, however, he manages to comply with the instructions to use Wishwater and forces the moon Kahani to move by the sheer power of his will (*HSS* 170-72). Through this act, he puts an end to the artificially maintained division between the dark and light parts of the moon. And when he finally wishes a happy ending for the story, that the sad city would remember its name, Kahani (or 'story'), this further results in a happy reunion with his mother, who has by then left Mr Sengupta/Khattam-Shud for good (*HSS* 210).

In the end, when Rashid's talent is restored, and peace has fallen upon Kahani, Rashid is once more able to demonstrate the use of stories by utilising his talent to the fullest. He tells the audience the same story the reader has just read, and in an elated way the unfolding of the story in the Valley of K of all that had happened induces the audience to turn against Mr Buttoo and force the dictator to escape and leave "the people of the Valley free to choose leaders they actually liked" (*HSS* 207). This is a victorious day for storytelling.

Comments have already been made as to the moral of the fable in *Haroun and the Sea of Stories*: stories as a way to truth, stories as a way to freedom. These add up to form a kind of an epistemology and an ethics for the tale. Yet further points might be made with regard to the importance of fiction. The first of these is an allegorical one and it has to do with the level of Rushdie's personal story, which this has been seen to be. In preparation for the war between the Chupwalas and the Guppees, the Chupwala 'Library,' or Army, behaves in what to Haroun seems to be a most disorderly manner. Butt protests to Haroun's doubts:

> But but but what is the point of giving persons Freedom of Speech, [...] if then you say they must not utilize the same? And is not the Power of Speech the greatest Power of all? Then surely it must be exercised to the full? (*HSS* 119).

We are told that it is as important to retain the freedom of speech for everyone as it is for great storytellers like Rashid/ Rushdie. If that freedom is not secured, if the source of stories becomes obscured through disuse, it will soon mean the end of all stories, no matter how great the storyteller.

Secondly, as pointed out, there is a specific warning against the threats to the storytelling powers that all sorts of Khattam-Shuds everywhere pose. In this context, Iff laments that the inhabitants of the palimpsest Kahani had failed in their responsibility:

> We are the Guardians of the Ocean, and we didn't guard it. [...] The oldest stories ever made, and look at them now. We let them rot, we abandon them, long before this poisoning. We lost touch with our beginnings, with our roots, our Wellspring, our Source. Boring, we said, not in demand, surplus to requirements. (*HSS* 146)

This is similar to the statement in *The Moor's Last Sigh*, where the Moor despairs over the multiplicity of Bombay which is lost because people have not been able to protect it (*MLS* 373). Like the freedom of speech, it is vital to preserve the hybridity of stories. There is indeed a mission in storytelling, because to lose the stories would mean an end to everything; it is, as mentioned, no trifling matter.

What happened to Snooty Buttoo in the Valley of K after Rashid's storytelling powers were restored, serves as a reminder of the importance which fiction can attain. Oppressive rulers can be overthrown by the sheer power of fiction, because it is capable of telling the truth about, exposing, oppression. Therefore, it is of fundamental importance that the sources of stories be protected. The reason why rulers like Khattam-Shud do not like stories at all is simple and laid out clearly when he answers Haroun's question:

> 'But why do you hate stories so much? [...] Stories are fun [...].'
>
> 'The world, however, is not for fun [...]. The world is for Controlling. [...] Your world, my world, all worlds [...]. They are all there to be Ruled. And inside every single story, inside every Stream in the Ocean, there lies a world, a story-world, that I cannot Rule at all. And that is the reason why. (*HSS* 161, the second ellipsis in the original)

Control over the world, everyone's worlds, their minds, people's souls what the rulers are after. What stories in there multiplicity then offer, it is claimed, is a counter-remedy to the ills of oppression.

Thirdly, there is also a somewhat smaller victory for love, as Haroun gives credit to the young (Wonderland-fashion) Page-soldier Blabbermouth's juggling skills. Haroun has been admiring his father's skill in juggling stories, and enamoured with the brave girl, tells her:

> I always thought storytelling was like juggling. [...] You keep a lot of different tales in the air, and juggle them up and down, and if you're good you don't drop any. So maybe juggling is a kind of storytelling, too. (*HSS* 109)

He wants to recognize the skill of the young girl in terms that are important for him, even though he cannot eventually convince her of the suitability of the parallel between juggling and storytelling. For Prince Bolo, Love had meant a single purpose, he wanted to save Princess Batcheat, when all the other Guppees rejoiced in argument. For Haroun love is different, it is reflected in storytelling. In this he follows his father, who considers stories to be primary. Haroun first saves the story waters (saving Rashid's skill at the same time) and then wishes back the name of the city Kahani, rather than desperately going after his lost mother. The result, however, is the more cheerful as even this third task is accomplished.

As a fourth point, if we consider Rashid who juggled with his tales, it is of no little importance that the women's stories, their storytelling in Rushdie's novels is very often described in terms other than writing. It may be Blabbermouth juggling (*HSS* 109), Mary of *Midnight's Children* pickling *(MC 458)*, Rani of Salman Rushdie, *Shame* embroidering shawls, or Uma of *The Moor's Last Sigh* creating selves (*MLS* 266).

And a fifth, last aspect, which is closely related to the power aspect discussed above, is worth taking up here, for it is a recurrent feature and a central one in the reconstruction of Rushdie's vision of fiction. It concerns the power of description:

> To give a thing a name, a label, a handle; to rescue it from anonymity, to pluck it out of the Place of Namelessness, in short to identify it-well, that's a way of bringing the said thing into being. (*HSS* 63)

This is an important statement, and if one considers its implications for fiction, they are vast. In this way, one can claim fiction to be a reality-constructing device, a sort of magical linguistic wand. It is also an ultimately optimistic way of looking at the world; but then again, we are told that "[b]elieve in your own eyes and you'll get into a lot of trouble" (*HSS* 63).

From the initially simple-looking story one could find profound statements on the significance of stories, and Dean Flower aptly if rhetorically notes that "What the story is really about is the story." In its fabulous, allegorical richness, *Haroun and the Sea of Stories* testifies to the basic principle that stories matter and nothing matters like stories. Now it is time to go on with the pursuit.

In *Haroun and the Sea of Stories*, it is the mechanical bird Hoopoe who (which) carries Haroun to and in the story-world. It is the Hoopoe, too, which (who) in another tale leads "all other birds through many dangerous places to their ultimate goal" (*HSS* 64). This allusion to Farid ud-Din Attar's *The Conference of the Birds* serves as a convenient link to another allegorical reading of a Rushdie novel, that of *Grimus*.

2. *Grimus*: "Fictions where a man could live"

2.1 Questions of Intertextuality

Grimus, Rushdie's first published novel, was not

enthusiastically received by the reviewers when it was first published in 1975. Rushdie's own subsequent estimation of the novel is likewise very low. Only when the book was published in the United States in 1979 did it begin to get some positive reviews. On this quite forgotten novel, Uma Parameswaran, then, notes the following:

> Had Rushdie not published any novel but *Grimus,* he would have been an echo of colonial writers in a postcolonial Commonwealth or a 'clever' but minor writer in the contemporary literature of Britain.

Because of the 'cleverness'-and despite the intellectual ambition-of the novel, it has never become a success and things might well have turned out as envisaged in the quotation above. The novel has also seldom been discussed in academic studies, although there have been some attempts, especially since Rushdie's international reputation began to grow. There are certainly, nevertheless, some interesting points to be made regarding this work.

To begin with, when one considers the issue of intertextuality, various sources and points of reference for *Grimus* have been suggested. Here the present writer is inclined to differ from Vishnu Salunkhe, who claims that "*Grimus* presents only a few aspects of India." Quite the contrary, the novel conveys many aspects of Indian cultures, as well as various other 'Eastern-Western' mythologies, histories, and texts. The word-play with the Amerindian plateau itself marks this, and Rushdie often returns to the idea of Columbus's displacement of India in the East/West paradigm. It is clear, though, that the India connection is less obvious here than in the later novels. To give an idea of the extent to which this intertextuality works, the following paragraphs collect as many as possible of the influences, parallels and sources deriving from various writers from many literary traditions and cultures which have been claimed for *Grimus* in its criticism.

Among the major parallel texts, the following can be mentioned: there is, first of all, Farid ud-din Attar's Persian poem *The Conference of the Birds,* which lends itself readily and openly to comparison, from quotations to thematic structure. Together with it goes, secondly, Ferdowsi's (or Firdausi's) *Shah-nama,* an earlier Persian epic text which for example introduces the mythical Simurgh (Simurg of *Grimus*). Thirdly, a further primary influence is Dante Alighieri's *Divine Comedy* with its motif of a descent and a quest. In both *Divine Comedy* and *Grimus* there is also a Virgil who acts as a guide, and hands this task in the end to Beatrice in Dante, or Media (and Bird-Dog as well) in Rushdie. Then we have an astounding medley of texts: Aesop's *Fables,* Miguel Asturias, Sir Francis Bacon's *New Atlantis,* R.M. Ballantyne's *The Coral Island,* Samuel Beckett, Jorge Luis Borges's stories "El Aleph" and "El Zahir," as well as "The Garden of Forking Paths," Lewis Carroll, Angela Carter's *The Infernal Desire Machines of Doctor Hoffmann,* Daniel Defoe's *Robinson Crusoe,* Umberto Eco's *The Name of the Rose* (although this was published only in 1980), T.S. Eliot, William Golding's *Lord of the Flies,* Ernst Hoffmann's *The Devil's Elixirs,* Mohammed Iqbal's *Shaheen* poems, Samuel Johnson's *The History of Rasselas, Prince of Abyssinia,* Franz Kafka, Anna Kavan's *Ice,* Omar Khayyam's *The Rubaiyat,* Stanley Kubrick's film *2001: Space Odyssey,* Doris Lessing's *Briefing for a Descent into Hell* and her *Canopus in Argos* series, Gabriel García Márquez, Flann O'Brien, William Shakespeare's *The Tempest,* R.L. Stevenson's *Treasure Island,* Tom Stoppard's *Rosencranz and Guildenstern Are Dead,* Jonathan Swift's *Gulliver's Travels,* J.R.R. Tolkien's *The Lord of the Rings,* Virginia Woolf's *Orlando*; *The Arabian Nights,* Arthurian romances, Menippean satire, *Panchatantra,* and *The Wandering Jew,* or Ahaseurus (of for example Eugène Sue).

There are also various other authors and works which can be credited with having contributed to the novel: Victor Hugo's *Notre Dame de Paris* in Ignatius Quasimodo Gribb and the hunchback figure, *Kama Sutra* of Vatsyayana, Samuel Coleridge's "Ancient Mariner" and "Kubla Khan," Rudyard Kipling's *Just So Stories,* Günter Grass's *Tin Drum,* Malcolm Lowry's *Under the Volcano,* Elias Canetti's *Auto-da-Fé,* Kurt Vonnegut's *Slaughterhouse 5,* Shakespeare's *Hamlet,* John

Keats's "Endymion," Homer's *Odysseus*, as well as numerous sacred texts, mythologies and legends: Chinese, Greek, Indian, Persian, Scandinavian, Native American, Christian, Hindu, Islamic, Sufi and Zoroastrian, to name but the obvious. There seems to be no end to the list of these intertexts.

One special feature in *Grimus* among Rushdie's novels may be noted here, namely the scarcity of cinematic references and allusions. If one compares this book with, say *The Satanic Verses*, there is a huge difference in that respect. But, then again, *Grimus* is much more meditative than the active and cinematic multitude of *The Satanic Verses*. It is also true that only at the time of *Grimus*'s publication, the post-World War II decline of the film industry was changing into a new growth.

With such a large real or assumed literary genealogy, the question of influence becomes superfluous. This being so, the question remains how successfully the various components are amalgamated to create a new whole. In the case of *Grimus*, the answer seems to be that it did not succeed. It demands such an amount of concentration and effort to make anything of the allusions. And most of the time they seem to evade or confuse readers, if one can judge by the scant criticism of the novel.

2.2 Science Fiction and Allegory

If intertextuality is the first point of interest in the discussion of *Grimus* here, allegory is the second. The novel has proved a difficult task for analysis; firstly, for the difficulties encountered in specifying it generically, and for example Rushdie has himself commented that "it doesn't fit very easily into any category." Furthermore, Deborah Madsen remarks that a "'multigeneric' text makes extremely problematic our inherited assumptions concerning the integrity of generic definitions," such as for example allegory. Secondly, all its non-topical, allegorical material has produced interpretative difficulties. There are several levels of interpretation for its allegory: the mystic Sufi search for the self (parallel to Attar's poem), the religious confrontation, the colonial/postcolonial containment, and the author-reader embrace.

The starting-point of the novel, in one of its four epigraphs, is the (in itself allegorical) 12th century Islamic mystical poem by Farid ud-din Attar, *The Conference of the Birds.* The Sufi quest alluded to through this inclusion would suggest a search for the meaning of life, or the emptying of the self. And appropriately enough, the main character, Flapping Eagle, sets forth on his pursuit as "an adaptable sort of man" (*G* 25), "an empty man, a Shell without a Form" (*G* 192) to go to the mythic mountain of Kâf, to find Simurg, or rather, and more grimly, Grimus. Ultimately he ends up becoming one with Grimus, in the same way as the thirty birds of Attar's poem find themselves to be Simurg.

It was a science fiction writing contest into which Rushdie entered his manuscript of *Grimus,* and this has proved to be something of a burden to the book, since it has been used as a demeaning label. It has been said that although *Grimus* is to be regarded as science fiction, there is not much technology in it, and what little there is is dubious. It may well have been misleading to look for technological futuristic explanations and James Harrison, too, admits the difficulty of connecting the science fiction qualities with any technological actualities whatsoever. He records a couple of points (that is, the references to weapons [*G* 211] and bombs [*G* 234]) which

> might well have persuaded readers that the novel was about the atomic genie that should never have been let out of the bottle. But it remains difficult to identify the Dimensions, the Stone Rose, or a combination thereof, at all specifically with any actual or potential scientific discovery.

For the present author likewise there seems very little evidence of such futuristic technology in *Grimus.* In fact, there is a somewhat Vonnegutian sarcasm with regard to machines and technology in general, for example when Flapping Eagle visits Phoenix for the first time: "I saw automobiles and launderettes and juke-boxes and all kinds of machines and people dressed in dusty clothes with a kind of despair in their eyes" (*G* 21); an attitude which is also somewhat anti-humanistic: "Free will really is an illusion, you know" (*G* 239). Furthermore, there is the ironic twist as Virgil conceptualises bicycles for Flapping Eagle and himself, apologising for the fact that "the mysteries of the internal combustion engine have always been beyond me" (*G* 84-85). There is at least a certain disillusionment with technology, if nothing more.

Rushdie was recognized as a science fiction writer in *The Encyclopedia of Science Fiction*, however, for *Grimus*. It was noted there that the book can be seen marginally as science fiction "in its use of *immortality* themes and in the interdimensional conflicts" (emphasis in the original). All these points considered, there seems ultimately little justification in regarding *Grimus* as science fiction in all but a marginal sense. If we agree to leave that line of argumentation aside, another one is ready to hand.

It has already been mentioned that in *Grimus*, Rushdie uses Attar's allegorical poem as a starting-point in the title and in the epigraphs. There are also direct references to the narrative of the poem: "There is a Sufi poem in which thirty birds set out to find the Simurg" (*G* 232-33; further references in *G* 209, and 197; also 208, where Grimus brings Virgil and Deggle "a bird to bury, a highly coloured bird of paradise," that is, Simurg). Therefore, with Attar's example in mind, a new *allegorical* (or, rather, a *metafictional*) reading of *Grimus* is offered here as a hypothesis, as a further gesture towards illustrating the arguments for the importance of fiction in Rushdie's novels. In this pursuit, we might find the Stone Rose to be the Rosetta Stone of *Grimus* (see *G* 208), helping us give a more coherent reading of the story. The following pages will also, it is hoped, suggest another explanation to the points referred to by Harrison above.

2.3 The Gorfs, the Endimions, the Divine Game of Ordering

Take first the 'Gorfs' and their idea of 'Endimions.' These have appeared difficult for interpreters. The Gorfs are enormous stone frogs (*G* 65), which fact is reflected in their name, an anagram of Frogs. To begin with, the simple stereotypical chauvinistic pun would seem to suggest that the

Gorfs ironically denote the French. They are after-a-fashion colonialist masters who exercise their power in subtle ways. The term 'colonialist' is used here in the specific sense defined by Albert Memmi as follows:

> A colonialist is [...] only a colonizer who agrees to be a colonizer. [...] [A]ccepting the reality of being a colonizer means agreeing to be a nonlegitimate privileged person, that is, a usurper. [...] He endeavors to falsify history [...], anything to succeed in transforming his usurpation into legitimacy.

In short, the Gorfs are such illegitimate colonialists, but in a proper postcolonial way, they have also become so disillusioned and disinterested that they finally allow Grimus to appropriate the Stone Rose, the instrument of their power. The catastrophe ensuing Grimus's inability to control the Effect through the use of the Stone Rose testifies to this indifference.

The above would not suffice to prove the Gorfs to stand for the French. As a further support for the present interpretation, it can be noted that they do not, after all, live on some faraway planet, but on palimpsest Earth, 'Thera,' in the palimpsest Universe, 'Nirveesu' (*G* 64). What is even more suggestive of it is that the Gorfic idea of the simultaneously existing Endimions or Dimensions could well denote the democratic ideals so forcefully put forward by the French Revolution: especially equality, but liberty and fraternity as well (see *G* 140 and 149). As such, there seems to be at least a shadow of these ideals in the Utopian (*G* 85 and 149), Communist (*G* 116 and 148-49), or, indeed, religious (*G* 100) Paradises, as conceptualised in the reversed, epic 'underwater Underworld' of Calf Island (with echoes of Atlantis, Robinson Crusoe's island, the Odyssey's Ithaca, More's Utopia, and the classical Ultima Thule among others) and particularly in the town of K. And as with the Gorfic planet, Virgil explains the existence of Calf Island in terms of Endimions, that "an infinity of dimensions might exist, as palimpsest, upon and within and around our own" (*G* 52-53).

Whether the Gorfs can reasonably be argued to represent the factual French colonialists or perhaps colonialism at large (if anything) will not change the fact that in the realm of the post/colonial world of *Grimus*, the Gorfs are more than anything else spectators; they look at how their exported ideas work in the Dimensions: "the ever stimulating spectator sport of observing other people's lives" (*G* 197). Even if they now seem to be content to watch, they nevertheless hold strongly to their dominion. The Gorfs' major occupation is the Divine Game, the language game of Ordering. In this game, they can manifest the power of language in their possession: "the vast mental powers of the Gorfs make it possible for them anagrammatically to alter their very environment and indeed their own physical make-up" (*G* 64-65). In the following some features of the Gorfs are analysed in terms of colonial issues.

The Gorf who mainly makes an appearance in the novel is "Our Gorf," the Gorf Koax. This Gorf had been chosen the titular head of the Gorfs, Magister Anagrammari, and he had developed the Divine Game further; he had

> moved towards heresy. He developed a minor branch of the Divine Game to such a point that it threatened the Game itself. It also gave the Gorfs the chance, at last, of measuring the extent of their brilliance or mediocrity against other civilizations. (*G* 66)

The Gorf Koax's heresy here corresponds well with the irreverence associated with Sufi mystics like Attar and Al-Hallaj, or the novel form as such, France being among the most important sources of its initiation. Moreover, while this innovation is useful, it severs "our Gorf's" relationship with the other Gorfs, and the Master Gorf, Dota, tells Flapping Eagle-Grimus that he has banished the Gorf Koax

> *who has settled irrelevantly in your Endimions. Should you meet him, kindly let him know that his gross Bad Order has led to his being banned from Thera [...]. He stands or falls with your Endimions.* (*G* 245; italics in the original)

In a way, Gorf Koax shares the fate of Flapping Eagle. The willingness on Gorf Koax's part to espouse features of a foreign, colonised culture leads this time to his expulsion, just as

Flapping Eagle was expelled by his own people for his unclean espousing of Unaxona culture. Purity has to be maintained.

The irony with which the colonial Gorfs are represented does not escape the reader: although the Gorfs are sightless, nearly immobile and totally isolated, they regard themselves as superior without any reservations. This could also be a highly self-ironic portrait, if one took the Gorfs to mean authors, which is a possible reading (compare this with the author-figure appearing in *The Satanic Verses* [*SV* 318]). They are not portrayed as monolithic, however, because at least the Gorf Koax wants to measure their civilisation with others. When Virgil asks why the Gorf Koax had wanted to remain on Calf Island, the answer is: "I liked it here" (*G* 93). With this answer, and his determination "to see Calf Island through to the end" (*G* 197), by taking the risk of perishing with the humans, this Gorf is rendered more human, and less oppressive. Virgil makes a similar comment to Flapping Eagle in relation to his search for the Elixir of Death: "Interesting [...] that you should think of death as such a humanizing force" (*G* 55).

The Gorf does not remain on Calf Island, or rather his presence is invisible because he does not want to get involved, although he wants to "meddle" with events on Calf Island (*G* 66-67). But Virgil is highly critical of the Gorf's presence and he realises something with which he can argue against the Gorf. In the emerging debate, Virgil comments:

> the Island did not include you in its conception, so by your own rules it would be a distortion if it were to use you in any Ordering process. Nor do we have any need of observers. (*G* 93)

The colonialist, persistent in his legitimation of his role as the creator of the colony, is proved to be at fault. Virgil manages to win the argument but cannot manage to order the Gorf Koax away in the end. No matter how much more human, and less oppressive, the Gorf is described to be, no power will surrender so easily.

But what then is the useful new branch of Ordering the Gorf

developed? This time there is a straight answer to the question in the text, in the form of another allusion to French thinking: "The minor branch was called Conceptualism [...] *'I think, therefore it is'*" (*G* 66; italics in the original), derived from René Descartes's famous dictum, *cogito, ergo sum*. The Gorf's genuine discovery is that this statement can be used to conceive other Endimions. To be able to control the new branch of the language game, the Gorf Koax finally conceptualised what is known as an Object, existing in all conceivable Dimensions: "An Object would exist in every single conceivable Endimions and it was only through contact with Objects that movement between the Endimions would be possible" (*G* 66); the Object in this case is the Stone Rose.

2.4 The Stone Rose

The Stone Rose, itself an oxymoron—and "actually not a rose at all" (*G* 241)-is the means of exploration, of crossing the Dimensions. It was made by the Gorfs "to link the Dimensions" (*G* 251; in fact, by Our Gorf [*G* 66]), all the "million possible Earths with a million possible histories, all of which exist simultaneously" (*G* 53). What is this Stone Rose? This is a crucial question, as the line of argumentation below depends on the answer to it. What is it that "enables you to travel [...] enables you to learn"? And much more, as the description close to the end of the book continues:

> With the Rose you can enter into, and become, a thousand thousand other people, live an infinity of lives, and acquire the wisdom and power to shape your own. [...] And one day [...] you can pass this supreme gift on to another, [...] give the Phoenix a new life, a new beginning. (*G* 251)

As we see, the Stone Rose is indeed something powerful, enabling one to become "a thousand thousand other people, live an infinity of lives." In a hypothetical way it may be asked, that would it be feasible to say that the Stone Rose signifies, not some futuristic scientific discovery, but fiction in general, or, even more specifically, the novel as a form? It has been claimed that it is precisely in fiction that one can enter other lives, other people.

The Stone Rose is forceful. In the Dimension in question, in the world of K, its power has, however, been misused. In order to control the inhabitants of K, Grimus, the patriarch of the island (in his colonial, religious, and familial roles) has presumed to take possession of the Stone Rose and to use it for his own purposes. Through this panoptic device he can keep the island under his surveillance: "Only if you were Grimus would you be fully conscious of what was happening on Calf Island" (*G* 67). This power Grimus denies the people of K by forbidding the Stone Rose, because "it had nothing to do with their reasons for being here. Immortality was their choice, not exploration. The Rose was mine" (*G* 235). Grimus takes the Stone Rose, the device of exploration, into his possession, promising them immortality instead.

We have now learned that the Stone Rose was conceptualised by the Gorf Koax to enable exploration of the potential existences in the Dimensions. The link between fiction (or the novel form) and the Stone Rose was already suggested and this is the crucial point in this allegorical reading. To examine this proposition, some other features of the allegory need first to be interpreted.

2.5 The Inner Dimensions, the Ion Eye, the Watercrystal, the Crystal of Potentialities

Immortality in K is based on obsession, a petrifying defence against the Effect, the frightening prospect of Potential Existences. This is not specific exclusively to the island, however, because there is obsession in the Axona culture and religion as well. Flapping Eagle is therefore able to comment that "life among the Axona prepared me in many ways for Calf Island. One of the ways was this: it taught Flapping Eagle the power of obsession" (*G* 24). Exile, the condition under which everyone on Calf Island lives, too, is connected with obsession. Thus, had Flapping Eagle's arrival not disturbed his thoughts, Virgil "would have reflected further, on ritual, on obsession, on the neuroses and displacement activities that exile creates" (*G* 15). Furthermore, politics is another aspect of obsession: "Moonshy differed from the rest only in choice of obsession. He was Opposition Man" (*G* 150). Obsession appears thus as a very common feature.

Flapping Eagle is unlike Attar's thirty birds, in that he is not looking for a king. He has his obsession, or "prime interest," however, and that is Grimus (*G* 124). After discovering that even the architect of K's protective philosophy of Obsessionalism, Ignatius Qasimodo Gribb, does not believe Grimus exists (*G* 131), Flapping Eagle nevertheless sets out "to find out as much as possible about Grimus, whether he was fact or fiction" (*G* 132).

But an obsession is not an end in itself, rather it provides a defence mechanism. What, then, is the Effect against which the people, and here the people of K especially, have to develop obsessions and Obsessionalism as their defence (see *G* 81, 149 and 218)? An immediate answer suggests itself in the fearsome Inner Dimensions. On several occasions, Virgil tries to explain these in terms of the human mind: "That's the tragedy of K. They're all scared of their own minds" (*G* 72), because one "never knows what universes may lie locked within one's mind" (*G* 55), and furthermore, "what the human race fears most is the workings of its own mind" (*G* 45). The people of K are not described as anything extraordinary, but rather as a mixture of contemporary people, from the revolutionary to the aristocrat, from the blacksmith/hunter to the cobbler/beggar. This condition of obsessions in K thus really reflects the ordinary human condition. Ignatius Gribb even defines obsession as "the supreme gift of the human race. To deny it is to deny our humanity" (*G* 161).

As one approaches these Inner Dimensions of the mind, one becomes vulnerable to the Dimension fever. And once one has acquired this condition, this fever, it is difficult to recover totally, because conquering the fever requires more than people are usually capable of. The torment of the fever is described in the following quotation:

> Lurking in the Inner Dimensions of every victim of the fever is his own particular set of monsters. His own devils burning in his own inner fires. His own worms gnawing at his strength. (*G* 84)

Here, one can acknowledge the proximity to psychology and the human psyche, the worms, devils and monsters being metaphors for fears, memories and suppressed desires. Similarly, as these monsters are the creation of one's own mind, they can only be controlled either by one's own power of will, or by chosen obsessions which keep the monsters of the mind repressed, in order to render life tolerable. Under Grimus, it has become increasingly difficult for the people of K to keep these monsters in check. Grimus has manipulated the Dimension fever to be his own shield, to protect himself from the people by blocking their entrance into his home with the fever's disturbing power.

Grimus begins to lose control of the tool of his power, the Stone Rose, and Virgil notes: "The trouble with Grimus [...] is he can't control the Effect" (*G* 71). The individual inner monsters meant to be controlled by each individual are becoming more universally threatening due to the intensified Dimension fever. Subsequently Grimus becomes dangerous to everyone: "At this time, in this place, this piece of knowledge is an untenably dangerous thing" (*G* 190). When the Stone Rose of the Gorfs should have been a tool for exploring, and particularly exploring the Inner Dimensions (of the human mind), it has now become an instrument for the patriarchal-colonial-religious power to keep the inhabitants of K under control.

If we were thoroughly to lay bare the allegory, there would still be a couple of less significant points to be explained, closely linked to the psychological aspects discussed above. They are the briefly mentioned Ion Eye, the Watercrystal and the Crystal of Potentialities. Of these, the Ion Eye is some sort of a method of looking for mental patterns, as especially in Freudian or Jungian psychoanalyses, suggested by the references to "Freudlein" and "Jungfrau" (*G* 25), or "Oxyput" insinuating Oedipus and Freud's famous interpretation of that myth (*G* 234). The Watercrystal is Virgil's diary through which Grimus had been able to learn about things such as Flapping Eagle's arrival. The Crystal of Potentialities, then, seems to be a sort of surveillance apparatus, perhaps a television, or some other kind of close-circuit crystal ball, which Grimus describes as follows: "In it I can examine many potential presents and futures and discover the key moments, the crossroads in time" (*G* 235). As these three do not emerge as fully developed ideas, it is impossible to come to any decisive conclusion as to their precise construct or significance in the allegory. But whatever they are, with the supplementary aid of these, Grimus is able to receive information on the inhabitants of K in order to govern them entirely.

2.6 Misuse of the Stone Rose

It is now time to return to the Stone Rose. When the Stone Rose with its supplementing devices becomes a weapon (*G* 211) or a bomb (*G* 234) to fulfil Grimus's "Grand Design" (*G* 234), even the Gorfs become concerned:

> *We are extremely perturbed about Grimus' misuse of the Rose. It was never intended to be a tool for intraendimions travel. Nor a magic box for the production of food. It is a flagrant distortion [...] to use the Rose to Conceptualize a packet of* (he searched for the right form) *coffee.* (*G* 245; italics in the original)

Thus the Gorfs take the Stone Rose seriously and think that it should not be trivialised by using it for purposes of travel and procuring foodstuffs. But unlike Virgil, in their pretentious colonialists' concern about the proper use of it, they are not interested in the other, more mischievous and tyrannical uses of the Stone Rose Grimus puts it to.

The reason why the Stone Rose does not function properly is that it has a piece missing. Nicholas Deggle (old Nick or the Devil [*G* 27]), Grimus's opponent, whom Flapping Eagle on his journey of centuries comes to know as Livia Cramm's "social whore" (*G* 29), had once been living on Calf Island, where he "broke that piece off the Stem" (*G* 191). He had wanted to destroy the whole object, but Grimus and Virgil would not let him do that. Instead, the two exiled Deggle from the island. But a piece from the stem of the Stone Rose was lost to the Devil, corrupting it, so Virgil, who had come to realise the ills of the misuse, suggests to Flapping Eagle to destroy the Rose:

> Dimension-Chaos in which we find ourselves [...] and indeed all Grimus's powers, spring from an object called

> the Stone Rose. [...] This is what must be destroyed. [...] It is possible that this Dimension cannot survive without the Rose. What is certain is that no-one will survive here, except for spiders, flies and animals, unless the Rose is broken. (*G* 191)

The oppressive Grimus gains all his power from the Stone Rose. It constrains people to live in Dimension-Chaos without a hope of ever emerging from it. And even more acutely, in Virgil's view, if the Stone Rose were not destroyed, human life would become impossible. Its destruction might reveal that their Dimension, their world, cannot survive without it, but certainly it cannot survive *with* it.

Together with the increasing Dimension-Chaos caused by Grimus's application of the Dimension fever to protect himself, there are further problems arising from the use of the impaired device. Towards the end of the novel, its use has resulted in existential problems, for there are now 'blinks' during which all human existence ceases for a moment, with grave consequences (*G* 163). What ensues is a struggle between Flapping Eagle and Grimus, or I-Eagle and I-Grimus. I-Eagle's conclusion is the following:

> Grimus misused the Rose [...]. The blinks are proof that it is both damaged and being stretched to breaking-point. We cannot continue to use it as Grimus did (*G* 251).

The power which the Stone Rose contains can be destructive and certainly Flapping Eagle thinks that Grimus has abused it. Grimus himself has become in his opinion "as twisted, as eaten away by power-lust, as its effect has stunted and deformed the lives of the people you brought here" (*G* 236). But could the Stone Rose have been used properly?

2.7 Proper Use of the Stone Rose

Multiplicity of voices, or Bakhtinian heterology, plays a part in *Grimus*, although it is not as explicit and predominant an aspect and issue here as in Rushdie's later novels. There is, however, a recognition of the related questions, here especially in Flapping Eagle's search for himself: "I am looking for a suitable voice to speak in" (*G* 32). The diversity of voices emerges in, for example, the varying narrative points of view of the novel. Although it is mainly narrated from the omniscient point of view, there are occasional first-person narrations: as in the case of Flapping Eagle-narrator ("my (his)" [*G* 16]), Dolores (*G* 57-58), Virgil (*G* 95-96), and Irina (*G* 179). This functions as a gesture allowing multiple points of view in the narrative. It is part of the democratic quality which the novel form is claimed to contain. In the novel, especially the Endimions stand for this kind of diversity. When this feature of reality is misused, it endangers the whole community, the whole universe. This is comparable to "Is Nothing Sacred?" where the oppressive closure of the little room of literature ends when the walls eventually tumble down.

Now, in relation to *Grimus*, if it is arguable, as claimed at the outset of the present explication, that the Stone Rose signifies, not some futuristic scientific discovery, but fiction in general, or, even more specifically, the novel as a genre, then it certainly reflects that multiplicity or heterology. And it is, indeed, claimed to have a comparable status as a form of knowledge:

> Grimus is in possession of a stupendous piece of knowledge: that we live in one of an infinity of Dimensions. To accept the nature of the Dimensions involves changing, entirely, our ideas of what we are and what our world is like. Thus rewriting the book of morality and priorities from the beginning. What you must ask yourself is this: is there such a thing as too much knowledge? If a marvellous discovery is made whose effects one cannot control, should one attempt to destroy one's find? Or do the interests of science override even those of society, and, indeed, survival? (*G* 189-90)

The Stone Rose is itself a key and the treasure, containing both the knowledge of and the means to enter the intradimensional worlds. The Stone Rose is here wittily connected with the discussion of whether scientific and more precisely technological discoveries and inventions can be judged on moral grounds. This link is perhaps the most influential in prompting readers to interpret the device as the atomic genie. But, as has been pointed out, there are very few arguments to sustain this explanation; another has to be formulated.

Clearly, one of the strengths of Rushdie's writing is the insistence on the power of language in governing and defining people. He shows time after time that the powerful fictions created by the religious, patriarchal and colonial authorities become the reality people live by and within. Here in this novel, the Gorfs, alien immobile stone frogs, have the power of control through their use of anagrams. Furthermore, the Gorfic notion of Conceptualisation empowers one to make things happen: "I think, therefore it exists." Grimus, who has learned how to employ this capacity, tells Flapping Eagle:

> In a sense, Flapping Eagle, I created you, conceptualizing you as you are. Just as I created the island and its dwellers with all the selectivity of any artist.
>
> -We existed before you found us, said Flapping Eagle. (*G* 233)

Flapping Eagle is not content with Grimus's view. The descriptive power of the colonialist cannot be claimed as the originating point of the existence of the colonised. Against these dominating fictions other counter-fictions are offered and claimed to be no less true. This feature is later developed more maturely in Rushdie's work, but it is there already in *Grimus*.

One might be tempted to claim the central point of Rushdie's writing to be the importance of language, and especially fictional language in the novel, and this characteristic is, indeed, that which Uma Parameswaran hints at in her discussion of word-play in *Grimus*:

> This could be the central metaphor of the novel: Creative power is; the diversity of life and values is due to what different people make of it, with it; all-pervading, all-embracing Simurg at one extreme and Grimus, a diabolical creator and controller, at the other.

There are also certain interlocked issues: these are post/colonial issues and religious issues; irreverent rebellion against origins, religion, coloniser. The contest with religion is aspiration for freedom: "To free myself, I must render Axona unclean," comments Flapping Eagle and rapes the god Axona (*G* 89). This counter-hegemonic status of the novel is, in *Grimus*, further illustrated by means of the figure of the brothel as sanctuary (*G* 185), very much as in *The Satanic Verses*.

For the Gorfs the Stone Rose is an instrument of power in its capacity to be of use in measuring between civilizations. Grimus has succeeded in gaining control of the device. In *Grimus*, then, we are indeed shown how this power can be wrenched from the colonialists, the Gorfs of this world. But, as we come to see, this does not happen without problems, because in Grimus's use it has become another kind of instrument of power altogether. The way in which Grimus uses the power of the Stone Rose is an indication of this problematic relationship. As Fawzia Afzal-Khan observes, "Grimus/Sispy becomes the prototype of the native-turned-neocolonizer." It is legitimate to ask whether Grimus is a native of Calf Island, having arrived there only thirty years earlier (*G* 209), but that is beside the point. In this respect, what matters more than what makes one a national is the fact that Grimus has obtained the Gorfs' power by confiscating the Stone Rose. And the subsequent fact that from this initial emancipatory move he has become another force of oppression.

Since human beings are so vulnerable to fictions we must be careful that no one gains absolute authority to determine our being. The liberating theme of the novel is that we must retain that power ourselves. This is in fact what Virgil had done before Grimus got the upper hand:

> With sufficient imagination, Virgil Jones had found, one could *create* worlds, physical, external worlds, neither aspects nor a palimpsest-universe. *Fictions where a man could live.* In those days, Mr Jones had been a highly imaginative man. (*G* 75, emphasis added)

It has been the purpose of this article to offer a reading of this novel from this initial standpoint, that fictions are necessary for life.

At the end of *Grimus* there is annihilation, a recurrent phenomenon in Rushdie's novels. As the power of definition has been wrenched once more from the oppressor, this time from Grimus by Flapping Eagle, the fictional reality Grimus created must consequently disappear. It is demonstrated that a dimension cannot exist without the imagination which makes it possible in the first place. Flapping Eagle's solution is to imagine a reality without the Stone Rose. But what follows is destruction instead of freedom: "Deprived of its connection with all relative Dimensions, the world of Calf Mountain was slowly unmaking itself" (*G* 253). But what in fact is it that is destroyed here?

In the end, we are given a world without the Stone Rose. But the Stone Rose is fiction and a world without fiction cannot exist, for it would be a world without Dimensions. The Gorf Koax had liked it on Calf Island and Virgil finally "understood how this hugely intelligent being would prefer the complex order of Calf Island" (*G* 93) to that of the bleak, flat Thera. We are not offered a new fiction to replace the unmade Calf Island, but we are left to imagine our own. If we take the tip, we will let the Stone Rose be neither violated nor destroyed. And then, "one day [...], you can pass this supreme gift on to another, [...] give the Phoenix a new life, a new beginning" (*G* 251). That would be a proper way to use it. (Furthermore, as a peculiar hint of the importance of authors which is an important theme in the later novels, the Stone Rose also incorporates Rushdie's initials).

It might well be that the reluctance with which *Grimus* seems to open to decipherment, has contributed to its poor reception. In being too demanding and enigmatic, the novel has resisted readings. With the complications mentioned, however, the allegorical reading given here might offer us a new way of approaching this as well as Rushdie's other novels. If in *Grimus*, Virgil had once been a man who could create worlds, "fictions where a man could live," in *The Satanic Verses* Jahilia is criticised precisely because it "had lost its old, shifting, provisional quality of a mirage in which men could live" (*SV* 359). Thus in *Grimus*, the knowledge of the dimensions as well as the means to enter them is circulated and the dangers of losing fictions is emphasised.

While it is argued that fiction is important as such, it is also true that it gives a platform on which to engage with important ethical issues; especially contemporary ones to which there is still insufficient distance to look at them more objectively; questions which are difficult and problematic like post/colonial and religious issues referred to above.

It is a somewhat unrewarding enterprise to offer allegorical readings because they cannot be exhaustive or ideal; they can always be denied relevance. It is nevertheless rather pleasing to see how an idea can be developed more and more towards completion by taking into account detail after detail. It has not been my task to draw a conclusion to *Grimus*, however, but to illustrate how the importance of fiction/the novel is argued for in Rushdie's works. If now, after the readings of *Haroun and the Sea of Stories* and *Grimus*, it were proposed that there is at least a kernel for fiction as an epistemology and an ethics in Rushdie's writing, the notion would not be altogether far-fetched. Whether one would want to turn it into a proper theory, is another question.

Notes

1. See Carolynn Van Dyke, *The Fiction of Truth: Structures of Meaning in Narrative and Dramatic Allegory* (Ithaca and London: Cornell UP, 1985) 9. Paul de Man attributes the decline of rhetorical figures such as those used, for example, in allegory "to the advent, in the course of the nineteenth century, of a subjectivistic critical vocabulary," "The Rhetoric of Temporality," in de Man, *Blindness and Insight: Essays in the Rhetoric of Contemporary Criticism*, 2nd rev. ed. (1983; London: Methuen, 1986.
2. On the importance of reading with regard to allegory and on the apparent generic conflict, K.M. Newton comments that "it could be argued that the decipherment of allegory is still not interpretation in the modern sense. [...] Yet a consideration of allegory reveals that interpretation is not merely a modern phenomenon but that it played a role in literary criticism even in the classical era. [...] Once the decision to read a text allegorically is taken it follows that it will be read differently and will take on a different meaning. The question of allegory is particularly central to literary interpretation because virtually

any literary text can be read as an allegory even though it may display no explicit signs of allegory," *Interpreting the Text: A Critical Introduction to the Theory and Practice of Literary Interpretation* (New York: Harvester Wheatsheaf, 1990) 3-4.

Very few texts have been described or discussed as allegorical at least since George Orwell's fabulous *Animal Farm* (1944). One can claim Philip Roth's *The Great American Novel* (1973) to be such an allegorical novel. His more psychological books, like *The Breast* (1972), have allegorical echoes as well, just like much psychoanalytical fiction. In science fiction one may find instances of allegory, too, for example in Ursula Le Guin's *The Left Hand of Darkness* (1969) or in the cold war era movie *Star Wars* (1977). Patrick Parrinder comments on this that "a large proportion of SF novels have something to say about the issues of knowledge and power. They tend to demand with a peculiar insistence to be read, in part, as social parables or fables," *Science Fiction: Criticism and Teaching* (London and New York: Methuen, 1980), 87. Rosemary Jackson notes, too, that the "other world" of Le Guin's "science fiction fantasies [...], however new or strange, is linked to the real through an *allegorical* association, as an exemplification of a possibility to be avoided or embraced" (emphasis added), *Fantasy: The Literature of Subversion* (1981; London and New York: Methuen, 1986) 43.

Finding extending definitions of allegory useless, Van Dyke distinguishes two forms of "postallegorical" literature. One is the kind of social and psychological literature which follows Marxian and Freudian lines of interpretation and the other is the postrealistic narrative by such writers as Hawthorne, Kafka, Mann, Beckett, Pynchon, and Nabokov, see 291-93.

3. Van Dyke, 16.
4. Van Dyke, 200.
5. J.A. Cuddon, *The Penguin Dictionary of Literary Terms and Literary Theory*, 3rd ed. (1991; London: Penguin Books, 1992) 22. In relation to fables, parables and myths, John MacQueen discusses the moral and religious dimensions of allegory in his book *Allegory*, The Critical Idiom 14 (1970; London: Methuen, 1978).
6. See Van Dyke 202-03.
7. See Van Dyke 290-93. On the changes in allegory towards the postallegorical, she comments that "what we have lost, losing thereby the ability to write allegory, is a certain perspective on reality-a readiness to seek the objects of mimesis in a realm irreducible to the sensible and the subjective," 293.
8. *Grimus* (London: Paladin, 1989; first published by Victor Gollancz, 1975). Subsequent references are given in parentheses, preceded by *G.*

9. *Haroun and the Sea of Stories* (1990; London: Granta Books, 1991). Subsequent references are given in parentheses, preceded by *HSS*.

10. Rushdie himself shies away from allegorical readings of his work because, as he says in the 1984 interview by Peter Craven, Michael Heyward and Penny Hueston, *Scripsi* 3.2-3 (August 1985): 108, in India, "allegory is a kind of disease [...]. Allegory asks readers to make a translation, to uncover a secret text that has not actually been written. In that sense I don't think my books operate as allegories."

11. Aron R. Aji, "All Names Mean Something: Salman Rushdie's *Haroun* and the Legacy of Islam," *Contemporary Literature* 36.1 (Spring 1995): 103-29.

12. Aji 103-04. On this question, Jean-Pierre Durix comments that "*Haroun* is obviously an allegory of Rushdie's personal situation, that of a writer silenced by forces identified with the enemies of books and of the imagination. Khattam-Shud can reasonably be interpreted as a recognizable representation of Ayatollah Khomeini," Durix, "Gardener of Stories: Salman Rushdie's *Haroun and the Sea of Stories*," *Journal of Commonwealth Literature* (1991): 114-22, Rpt. *Reading Rushdie: Perspectives on the Fiction of Salman Rushdie*, ed. M.D. Fletcher, *Cross/Cultures: Readings in Post/Colonial Literatures in English* 16 (Amsterdam and Atlanta: Rodopi, 1994) 345. Even more pointedly, G.R. Taneja remarks that "*Haroun and the Sea of Stories* can hardly be read as *anything* other than an allegory of Rushdie's present predicament" (emphasis added), "Facts of Fiction: *Haroun and the Sea of Stories*," *The Novels of Salman Rushdie*, ed. G.R. Taneja and R.K. Dhawan (New Delhi: Indian Society for Commonwealth Studies, 1992) 198.

13. This bears a striking resemblance to the opening of Ford Madox Ford's *The Good Soldier: A Tale of Passion*: "This is the saddest story I have ever heard" (1946; Harmondsworth: Penguin, 1985).

    In the context of Rushdie's novels, it also merits to mention Dowell, the narrator of Ford's novel, for he displays similar characteristics as for example Saleem Sinai of *Midnight's Children*. As an illustration of this, at one point Dowell comments: "I console myself with thinking that this is a real story and that, after all, real stories are probably told best in the way a person telling a story would tell them. They will then seem most real," 167. Randall Stevenson links the unreliability of Dowell with modernist fiction, commenting that it fosters such scepticism which "installs in the fiction an epistemological doubt, an uncertainty about how completely or truthfully the world can be known or communicated through any individual's idiosyncratic vision of it," *Modernist Fiction: An Introduction* (Hemel Hempstead: Harvester Wheatsheaf, 1992) 26-27.

14. In the political context of Snooty Buttoo, this then serves as an ironic reference to similar titles of political leaders and dictators such as for example "Genius of the Carpathians" and "Danube of Thoughts" for

Nicolae Ceaucescu of Romania, who was executed at the end of 1989 after a popular uprising. Trond Gilberg writes that: "The Ceausescu personality cult has reached heights that are ridiculed outside the borders of Romania. The General Secretary is variously described as the greatest thinker, philosopher, statesman, and scientist the world has ever seen," *Nationalism and Communism in Romania: The Rise and Fall of Ceausescu's Personal Dictatorship* (Boulder and Oxford: Westview Press, 1990) 54. More on Ceaucescu's personality cult, in Mary Ellen Fischer, *Nicolae Ceaucescu: A Study in Political Leadership* (Boulder and London: Lynne Rienner Publishers, 1989) 160-61. While Ceaucescu is one of the most recent examples, there have of course been a host of other politicians with an ornate personality cult around them: Mao Zedong, Josef Stalin, Kim Il Sung and so on.

15. Compare this with the similar quest in *The Moor's Last Sigh* (New York: Vintage Books, 1997; first published by Jonathan Cape, 1995) 381. Subsequent references are given in parentheses, preceded by MLS. The encrypted name of Rushdie's son, Zafar, in the epigraph to *Haroun and the Sea of Stories* would also suggest a more autobiographical reading, especially the last lines: "As I wander far from view/Read, and bring me home to you" (*HSS* 11); also compare with David Sheff, "Playboy Interview: Salman Rushdie," *Playboy* 43.4 (April 1996): 59.

16. *The Satanic Verses* (London: Viking/Penguin, 1988) 214-15. Subsequent references are given in parentheses, preceded by *SV*.

17. There is the further layer of personal allegory, as for example in the following quotation: "one cannot help but make a connection between Khattam-Shud and Rushdie's own chief persecutor, Khomeini, the voice of the *fatwa* that seeks to impose the most final of silences on Rushdie's utterances," Catharine Cundy, "Through Childhood's Window," *Reading Rushdie* 338.

18. The title reflects the eleventh-century Sanskrit collection *Katha Sarit Sagara* by Somadeva, which Snooty Buttoo mentions to Rashid and Haroun (*HSS* 51), see Dean Flower, "Not Waving but Drowning," *The Hudson Review* 44:2 (Summer 1991): 319.

19. *The Wizard of Oz: A Short Text about Magic* (1992; London: British Film Institute, 1993). Subsequent references are given in parentheses, preceded by *WO*.

20. Without going too much into detail, it may be noted for example that they both begin with a sad place; Dorothy's Kansas is a monochrome emptiness, Haroun's sad city had even forgotten its name.

21. Roland Barthes, "The Death of the Author," *Image-Music-Text*, trans. Stephen Heath (1977; New York: Noonday Press, 1991; orig. in 1968), 145.

22. *Midnight's Children* (London: Picador, 1982; first published by Jonathan Cape, 1981) 256. Subsequent references are given in parentheses,

preceded by *MC*. The importance of childhood in Rushdie's novels is discussed for example in Cundy's "Through Childhood's Window" 336-41.

23. *Shame* (London: Picador, 1984; first published by Jonathan Cape, 1983, 190-95.
24. This point is developed in my "*Shame*: Necklace of Stories," *Postcolonialism and Cultural Resistance*, ed. Jopi Nyman and John A. Stotesbury (Joensuu: University of Joensuu, Faculty of Humanities, 1999) 117-22.
25. The feature of naming, or description, is an important one in postcolonial as well as in feminist criticism, see the discussion in chapter III with relation to *Shame*.
26. Flower 319.
27. See Farid ud-Din Attar, *The Conference of the Birds* (*Manteq at-Tair*) trans. Afkham Darbandi and Dick Davis (Harmondsworth: Penguin, 1984).
28. See for example the 1982 "Interview with Salman Rushdie," by Jéan-Pierre Durix, Kirsten Holst Petersen, Jacqueline Bardolph, Anna Rutherford and Carole Durix, *Kunapipi* 4.2 (1982): 25, where he describes it as "too clever for its own good," and the 1984 *Scripsi* interview, 125, where he comments that "I feel very distant from it, mainly because I don't like the language it is written in."
29. Uma Parameswaran, "Salman Rushdie in Indo-English Literature," *The Journal of Indian Writing in English* 12.2 (July 1988): 15-25. Rpt. Parameswaran, *The Perforated Sheet: Essays on Salman Rushdie's Art* (New Delhi: Affiliated East-West Press, 1988) 13.
30. Vishnu B. Salunkhe, "Salman Rushdie and India," *The Novels of Salman Rushdie* 192. Of Indian, or Hindu aspects, one could mention the Calf Island as *lingam* and the sea as *yoni* (*G* 55-56), the Calf Island itself suggesting approximity with the Sacred Cow, and the Giant Turtle as an avatar of Vishnu (*G* 50).
31. Kathryn Hume remarks that the use of 'Indian' here "is just a punning marker of marginalization to white Anglo culture," "Taking a Stand while Lacking a Center: Rushdie's Postmodern Politics," *Philological Quarterly* 74.2 (Spring 1995): 211.
32. See Ferdowsi's *The Epic of Kings: Shah-Nama, the National Epic of Persia by Ferdowsi*, trans. Reuben Levy (London: Routledge and Kegan Paul, 1967). It is also this poem which recounts the story of Rostam, who features in some versions of the dust jacket of *The Satanic Verses*.
33. See Catharine Cundy, "'Rehearsing Voices': Salman Rushdie's *Grimus*," *The Journal of Commonwealth Literature* 27.1 (1992): 131; rpt. *Reading Rushdie* 45-54.
34. See Ib Johansen, "The Flight from the Enchanter: Reflections on Salman Rushdie's *Grimus*," *Kunapipi* 7.1 (1985): 24.

35. For example, in the following studies these references are set out (referred works or authors in parentheses): Timothy Brennan, *Salman Rushdie and the Third World: Myths of the Nation* (Houndmills: Macmillan Press, 1989) (Ferdowsi, Dante, Kafka, *The Arabian Nights*, Eliot, Khayyam); Catharine Cundy, "'Rehearsing Voices'" (Dante, Attar, Johnson); James Harrison, *Salman Rushdie*, Twayne English authors series: 488 (New York: Twayne Publishers, 1992) (Borges); Ib Johansen, "The Flight from the Enchanter," 20-32 (Márquez, Asturias, Menippean satire, Shakespeare, Dante, Attar, Tolkien, Kubrick, Kavan, Lessing, Hoffmann, Carter); Suzanne Kiernan, "A Language for Oppression," *The Age Monthly Review* 1.9 (1982): 7-9 (Beckett); K.V.S. Murti, "Bacchus and Buddha: Salman Rushdie and R.K. Narayan," *The Novels of Salman Rushdie* 157-68 (Swift, Woolf, Bacon, Stevenson, Defoe, Ballantyne, Golding, Dante); Uma Parameswaran, "Handcuffed to History: Salman Rushdie's Art," *ARIEL* 14.4 (October 1983): 34-45, rpt. Parameswaran, *The Perforated Sheet*, 1-11 (*The Wandering Jew*, Arthurian romances, Tolkien); Parameswaran, "New Dimensions Courtesy of the Whirling Demons: Word-Play in *Grimus*," in Parameswaran, *The Perforated Sheet*, 55-66, rpt. *Reading Rushdie* 35-44 (Márquez, Kafka, Eliot, Carroll, Kafka, Stoppard, *The Arabian Nights*, Borges); Barbara Ozieblo Rajkowska, "The Reality of the Alien: an Exploration of Salman Rushdie's Novels," *Revista canaria de estudios ingleses* 13/14 (April 1987): 9-27 (Eco); Sushila Singh, "*Haroun and the Sea of Stories*: Rushdie's Flight to Freedom," in *The Novels of Salman Rushdie* 209-16 (Aesop, *Panchatantra*); Syed Mujeebuddin, "Warped Mythologies: Salman Rushdie's *Grimus*," *ARIEL* 25.4 (October 1994): 135-51 (Iqbal, Attar, Dante); Anthony Thwaite, "Games People Play," *The Observer* 9 Feb. 1975: 28 (O'Brien). One surprising omission from these lists is Herman Hesse's *Das Glusperlenspiel* (1943), with its affinity to the Gorfic Game of Ordering, see *The Glass Bead Game*, trans. Richard and Clara Winston (1960; Harmondsworth: Penguin, 1981).

36. On the mythical variety, for example Colin Smith notes that "*Grimus* dances allusively through the worlds of Persian, Nordic and Indian mythology [...]. Rushdie's fictional model, which aims to expose the human causes of re-emergent historical patterns, deliberately sets itself in the broadest possible tradition, in which Eastern and Western myth-making merge," in "The Unbearable Lightness of Salman Rushdie," *The New Literatures in English*, vol. 1, ed. Dieter Riemenschneider, Critical Approaches to the New Literatures in English (Essen: Blaue Eule, 1989) 105.

37. The growing popularity of movies in the 1970s has to do with new modes of production, release and distribution, the effect of which can be seen in "the unprecedented success of the first 'megablockbusters,' *Jaws* (1975) and *Star Wars* (1977)," Stephen Powers, David J. Rothman and Stanley Rothman, *Hollywood's America: Social and Political Themes in Motion Pictures* (Boulder, CO and Oxford: Westview Press, 1996) 29.

38. Fawzia Afzal-Khan describes it as "a mishmash of myth, fantasy, and science-fiction," in "Post-modernist Strategies of Liberation in the Works of Salman Rushdie: The Subject/Object Dialectic and Manichean Imperialism," *Journal of South Asian Literature* 23.1 (Winter/Spring 1987): 142. Rushdie himself records having chosen the science-fiction mode for exploration of ideas, but it turned out to be "a fantasy in a sense I now disapprove of, a fantasy without any roots in the discernible world," interview in *Scripsi* 125.
39. In the 1982 "*CA Interview*" by Jean W. Ross, *Contemporary Authors*, vol. 111, ed. Hal May (Detroit, MI: Gale Research Co., 1984) 415.
40. Deborah L. Madsen, *Rereading Allegory: a Narrative Approach to Genre* (New York: St. Martin's Press, 1995) 1.
41. An evaluative postcolonial reading was perhaps first attempted in Johansen: "In *Grimus* the clash between different systems of values and between the people of the *third world* and their *European* colonizers is largely carried out in *metaphorical* terms, as part of a literary experiment with time, space, and language" (emphases in the original), 30. This is followed by Cundy, 1992, 134-5. Syed Mujeebuddin claims, however, that "*Grimus* falters in its failure to countenance postcolonial concerns" 148.
42. Although some studies, among them M. Madhusudhana Rao's in many ways unsatisfactory and inaccurate *Salman Rushdie's Fiction: A Study (Satanic Verses Excluded)* (New Delhi: Sterling Publishers, 1992), try to discuss the novel in technological terms (see for example 100-02), others are not so convinced; for example R.K. Dhawan comments that "there are no spaceships in it; the most predominant element of the book is fantasy," "History and the Novel: Some Significant Statements in *Imaginary Homelands*," in *The Novels of Salman Rushdie* 261.
43. Harrison 37-8.
44. *The Encyclopedia of Science Fiction*, ed. Peter Nicholls (London: Granada, 1979) 510; rev. ed, eds. John Chute and Peter Nicholls (London: Orbit, 1993) 1035.
45. Albert Memmi, *The Colonizer and the Colonized*, trans. Howard Greenfeld (1965; London: Souvenir Press, 1974) 45 and 52; orig. *Portrait du Colonisé précédé du Portrait du Colonisateur* (1957).
46. Albert Memmi refers specifically to the Tunisian situation. Forty years later, this issue seems immensely tragic in the Algerian context.
47. Here there is a remarkable allusion to Aristophanes's play "The Frogs" (*Batrakhoi*), in which the choir of frogs sings repeatedly: "Brekekekex, ko-ax, ko-ax," see *Five Comedies of Aristophanes: The Birds, The Frogs, The Clouds, The Wasps, Lysistrata*, trans. Benjamin Bickley Rogers (New York: Doubleday, 1955) 91. Several affinities between *Grimus* and 'The Frogs' could be established; suffice it here to mention the following details from the play: the underworld of Hades, Dionysus's contest with

the frogs, the monster, rebellion, griffin-eagles and the Athenian democracy which was weighed in the poetry contest between Euripides and Aeschylus.

Another one of Aristophanes's plays relevant in this context is "The Birds" (*Ornithes*), featuring above all the hoopoe, 8-33; among the flight of other birds, there is also a mention of an orphan bird and an eagle, see 57.

48. Koax could also denote a 'hoax,' a Zen 'koan,' a 'coax' cable, or even anagrammatically 'ax(e) ok,' referring to the Axona, 'axe owner.'

    Al-Husayn ibn Mansur al-Hallaj was cruelly executed in Baghdad in AD 922. His views on the unity of man and God prompted opposition, and "to some he appeared blasphemously to contradict Islam's fundamental understanding of the transcendence of God and even to threaten the social order"; editor's comments to "Al-Hallaj: the Crucifixion of a Mystic," in *Anthology of Islamic Literature: from the Rise of Islam to Modern Times*, ed. James Kritzeck (1964; New York: New American Library, 1975), 96.

49. Compare this with Shakespeare's *Romeo and Juliet*: "What's in a name? That which we call a rose / By any other word would smell as sweet," II.ii, *The Riverside Shakespeare* (Boston : Houghton Mifflin, 1974) 1068. See also Gertrude Stein's *Sacred Emily*, and its "Rose is a rose is a rose is a rose."

50. On the question of the relationship between art and religion, there is an interesting detail in this passage in the comment that obsession "writes novels and moves mountains" (*G* 161).

51. Compare this with Rushdie's explanation of why he does not like *Grimus*: "I don't hear my voice in *Grimus*," in "Interview with Salman Rushdie," by Kumkum Sangari, *The Book Review* 8.5 (March-April 1984): 253.

52. "Is Nothing Sacred?" The Herbert Read Memorial Lecture, Feb 6, 1990, read by Harold Pinter, published in *Granta* 31 (Spring 1990): 99-111; quoted from the reprint in *Imaginary Homelands: Essays and Criticism 1981-1991* (London: Granta Books, 1991) 429.

53. Story-telling is crucial here, although the novel form is emphasised by Rushdie in "Is Nothing Sacred?" where he proposes "the novel as the crucial art form of [...] the post-modern age," in *Imaginary Homelands* 424. While Rushdie himself is no poet (having so far only two poems to his credit), there are also important references to poetry in many of his books: there is Virgil in *Grimus*, Omar Khayyam Shakil in *Shame*, Jumpy Joshi and Baal as well as Bhupen Gandhi in *The Satanic Verses*. (The last three poets are important figures of resistance to existing authorities.) There is also a reference in Grimus to "a tradition of scientist-poets" (*G* 75). On the reverence accorded poets in India and Pakistan, Rushdie comments that "I did not think I had ever seen a people, even in India and Pakistan where poets were revered, who

valued poetry as much as the Nicaraguans," *Jaguar Smile: A Nicaraguan Journey* (New York: Penguin, 1988; first published by Pan Books, 1987) 40.

54. Parameswaran, "New Dimensions" 58.
55. Afzal-Khan 146.
56. This passage gave the inaugurating line—"Fictions where a man could live"—for my study *Fictions to Live In: Narration as an Argument for Fiction in Salman Rushdie's Novels* (Frankfurt/M: Peter Lang, 1998).
57. That the Gorfs would not do anything like this is interesting. One could ask whether this is an occasion of the scholastic problem, "is the omnipotent God able to create so large a stone that he cannot lift it," or whether it refers to the Creator/colonialist who has left the creation/colony to solve its own problems, without intervening.

Works Cited

Afzal-Khan, Fawzia. "Post-modernist Strategies of Liberation in the Works of Salman Rushdie: The Subject/Object Dialectic and Manichean Imperialism." *Journal of South Asian Literature* 23.1 (Winter/Spring 1987): 137-45.

Aji, Aron R. "All Names Mean Something: Salman Rushdie's *Haroun* and the Legacy of Islam." *Contemporary Literature* 36.1 (Spring 1995): 103-29.

Aristophanes. *Five Comedies of Aristophanes: The Birds, The Frogs, The Clouds, The Wasps, Lysistrata.* Trans. Benjamin Bickley Rogers. New York: Doubleday, 1955.

Attar, Farid ud-Din. *The Conference of the Birds.* Trans. Afkham Darbandi and Dick Davis. Harmondsworth: Penguin, 1984. Orig. *Manteq at-Tair* in ca. 1177.

Barthes, Roland. "The Death of the Author." Trans. Stephen Heath. In Barthes, *Image-Music-Text.* 1977. New York: Noonday Press, 1991. 142-48. Orig. in 1968.

Brennan, Timothy. *Salman Rushdie and the Third World: Myths of the Nation.* Houndmills: Macmillan Press, 1989.

Cuddon, J.A. *The Penguin Dictionary of Literary Terms and Literary Theory.* 3rd ed. 1991. London: Penguin Books, 1992.

Cundy, Catharine. "'Rehearsing Voices': Salman Rushdie's *Grimus." The Journal of Commonwealth Literature* 27.1 (1992): 128-38. Rpt. Fletcher, *Reading Rushdie,* 45-54.

____. "Through Childhood's Window: *Haroun and the Sea of Stories.*" In Fletcher, *Reading Rushdie,* 335-41.

de Man, Paul. "The Rhetoric of Temporality." In de Man, *Blindness and Insight: Essays in the Rhetoric of Contemporary Criticism.* 2nd rev. ed. 1983. London: Methuen, 1986. 187-228. Orig. in 1969.

Dhawan, R.K. "History and the Novel: Some Significant Statements in *Imaginary Homelands.*" In Taneja and Dhawan, *The Novels of Salman Rushdie.* 255-67.

Durix, Jean-Pierre. "Gardener of Stories: Salman Rushdie's *Haroun and the Sea of Stories.*" *The Journal of Commonwealth Literature* (1991): 114-22. Rpt. Fletcher, *Reading Rushdie,* 343-51.

Van Dyke, Carolynn. *The Fiction of Truth: Structures of Meaning in Narrative and Dramatic Allegory.* Ithaca and London: Cornell UP, 1985.

Ferdowsi. *The Epic of Kings: Shah-Nama, the National Epic of Persia by Ferdowsi.* Trans. Reuben Levy. London: Routledge and Kegan Paul, 1967.

Fischer, Mary Ellen. *Nicolae Ceaucescu: A Study in Political Leadership.* Boulder and London: Lynne Rienner Publishers, 1989.

Flower, Dean. "Not Waving but Drowning." *The Hudson Review* 44.2 (Summer 1991): 317-25.

Ford, Ford Madox. *The Good Soldier: A Tale of Passion.* 1946. Harmondsworth: Penguin, 1985. Orig. in 1915.

Gilberg, Trond. *Nationalism and Communism in Romania: The Rise and Fall of Ceausescu's Personal Dictatorship.* Boulder and Oxford: Westview Press, 1990.

Al-Hallaj, Al-Husayn ibn Mansur. "Al-Hallaj: the Crucifixion of a Mystic." Trans. Eric Schroeder. In *Anthology of Islamic Literature: from the Rise of Islam to Modern Times.* Ed. James Kritzeck. 1964. New York: New American Library, 1975. 96-104.

Harrison, James. *Salman Rushdie.* Twayne English authors series: 488. New York: Twayne Publishers, 1992.

Hesse, Herman. *The Glass Bead Game.* Trans. Richard and Clara Winston. 1960. Harmondsworth: Penguin, 1981. Orig. *Das Glasperlenspiel* in 1943.

Hume, Kathryn. "Taking a Stand while Lacking a Center: Rushdie's Postmodern Politics." *Philological Quarterly* 74.2 (Spring 1995): 209-30.

Jackson, Rosemary. *Fantasy: The Literature of Subversion.* 1981. London and New York: Methuen, 1986.

Johansen, Ib. "The Flight from the Enchanter: Reflections on Salman Rushdie's *Grimus.*" *Kunapipi* 7.1 (1985): 20-32. Rpt. Fletcher. *Reading Rushdie.* 23-34.

Kiernan, Suzanne. "A Language for Oppression." *The Age Monthly Review* 1.9 (Sept. 1982): 7-9.

Kuortti, Joel. *Fictions to Live In: Narration as an Argument for Fiction in Salman Rushdie's Novels.* Frankfurt/M: Peter Lang, 1998. Wien: Peter Lang, 1998.

____. "*Shame*: Necklace of Stories." In *Postcolonialism and Cultural Resistance,* ed. Jopi Nyman and John A. Stotesbury. Joensuu: University of Joensuu, Faculty of Humanities, 1999. 117-22.

Madsen, Deborah L. *Rereading Allegory: a Narrative Approach to Genre.* New York: St. Martin's Press, 1995.

Memmi, Albert. *The Colonizer and the Colonized.* Trans. Howard Greenfeld. 1965. London: Souvenir Press, 1974. Orig. *Portrait du Colonisé précédé du Portrait du Colonisateur* in 1957.

Murti, K.V.S. "Bacchus and Buddha: Salman Rushdie and R.K. Narayan." *The Commonwealth Review* 1.2 (1990). 157-68. Rpt. Taneja and Dhawan, *The Novels of Salman Rushdie.* 157-68.

Newton, K.M. *Interpreting the Text: A Critical Introduction to the Theory and Practice of Literary Interpretation.* New York: Harvester Wheatsheaf, 1990.

Nicholls, Peter, ed. *The Encyclopedia of Science Fiction.* London: Granada, 1979. 510. Rev. ed. Ed. John Chute and Peter Nicholls. London: Orbit, 1993. 1035.

Parameswaran, Uma. "Handcuffed to History: Salman Rushdie's Art." *ARIEL* 14.4 (Oct. 1983): 34-45. Rpt. Parameswaran. *The Perforated Sheet.* 1-11.

____. "New Dimensions Courtesy of the Whirling Demons: Word-Play in *Grimus.*" In Parameswaran, *The Perforated Sheet.* 55-66. Rpt. Fletcher, *Reading Rushdie.* 35-44.

____. *The Perforated Sheet: Essays on Salman Rushdie's Art.* New Delhi: Affiliated East-West Press, 1988.

____. "New Dimensions Courtesy of the Whirling Demons: Word-Play in *Grimus.*" Parameswaran. *The Perforated Sheet.* 55-66. Rpt. Fletcher. *Reading Rushdie.* 35-44.

____. "Salman Rushdie in Indo-English Literature." *The Journal of Indian Writing in English* 12.2 (July 1984). 15-25. Rpt. Parameswaran, *The Perforated Sheet.* 12-20.

Parrinder, Patrick. *Science Fiction: Criticism and Teaching.* London and New York: Methuen, 1980.

Powers, Stephen, David J. Rothman and Stanley Rothman. *Hollywood's America: Social and Political Themes in Motion Pictures.* Boulder, CO and Oxford: Westview Press, 1996.

Rajkowska, Barbara Ozieblo. "The Reality of the Alien: an Exploration of Salman Rushdie's Novels." *Revista canaria de estudios ingleses* 13/14 (April 1987): 9-27.

Rao, M. Madhusudhana. *Salman Rushdie's Fiction: A Study* (*Satanic Verses Excluded*). New Delhi: Sterling Publishers, 1992.

Rushdie, Salman. "CA Interview." By Jean W. Ross in 1982. *Contemporary Authors,* Vol. 111. Ed. Hal May. Detroit, MI: Gale Research Co., 1984. 414-17.

____. *Grimus.* London: Paladin, 1989. First published by Victor Gollancz, 1975.

____. *Haroun and the Sea of Stories.* 1990. London: Granta Books, 1991.

____. "Interview with Salman Rushdie." By Peter Craven, Michael Heyward and Penny Hueston. *Scripsi* 3.2-3 (Aug. 1985): 106-26.

____. "Interview with Salman Rushdie." By Kumkum Sangari. *The Book Review* 8.5 (March-April 1984): 247-53.

____. "Interview with Salman Rushdie." By Jéan-Pierre Durix, Kirsten Holst Petersen, Jacqueline Bardolph, Anna Rutherford and Carole Durix. *Kunapipi* 4.2 (1982): 17-26.

____. "Is Nothing Sacred?" The Herbert Read Memorial Lecture, Feb 6, 1990, read by Harold Pinter, published in *Granta* 31 (Spring 1990): 99-111; in Rushdie. *Imaginary Homelands: Essays and Criticism 1981-1991*. London: Granta Books, 1991. 415-29.

____. *The Jaguar Smile: A Nicaraguan Journey*. New York: Penguin, 1988. First published by Pan Books, 1987.

____. *Midnight's Children*. London: Picador, 1982. First published by Jonathan Cape, 1981.

____. *The Moor's Last Sigh*. New York: Vintage Books, 1997. First published by Jonathan Cape, 1995.

____. "Playboy Interview: Salman Rushdie." By David Sheff. *Playboy* 43.4 (April 1996): 49-62 and 165.

____. *The Satanic Verses*. London: Viking/Penguin, 1988.

____. *Shame*. London: Picador, 1984. First published by Jonathan Cape, 1983.

____. *The Wizard of Oz: A Short Text about Magic*. 1992. London: British Film Institute, 1993.

Salunkhe, Vishnu B. "Salman Rushdie and India." In Taneja and Dhawan, *The Novels of Salman Rushdie*. 185-94.

Shakespeare, William. *Romeo and Juliet*. In *The Riverside Shakespeare*. Boston: Houghton Mifflin, 1974.

Singh, Sushila. "*Haroun and the Sea of Stories*: Rushdie's Flight to Freedom." In Taneja and Dhawan. *The Novels of Salman Rushdie*. 209-16.

Smith, Colin. "The Unbearable Lightness of Salman Rushdie." *The New Literatures in English*. Vol. 1. Ed. Dieter Riemenschneider. Critical Approaches to the New Literatures in English. Essen: Blaue Eule, 1989. 104-15.

Stevenson, Randall. *Modernist Fiction: An Introduction*. Hemel Hempstead: Harvester Wheatsheaf, 1992.

Syed, Mujeebuddin. "Warped Mythologies: Salman Rushdie's *Grimus*." *ARIEL* 25.4 (Oct. 1994): 135-51.

Taneja, G.R. "Facts of Fiction: *Haroun and the Sea of Stories*." In Taneja and Dhawan. *The Novels of Salman Rushdie*. 197-208.

Taneja, G.R. and Rajinder Kumar Dhawan, eds. *The Novels of Salman Rushdie*. New Delhi: Indian Society for Commonwealth Studies, 1992.

Thwaite, Anthony. "Games People Play." *The Observer* 9 Feb. 1975: 28.

3

THE (UN)MAKING OF SALADIN CHAMCHA: RUSHDIE'S SUBVERSION OF THE *BILDUNGSROMAN*[1]

SHAUL BASSI

> "I am Born." This is the title of the first chapter of *David Copperfield,* and in a good four of our six novels *Tom Jones, Jane Eyre, David Copperfield* and *Great Expectations,* the heroes' childhood, if not always their birth, is granted an emblematic and lasting prominence. It is the first of the many differences between the English "Bildungsroman" and the continental one (Moretti 1987: 182).

> It is significant that many of the postcolonial novels that chart [the] process of *Bildung* for the individual self and the nation [...] begin with a death rather than with the more conventional birth of the *Bildungsroman* protagonist (Lima 1993: 441).

"To be born again [...] first you have to die": death and birth traverse each other in the opening of Salman Rushdie's *The Satanic Verses,* as the two protagonists Saladin Chamcha and Gibreel Farishta fall from the sky after the explosion of their airplane and land unharmed on the shores of Britain.

The encounter between postcolonial authors and *Bildungsroman* was almost inevitable: no genre could better serve the purpose of narrating complex hybrid cultural legacies and negotiate within them new forms of identity (Lima 1993: 433, 440). And yet this encounter was vitiated by an original sin: in the classical Victorian novel of apprenticeship, the success of the European hero depended on the riches accumulated in the colonies at the expense of the natives (Said 1994: 73ff).

The death to which Maria Helena Lima refers in our opening quotation depends on the state of impoverishment and devastation in which the "triumph" of the West has left the colonies. This denounces the radical difference between European and postcolonial space. The former is a space of possibilities (of which the colonies are an ideal extension), where the hero, albeit facing numerous vicissitudes, is free to construct his fortunes and his self. In the postcolonial space, deprived of its resources and left in dire social and political conditions, one can optimistically aim at reconstructing.

The Rushdian incipit, with its fantastic non-death which turns into a rebirth, seems to combine the English and postcolonial models. Pursuing this hypothesis, I would like to read the story of Saladin Chamcha as a dialogue between the writer and the tradition of *Bildungsroman*, on the basis of the precious typological and morphological observations on the English novel of education by Franco Moretti in his seminal study of this genre (1987; 1999).

In the revised Italian edition, Moretti responds to those who have criticized the euro- and male-centrism of his analysis by simply admitting to the limits of his own competence and, more crucially, drawing precise historical and geographical boundaries for the *Bildunsgroman* as he intends it. A genre which he considers quintessentially European and "declared impossible" by the outbreak of World War I (1999: xiv-xv, 257). I argue that thanks to the postcolonial time-lag of modernity theorized by Homi Bhabha (1994: 246-56), Chamcha starts as a belated follower of the Western promises of the *Bildungsroman* and ultimately fails because his world is no longer that of Dickens or Thackeray.

Let us begin by summarizing the facts of Saladin's life before his fatal fall in the linear form of the Victorian novel, piecing them together from the narrator's flashbacks.

Salahuddin Chamchawala was born in Bombay around the middle of the 20th century, together with Independent

India. His childhood is marked by his domineering father, a rich nationalistic philantrope who exerts a rigid control over his son, as when he confiscates some money that the boy had found by chance or when he catches him, quite literally, with his pants down.

Salahuddin then develops an intense hatred for his environment and dreams of escaping to London, which in his imagination is the capital of riches and the antithesis of the squalid and vulgar Bombay. One day the thirteen-year old boy is sexually harassed, and the feeling of shame which prevents him for disclosing the event projects him even closer to his longed-for destination.

The dream comes true when the father offers him to educate in England. He escorts him to London and unexpectedly returns him the subtracted money, but leaves him to support himself on his own. The impact with British school takes the shape of a kipper, a mysterious fish that will keep Salahuddin occupied for ninety minutes, without any of his new schoolmates coming to his aid.

Despite everything, his determination brings him over high school and college, and, save some sporadic homecomings that simply allow his frail mother to witness disconcertedly the transformation of his enstranged son, he becomes a true Englishman. Eventually Salahuddin Chamchawala truns into Saladin Chamcha, adopting a name which is more compatible with English phonetics. To put down deeper roots in his new homeland, he also takes the final, logical step: Saladin marries an English woman, Pamela Lovelace.

Saladin's inveterate anglophilia, far from being a simple childish eccentricity, is the late fruit of that project of social engineering devised by the British in 19th-century India. To mediate between them and the masses, otherwise not controllable, they aimed at creating a class of people who were supposed to be, in the famous words of T. B. Macaulay, "Indian in blood and colour, but English in taste, in opinions, in morals, and in intellect" (cit. in Kalinnikova 1982: 2). Saladin's name is itself significant, as Rushdie explained in an interview a long time before the publication of the novel:

> Colloquially, a *Chamcha* is a person who sucks up to a powerful people, a yes-man, a sycophant. The British Empire would not have lasted a week without such collaborators among its colonized peoples. You could say the Raj grew fat by being spoon-fed. Well, as we all know, the spoon-feeding ended, or at least ceased to be sufficiently nourishing, and the British left. But the effects of the Empire linger on (1982: 8).

The England admired by Saladin is surely a mythical England, an idealized image of the "mother land" created *ad hoc* for the subjects of the Empire. It has been amply demonstrated how English literature was used to transmit to the Indian higher classes the main Western and Christian values, where the teaching of the Bible would have offended the religiousness of Hindus and Muslims. It is not by chance that its first academic appearance took place in Bengal, before it was introduced at London University College (Viswanathan 1989; Rajan 1992; Chandra 1992).

It is at this point that I would like to venture the hypothesis that Saladin may have been a reader of English novels of education, and that he may have tried to model his life on their exemplary plots: he leaves the paternal house, suffers a stern education made harsher by financial hardship, but finally finds an English job and takes an English wife.

If things went like in Dickens's books (on his presence in *The Satanic Verses* see Hennard Dutheil 1999: 63-79), the wedding would sanction the accomplishment of the education, it would constitute that "'pact' between the individual and the world," that "metaphor for the social contract" that guaranteed to the Victorian hero familial and economic stability (Moretti 1987: 22). Events for Saladin, however, take a very different route. The bankrupt of the marriage represents a check of the project of *Bildung* that Saladin had been cultivating since adolescence and his acting and dubbing career follows the ups and downs of show business.

Many postcolonial narratives relate how many immigrants become disillusioned with their European experience and return home to rediscover their native culture. Saladin seeks relief from his existential crisis in a trip to Bombay, where a group of friends and an extemporaneous lover try to win him back to his Indianness. But this temporary homecoming solves none of his personal dilemmas: the Great Socialization which the *Bildungsroman* promises and promotes (Moretti 1999: 258) is no more possible in India than in Britain. Saladin heads back to London, embarking on the plane which will be blown up by Kashmir separatists.

Upon his landing to Britain after the fall, Saladin is arrested as illegal alien and brutalized by the police. He then undergoes a strange metamorphosis that turns him into a goatish monster and causes his internment in a sinister clinic for "mutants." After taking part in a collective getaway, he finds shelter in the attic of a London café, run by a family of Asian immigrants. Onlyeth their help and at the end of a long interior travail will Saladin be able to repossess his human semblance.

The main thesis of this essay is that in this postlapsarian stage, Rushdie deconstructs Chamcha's English "apprenticeship" manipulating and deforming many of the founding elements of the classical novel of formation, demonstrating how and why they cannot apply to the postcolonial individual.

This may sound as an anachronistic operation, since the 19th-century *Bildungsroman* had already been reconfigured by successive traditions (suffice to think of early 20th-century avant garde). The crucial difference lies in the fact that the previous models of *anti-bildungsroman* expressed a lack of confidence in the idea of progress inherent in the original. So their (anti-)heroes traversed life without learning, without advancing, remaining at the point where they had started, which still was a relatively privileged social position (Moretti 1999: 257ff). This possibility is not available to the postcolonial subject, for reasons that a detailed list of Rushdie's deformations will clearly show.

Youth. Youth is the age that the *Bildungsroman* elects to key moment of life and "symbolic form of modernity" (Moretti 1999). For Saladin, youth turns out to be the age of utopias and false promises when he endorses values that will miserably fall apart when he is forty.

History. The great historical events, from the French Revolution to the 1848 uprisings, were always marginal in the plots of novels of education, exorcized or eluded to grant to the hero safe unlimited space for his (self-)exploration (Moretti 1987: 12). On the contrary, history tracks Saladin down: the terrorist attack by the Kashmir separatists sucks him in the whirlpool of Indian politics and starts his misadventures. The inextricable link between individual and History is at the centre of Rushdian narrative since *Midnight's Children,* whose protagonist is born "handcuffed" to History. A metaphor which suggests the violent enforcement of the law which we will presently discuss.

Mobility. The classical European hero was mobile by definition and his movements took the form of "travel and adventure, wondering and getting lost, 'Boheme' and 'parvenir'" (Moretti 1987: 4), in any event a necessary and often desired exploration. Postcolonial mobility means migration, exile, escape from war and persecution. Saladin falls from the sky, is transported in a prison-van, is interned in a special clinic, is involved in a getaway, and finally secluded in a small café. As much as the classic hero is master of his own destiny, Saladin remains wholly subordinate to it until he breaks the spell of his idealized *Bildung*.

The Law. Moretti has observed that the law dominates the horizon of English novels of education, which "do not simply state that everyone 'has a right' to justice; they mantain instead that everyone, in fact, *receives* justice" (1987: 213). The happy ending is always sanctioned by a tribunal which acknowledges the identity of the hero, his social status and usually bestows on him a substantial unexpected inheritance. The Law that manifests itself to Saladin after his landing is a brutal and violent police force that arrests, beats, jails him, and, above all, refuses to recognize him as a "citizen" because of his ethnic difference. When he tries to identify himself as the star of a popular TV show—"Don't any of you watch TV? Don't you see? I'm Maxim. Maxim Alien.'—a policeman replies: "So you are. And I am Kermit the Frog" (140).

This episode bears out the observation of Hannah Arendt, for whom the western notion of human rights depends on citizenship and does not apply to those individuals (refugees, immigrants, illegal aliens) who fall outside the parametres of the nation state and precisely for this reason would most require protection from violations (1975: 267-302).

Metamorphosis. In the English novel "conservation" seems to be the most important value and its centrality "generates an equally inevitable repugnance to change" (Moretti 1987: 8). Chamcha, whose assonance with Kafka's Samsa rings a loud intertextual bell, is subject to the most radical form of change: physical metamorphosis. He turns into a sort of satyr with horns, hooves and an embrassingly big phallus. This example of Rusdhie's often misinterpreted "magical realism" (Bassi, 1999) foregrounds the vulnerability of the body to the modern disciplinary power of the state.

The Villain. The theme of metamorphosis is connected to another distinct feature of the English novel, where "[b]etween the insipid normality of the hero, and a stable and a thoroughly classified world, no spark will ever flash" (Moretti 1987: 200). Hence the need of a *villain,* an antagonist who comes from the outside to break the social order by embodying all its negative values (Frankenstein, Dracula, Mr. Hyde, etc.). Saladin, who dreamt of being the hero, finds himself in the role of its opposite. He ends up representing the quintessential villain of the society he had idealized: devilish, bestial, lascivious, stinking, sensual—a creature which embodies all the western stereotypes of the ethnic Other. After all he has the name of an ancient foe of the West: "when the French general Gouraud entered Damascus in 1920, he proceeded immediately to the tomb of Salah al-Dîn al-Ayoubi, who had defeated the Europeans in the Third Crusade, and announced gloatingly: 'Nous revoilà, Saladin!'" (Kabbani 1986: 5).

The Narrator. The traditional Victorian narrator was heterodegetic, omniscient and lavishly offered psychological and moral judgments on his characters. He "awaited" them as a member of the society in which they were gradually integrating. The narrator of *The Satanic Verses* is somehow kin to this antecedent, at least in his self-confidence: "I know the truth, obviously. I watched the whole thing. As to omnipresence and -potence, I'm making no claims at present, but I can manage this much, I hope" (10). But for a paradox which is solely apparent, he is much less sure of his own identity as demonstrated in his first aside: "Who am I? / Who else is there?" (4); and a few pages later: "Who am I? / Let's put it this way: who has the best tunes?" To understand oneself, the narrator, seems to suggest, one has to interrogate one's relationship with others and with language.

Identity. In a way all the previous themes merge in the grand theme of identity, since the *Bildungsroman* is the story of an identity in the making. Lukacs asserts that "the novel tells of the adventure of interiority; the content of the novel is the story of the soul that goes to find itself, that seeks adventures in order to be proved and tested by them, and by proving itself, to find it own essence" (1978: 89). This definition, written as part of Lukacs's response to World War I—which for Moretti marks the end of the *Bildungsroman*—endorses the notion of an *essentialist* subject who believes in "secure authorial intention, individual autonomy, integral self-determination, and universal law" (Barney 1993: 360). A subject for whom language is an instrument to *express, describe* and *comment* the world.

Many of these assumptions are echoed by Saladin when, on the verge of his crisis, he recites to himself a lithany of his vacillating principles:

> I am a real man, he told the mirror, with a real history and a planned-out future. I am a man to whom certain things are of importance: rigour, self-discipline, reason, the pursuit of what is noble without recourse to that old crutch, God. The ideal of beauty, the possibility of exaltation, the mind. I am: a married man. But in spite of his litany, perverse thoughts insisted on visiting him (135-36).

Modernist and postmodernist literature, philosophy and psychoanalysis have deconstructed this ideal self piece by piece, and Rushdie wittily captures many of the issues of the post-structuralist critique of the subject that reached its peak in the 1980s. Man has no essence, being less a unity than a field of conflicting forces; he is never identical because it is continuously reinvented in each new horizon where he is placed; he considers himself as universal without perceiving his own social, ethnic, sexual and cultural relativity and situatedness; he is never external to the world and therefore cannot judge it objectively. His memory does not retrieve the past in a transparent and fluid manner but processes and edits it into a narrative form and his language shapes, influences and produces his perception of the world. His identity, in short, is not self-defined but interpellated by ideology and guided, if not controlled, by the various dispositives of power of society and the state.

In his first portrait of the character, Rushdie curiously weaves together the two rival conceptions of the self.

> Mr Saladin Chamcha had constructed this face with care—it had taken him several years to get it just right—and for many years now he had thought of it simply as *his own*—indeed, he had forgotten what he had looked like before it. Furthermore, he had shaped himself a voice to go with the face [...] (33).

An *invented* and *constructed* identity is impressed in Saladin's conscience as if it had always been lodged there as "true self." Later the reasons for this operation are clarified:

> A man who sets out to make himself up is taking on the Creator's role, according to one way of seeing things; he's unnatural, a blasphemer, an abomination of abominations. From another angle, you could see pathos in him, heroism in his struggle, in his willingness to risk: not all mutants survive. Or, consider him sociopolitically: most migrants learn, and can become disguises. Our own false descriptions to counter the falsehoods invented about us, concealing for reasons of security our secret selves (49).

Following another classic model such as *Tom Jones*, three women characters are made to represent three interpretations of the dilemma of identity. The English wife Pamela, chronically depressed, is incapable of thinking herself out of her identity which is static, self-referential and evokes the collective crisis of the 1960s generation. As soon as she has learned of his husband's death, she jumps in the arms of a friend, committing (unknowingly?) that adultery which was inconceivable in the English *Bildungsroman*.

At her antipodes stands Zeenat Vakil, a successful Indian doctor, a warm, positive character who attempts to reconcile Saladin with India. "Tonight [...] we cracked your shell" (56), she tells him after a night of love. Her rhetoric is that of the "true [Indian] self" around which a fictitious personality has calcified and needs to be removed.

The third woman is Mimi Mamoulian, who is a colleague of Saladin. Mimi, who is Armenian and Jewish, is the perfect migrant who has learnt to accept her own condition with irony and with no apparent conflicts. When half-jokingly she suggests that they should get married, Saladin responds: "You're Jewish.' ... 'I was brought up to have views on Jews.'" She retorts: "So I'm Jewish,' [...]. 'You're the one who's circumcised. Nobody's perfect'" (60). Saladin is obsessed by self-definition which also consists in rigidly discriminating between self and other, and the Jew is Other both for Christians and Muslims. Mimi's quip reveals to him that a sign of that alterity which he strives to keep at distance is marked on his very body. Shortly after, that feared alterity will swallow him completely turning him into a monster.

The theme of identity surfaces in the pivotal episode of the clinic for mutants, where Saladin meets the Manticore. Borges informs us that the manticore is an anthropophagous creature, with the head of a tiger and three rows of teeth (Borges-Guerrero 1966). Here such bloodthirsty animal appears as a victim of the system who can explain his metamorphosis in these terms: "'They describe us,' the other whispered solemnly. 'That's all. They have the power of description, and we succumb to the pictures they construct'" (168). In this Foucauldian nightmare, forces that transcend the individual can control him to the extent of modifying his very body and turning him into a monster. Moretti describes the rising presence of institutions in the *Bildungsroman*, which gradually erode the space of the individual (1999: 258). Here the institution encroaches the very borders of the human body in an instance of that biopolitics which has characterized the 20th century and culminated in the Nazi concentration camp (Agamben 1995).

But stressing the fact that such a process can occur only if the victim cooperates, the Manticore leaves a decisive opening for the freedom of the individual to determine his own fate.

After fleeing from the clinic, Saladin finds refuge in the Shaandaar Café, a peripheral B&B run by an immigrant family from Dhaka. This may be one of the *neutralized spaces* which, according to Moretti, are the background of education novels (1999: 258). We may say that the European dinner gives way to the Asian breakfast, as the ritual that allows the individual to find his way in life.

The father Muhamad Sufyan is a former teacher who emigrated for political reasons. He loves to quote from Darwin, Apuleius, and above all Ovid and Lucrece, with their opposing ideas on metamorphosis and identity (276). It is at once an ironical and realistic that the high culture from which the young protagonists of the *Bildungsroman* would take their intellectual nourishment, is preserved in postmodern London by an Asian teacher demoted to coffeehouse owner. Sufyan's adolescent daughters, who wear blue-jeans and speak a disarticulate slang, represent a new generation for whom ethnic and other differences are flattened in the new urban mass culture. They are not shocked by Saladin's beastly appearance: "It's just we've been thinking, know what I mean, and well it'd just be awful if you weren't, but you are, 'course you are, so that's all right," (Mishal). Brilliant [...] Magic. You know. *Extreme*" (Anahita) (258). Is this an instinctive spirit of tolerance or the endemic inability of distinguishing between simulation and reality of the MTV generation?

On the backdrop of Saladin's captivity, London is shaken by violent social and ethnic turmoils, the last aftermath of colonialism which now reverberates in the Western metropolis.

Deemed dead, betrayed by his wife, imprisoned in an animalesque body, Saladin has to reconsider his values:

> I am by nature an inward man, he said silently into the disconnected phone; I have struggled, in my fashion, to find my way towards an appreciation of high things, towards a small measure of fineness. On good days I felt it was within my grasp, somewhere within me, somewhere within. But it eluded me. I have become embroiled, in things, in the world and its messes, and I cannot resist. The grotesque has me, as before the quotidian had me, in its thrall. The sea gave me up; the land drags me down (260).

Interiority, a cardinal value in the *Bildungsroman*, turns out to be a chimera. Saladin then yields to his own condition of impure, hybrid, mutable and grotesque being: "*I am*, he accepted, *that I am*" (289). Recuperating this Biblical phrase, Rushdie also reverses the notorious words of Iago ("I am not that I am," *Othello* 1.1.64), the proto-bourgeois and proto-racist character who builds his own identity in contrast to the "barbarian" Othello.[2]

According to the philosophers Lakoff and Johnson "A large part of self-understanding is the search for appropriate personal metaphors that make sense of our lives [...]. The process of self-understanding is the continual development of new life stories for yourself" (1980: 233). More recently, Antal Borbely has offered psychoanalytical support to this view: "when individuals are able to integrate strong emotional experiences, they do so with increased recourse to metaphorical processes," which are opposed to "idiomatic, rigid analogical thinking" (1998: 930). We could paraphrase these observations by saying that Saladin initially made his identity depend analogically on the narrative and rhetorical patterns of the *Bildungsroman* and only when is he able to conceive alternative metaphors, to translate his own mind, he finds a way out of the translational state of his body and regains his human form.

Home. The traditional hero would leave his home in search of himself only to find that the "truth" was just in what he had left behind, and so he would return there. How come, then, that after having subverted the main parameters of the *Bildungsroman, The Satanic Verses* closes with the most classical homecoming and Saladin's reconciliation with his dying father?

The answer perhaps lies in the non-definitive nature of this homecoming, which does not mark the reintegration of the hero in his place of origin and the subsequent fetishization of ethnic identity. The return is an unavoidable stage because one needs to come to terms with his own roots, but Saladin does not find in Bombay any ultimate truth. After his father's death, his friend Zeeny exclaims "Let's get the hell out of here," and Saladin answers "I'm coming" (547). These are his final words in the novel.

> Writing about "literature and life" Gilles Deleuze suggests that Sanity as literature, as writing, consists in inventing an absent people which is needed. It pertains to the fabulating function to invent a people. One does not write with his memories unless he makes of them the collective origin or destination of a people to come, still buried under its betrayals and repudiations (1993: 14, my translation).

Saladin Chamcha represents a world to come, born of the death of the Empire, out of a cataclismatic clash of civilizations, a world made of cultural fragments that struggle to find a new balance in the age of globalization.

A late epigone of David Copperfield, Chamcha walks the road of the *Bildungsroman* in reverse, moving from the illusion of an autonomous and self-sufficient subjectivity to the recognition that every individual is enmeshed—even though by no means powerless—in our modern disciplinary society.

The deformation of the *Bildungsroman* by Rushdie may be another chapter of the project theorized by Homi Bhabha:

> the postcolonial translation of modernity rests in its performative, deformative structure that does not simply

> revalue the contents of a cultural tradition, or transpose value 'cross-culturally.' The cultural inheritance of slavery of colonialism [...] is to introduce another locus of inscription and intervention, another hybrid, 'inappropriate,' enunciative site (1994: 241-42).

Where Saladin would have gone after leaving his house in Bombay and where Rushdie would have gone after *The Satanic Verses* in his exploration of postcolonial identity are questions whose significance has been dramatically changed by the *fatwa* against the writer.

Notes

1. An earlier version of this essay was published in Italian as "*The Satanic Verses* come romanzo di (de)formazione," in *Anglistica e...: metodi e percorsi comparatistici nelle lingue, culture e letterature di origine europea.* Volume I: *Transiti letterari e culturali. Atti del XVIII Convegno dell'Associazione Italiana di Anglistica, Genova,* edited by Giuseppe Sertoli and Goffredo Miglietta, Edizioni Università di Trieste, Trieste, 1999.
2. Saladin's statement is followed by the word 'Submission,' which may stand for the acceptance of the new condition but is also the translation of 'Islam.' An allusion to another fundamental component of Saladin's identity which we can now only mention in passing.
3. Cfr. Lima 1993: 454. From a postcolonial perspective the house offers "an illusion of coherence and safety based on the exclusion of specific histories of oppression and resistance and on the oppression of differences even with oneself." B. Martine C. T. Mohanty, cit. in Lima, 1993: 439.

Works Cited

Agamben, Giorgio. 1995. *Homo Sacer*. Torino: Einaudi.

Arendt, Hannah. 1975. *The Origins of Totalitarianism*. London: Harcourt, Brace and Company.

Barney, Richard A. "Subjectivity, the Novel, and the *Bildung* Blocks of Critical Theory." *Genre* 26 (Winter): 359-75.

Bassi, Shaul. 1999. "Salman Rushdie's Special Effects." *Coterminous Worlds: Magical Realism and Postcolonial Anglophone Literature*. Ed. Elsa Linguanti et al. Rodopi, Amsterdam & Atlanta: Cross/Cultures. 47-60.

Bhabha, Homi K. 1994. *The Location of Culture*. London: Routledge.

Borbely, Antal F. 1998. "A Psychoanalytic Concept of Metaphor." *International Journal of Psychoanalysis* 79: 923-36.

Borges, Jorge Luis-Monica Guerrero. 1966. *Manual de zoologia fantastica.* Mexico: Fondo de Cultura Economica.

Chandra, Sudhir. 1992. *The Oppressive Present: Literature and Social Consciousness in Colonial India.* Delhi: Oxford UP.

Deleuze, Gilles. 1993. *Critique et clinique.* Paris: Minuit.

Hennard Dutheil de la Rochère, Martine. 1999. *Origin and Originality in Rushdie's Fiction.* Bern: Peter Lang.

Kabbani, Rana. 1986. *Europe's Myths of Orient.* London: Pandora Press.

Kalinnikova, Elena J. 1982. *Indian-English Literature: A Perspective.* Ghaziabad: Vimal Prakashan.

Lakoff, George-Mark Johnson. 1980. *Metaphors We Live By.* Chicago: U of Chicago P.

Lima, Maria Helena. 1993. "Decolonizing Genre: Jamaica Kincaid and the *Bildungsroman.*" *Genre* 26 (Winter): 431-59.

Lukács, György. 1978. *The Theory of the Novel.* London: Merlin Press.

Moretti, Franco. 1987. *The Way of the World: The Bildungsroman in European Culture.* London: Verso.

Moretti, Franco. 1999. *Il romanzo di formazione.* Rev. Ed. Torino: Einaudi.

Rajan, Rajeswari S. 1992. *The Lie of the Land: English Literary Studies in India.* Delhi: Oxford UP.

Rushdie, Salman. 1982. "The Empire Writes Back with a Vengeance." *The Times* 3 July.

____. 1988. *The Satanic Verses.* London: Viking.

Said, Edward. 1994. *Culture and Imperialism.* London: Vintage.

Viswanathan, Gauri. 1989. *Masks of Conquest: Literary Study and British Rule in India.* New York: Columbia UP.

4

Pessoptimism: Satire and the Menippean Grotesque in Rushdie's *Midnight's Children*

JOHN CLEMENT BALL

In October 1988, Salman Rushdie cracked a joke during a panel discussion at Toronto's International Festival of Authors. With Indira Gandhi's assassination and Zia ul-Haq's recent airplane crash presumably on his mind, Rushdie remarked that his novels had featured a select group of politicians and that most of them had subsequently died. "Many met violent ends," he said, "I've come to believe maybe this is a service I could perform" (Rushdie, Remarks). This quip by a popular and influential author—whose construction by himself and his admirers as a secular, postmodern, postcolonial, Third World, cosmopolitan migrant makes him the very model of a valorized contemporary subject—ironically makes the writer in opposition sound like a very ancient figure: the fearsome curser-satirist of Robert C. Elliott's influential study *The Power of Satire*, a person whose words were seen by "primitive" peoples to have the power to kill. Versions of such a figure populate Rushdie's novels. In *Shame*, Old Mr. Shakil and Iskander Harappa spew multi-directional oaths, calling death upon enemies local and foreign. Gibreel as angel of destruction does the same to London in *The Satanic Verses*, and Baal, the satirist of Jahilia in that novel, composes "assassination songs" against murdered men's killers (Rushdie, *Satanic* 98). But however noisy and fearsome they may be, however morally correct their objections to the status quo, such characters are inevitably compromised in Rushdie's narratives. They are variously shown to be delirious or desperate, out of synch with their times. The most concrete achievement of their ravings and curses is usually to hasten their own deaths.

Perhaps the jesting tone in which Rushdie allied himself with Elliott's "primitive" satirist was an expression of uneasy ambivalence about the role. In awe (or mock-awe) at the "success" of his previous satiric representations, Rushdie might nonetheless have had reason to wonder about the consequences of his latest satiric attack: would he hit another target, or bring on his own death? *The Satanic Verses* had just been published, a novel whose biggest target was not a politician, or even a national political culture, but an international faith. It was already controversial for being deemed officially unwelcome in India. (Rushdie had a joke for this too, that day. When asked why Rajiv Gandhi had banned the book, he said that perhaps it was because in a previous novel "I was rude to his mother" [Rushdie, Remarks]). While *The Satanic Verses* was seen by many Muslims as a violent assault on sacred tradition, the real death-blow came not from Rushdie's text but from the words of the Ayatollah Khomeini. As Srinivas Aravamudan describes the logic of what became "the Rushdie affair,"

> The satirist's arrow, once it is defined as *literal*, as well as performative—through the workings of defamation or blasphemy—is often matched with a countershaft designed to accordingly damage the originator of the verbal attack. But the respondent in this war game can choose to raise the stakes, adopting more violently persuasive means. (Aravamudan 17)

It was not Rushdie's text but the words pronouncing the *fatwa* against him that held the real power, as Aravamudan notes: "[the question] 'what can Khomeini do?' is entirely inseparable from 'what does Khomeini say?'" (Aravamudan 18). Through this rebound effect, the satiric words of Rushdie's novel provoked the most notorious literary event of our time, and the author was left hoping the Ayatollah's murderous words would be of the ineffectual sort and not cause his own "violent end."

Rushdie has always been ambivalent about satire; before and after the *fatwa* he has alternately embraced and resisted association with it. But while this paper does not attempt to steer its discussion of satire through the treacherous waters of the *Satanic Verses* debate, it does hope to demonstrate a very particular kind of ambivalence in Rushdie's earlier novel, *Midnight's Children*—one created by two countervailing types of satiric energy, and by the contrasting images of the body that most vividly show the differences between them. In all of Rushdie's novels thematic and political cross-currents are manifest as generic tensions. Many of the interpretive questions swirling around the work of an author so often labelled a "satirist" can be usefully addressed by probing beyond the illusion of transparent meaning implied by casual uses of this signifier, and asking what kinds of "satire" Rushdie's first major book actually contains.

In two famous essays Rushdie associates the writing of which he approves—and his own directly or by implication—with satire. "Outside the Whale" argues for recognition of the sociopolitical, referential contexts of all "works of art," proceeding to challenge George Orwell's "quietist option" for the writer (Rushdie, "Outside" 92, 97). Rushdie insists that writers take sides in debates and make "as big a fuss" as possible about injustices and oppressions; using "comedy, satire, deflation," the artist must not be "the servant of some beetle-browed ideology," but rather "its critic, its antagonist, its scourge" (Rushdie, "Outside" 98, 99). In *The Satanic Verses*, the satirist Baal describes his work, "[a] poet's work," in similar terms: "To name the unnamable, to point at frauds, to take sides, start arguments, shape the world and stop it from going to sleep" (*SV* 97). Satire, in such statements, becomes the very essence of responsible art. "In Good Faith," Rushdie's post-*fatwa* response to attacks on his novel, defends the artist's "freedom to challenge, even to satirize all orthodoxies, including religious orthodoxies" (Rushdie, "In Good" 396). He denies that satire is an alien, unfamiliar mode to Islamic culture that can therefore be read only literally as blasphemy, yet feels he must contextualize the "forceful, satirical" language of the character Salman the Persian as the product of Gibreel's destabilized dreaming mind (Rushdie, "In Good" 399). His own purpose in writing the book was not to offend against Islam, he says; "dispute was intended, and dissent, and even, at times, satire, and criticism of intolerance, and the like" (Rushdie, "In Good" 414). Here Rushdie appears comfortable with the idea of his writing as intentional satire (if not with its reception as such).

But if oppositional referentiality makes him a satirist, elsewhere Rushdie asserts that his work's social and political grounding makes him a realist, even a naturalist. While *Shame* may be "as black a comedy as it's possible to write," he says, it is so "not for easy satirical reasons, but for naturalistic reasons. Because that seemed to be the only way that one could come somewhere close to describing the world that was there" (Rushdie, "Midnight's" 15). Here Rushdie asserts the fidelity of his representations against a literary snobbism that might discredit "easy satirical" techniques of caricature, fanciful exaggeration, and symbolic violence. He says that only in the West are his novels seen as fantasies, and only Westerners are likely to forget that *Shame* is about a real place and real dictators. In India, he proudly observes, nobody talks about *Midnight's Children* "as a fantasy novel; they talk about it as a novel of history and politics" (Rushdie, "Midnight's" 15).

From a theoretical standpoint, none of this is very rigorous (nor should we necessarily expect it to be). Rushdie uses "realistic" and "naturalistic" loosely, as synonyms for "referential." And referentiality has always been a component of satire, easy or otherwise. It is also a popular option for fantasy, if only as the recognizable context against which the fantastic appears *as* fantastic (Todorov, *Fantastic* 25). Rushdie's ambivalence about satire transcends the "kill-or-be-killed" fate that faces the ancient curser-satirist. It can be read as an expression of a time-honoured ambiguity inherent in the protean manifestations and shadowy generic status of satire. If satire is principled dissent against specific instances of terror, injustice, authoritarian coercion, shameful behaviour, then yes, Rushdie writes it. If satire is cheap-shot caricatures, a will to power over easily conjured phantasms, then no, it is not a term he would have us use.

Rushdie's critics often link his novels with satire and the satiric. Typically, they presume a conventional definition of satire as a playfully didactic mode of referential attack using various deforming techniques of representation and rhetoric. Target-specific satiric jabs are certainly prevalent in all of Rushdie's work, yet it is hard not to agree with James Harrison when he argues that overemphasizing Rushdie's activity as a satirist may limit other interpretive possibilities. Although Harrison favours a reading of *Shame* as "a satire" with "close to a single satiric purpose—almost a single target" (Harrison 5), he argues that its predecessor cannot be adequately accounted for under that rubric. *Midnight's Children*, despite its very "angrily written" Book Three, and despite many incidental "rapier thrusts [...] en passant" towards specific Indian phenomena in Books One and Two, is not predominantly satiric in tone: "The targets for such satire are too scattered, and there is too much else going on" (Harrison 46, 48).

This view is preferable to Tariq Ali's early reading of *Midnight's Children* as "centrally an attack on clearly identifiable targets: the indigenous ruling classes in South Asia"—"a devastating political indictment" characterized by "pessimism and nihilism" (Ali 87, 93). To Ali one is compelled to respond, "Is that all? Is the novel *only* pessimistic, *only* an attack, and *only* on the ruling classes?" Ali dismisses Rushdie's own view that the book's apparent despair and pessimism are countered by its "optimistic" inscription of "the Indian talent for non-stop self-regeneration" through its teeming density of stories (Rushdie, "Imaginary" 16). However, versions of this "positive" reading are forwarded by many other critics, and a recurring debate over *Midnight's Children* concerns whether it is best seen as celebration or critique, as ultimately optimistic or pessimistic about the overarching referent behind its fictions: post-independence India.

The temptation here, as with all polarities, is to seek a middle ground. In a recent article Neil ten Kortenaar, acknowledging the novel's "paradoxical" reception "as both a celebration of India and a withering satire on the very possibility of the nation-state" (ten Kortenaar 41, 57), performs a subtle and compelling reading of its historical allegory that challenges Timothy Brennan's view of Rushdie as one of the Third World's "satirists of nationalism and dependency" (Brennan 81). Showing in detail how Rushdie's allegory literalizes conventional metaphors of national history, ten Kortenaar argues that such metaphors, once exposed as the fictions they are, can nevertheless offer a form of "truth." In his view, "Rushdie's novel explodes the notion of the nation having a stable identity and a single history, then invites a sceptical, provisional faith in the nation that it has exploded" (ten Kortenaar 41-42). It is a critique that ultimately affirms.

While ten Kortenaar's may be the most nuanced reading yet of the novel's allegorical gestures, the same critical paradox may be approached through a different generic category. Allegory is undoubtedly central to the novel's meanings, but there are many other genres, sub-genres and modes at work, including autobiography, epic, bildungsroman, picaresque, "magic realism," fantasy, and satire. As a generic medley, Rushdie's novel can be reconfigured through the lens of a subsuming and controlling genre: the Menippean satire. Not only does *Midnight's Children* fit the chief characteristics of this genre (most notably theorized by Mikhail Bakhtin), but the question of whether it optimistically celebrates or satirically negates the nation can be seen as a function of a generic tension between Menippean satire and a more conventional "negative" satire involving referential attack. That tension, revealed in large part through contrasting images of the grotesque body, results in an ambivalent, at times conflicted vision of national history best captured in a neologism Rushdie once borrowed from Edward Said (who in turn borrowed it from the Palestinian novelist Emile Habiby): "pessoptimism" (Rushdie, "On Palestinian" 168; Said 26).

Midnight's Children exemplifies many features of Menippean satire (or "menippea") as discussed by Bakhtin. When Saleem narrates his familial and personal histories, he aspires to "encapsulate the whole of reality" (*MC* 75)—the multiplicitous reality of the Indian subcontinent that he claims to contain within him and to reflect metaphorically through his life. He fears absurdity, and seeks the meaning and purpose of his life history as well as, by extension, his nation's. Likewise, Bakhtin's Menippean satire, also called "encyclopedic satire" (Payne 5), is characterized by "an extraordinary philosophical universalism and a capacity to contemplate the world on the broadest possible scale. The menippea is the genre of 'ultimate questions'" (Bakhtin, *Problems* 115). It deals with topical issues, addressing the ideologies of the day, and arises in periods of social change, "when national legend was already in decay, [...] in an epoch of intense struggle among numerous and heterogeneous religious and philosophical schools and movements" (Bakhtin 119). Rushdie's 63-year narrative begins in 1915, the year of Mohandas Gandhi's return from South Africa to join nationalist agitation, and ends in 1978, shortly after the end of Indira Gandhi's Emergency. Its chronological centrepoint and thematic focus is the moment of independence in 1947, when an imposed and hierarchical imperial order gave way to a postcolonial democratic self-rule. Menippean satire is a "utopian" genre (Bakhtin 118) and Rushdie captures the utopian spirit of freedom, optimism, and newness of the transitional period through images of celebratory crowds, of Saleem's birth and growth and adoration by his family, and also through an exuberant, transgressive narrative style reflective of the multiplicitous energies of carnival.

Menippean satire in Bakhtin's account is based on his theory of "carnival" as a liberating, subversive challenge to the political status quo. Carnival (as social event and transcendent principle) represents a utopian transgression of ossified hierarchies; its literary manifestation, the Menippean satire, is thus a positive, future-oriented genre in which pluralism and festive laughter represent signs of renewal, hope, and incipient democracy. Rushdie establishes such principles as working norms in portraying newly independent India's proliferating possibilities. Bakhtin's privileging of discovery over certitude, participation over detachment, unstable "becoming" and transformation over official authority's stasis and negation are echoed by Rushdie's own preferences. The colourful "carnivalization of speech" (Bakhtin, *Rabelais* 426) that Saleem's polyphonic medley of discourses and languages achieves makes his monologue a "microdialogue," which Bakhtin sees as possible when a voice incorporates a multiplicity of mutually conflicting and interrupting voices (Bakhtin, *Problems* 75). Indeed, embedded genres and a mixed style are key features of Menippean satire. Saleem's physical, spiritual, and mental mutability establishes identity and character as process. Like the heroes of the Dostoevsky novels that are Bakhtin's privileged specimens of post-Rabelaisian Menippean satire, Saleem's richness as a character is a direct function of the fact that he "never coincides with himself" (Bakhtin, *Problems* 59). For if, as Saleem constructs his identity, "I am the sum total of everything that went before me, of all I have been seen done, of everything done-to-me [...] everyone everything whose being-in-the-world affected was affected by mine" (*MC* 370), then that identity will be not only multiple but changing constantly. In the essays collected in *Imaginary Homelands*, Rushdie regularly voices his approval of such Bakhtin-friendly concepts as hybridity, pluralism, impurity, transformation, and newness. He prefers questions to answers, and opposes absolutism in favour of provisional, indeterminate truths. He insists on a social grounding and social mandate for art, and believes, like Bakhtin, that "the novel is one way of denying the official, politicians' version of truth" (Rushdie, "Imaginary" 14).

Menippean satire for Bakhtin involves "an *extraordinary freedom of plot and philosophical invention*"; it boldly uses the fantastic and extraordinary for "the provoking and testing of a philosophical idea, a discourse, a *truth*" (Bakhtin, *Problems* 114). Saleem proposes that events such as the telepathic Midnight Children's Conference have allegorical or symbolic value intimately bound to the truths he wants to confirm. In comments that seem custom-made for *Midnight's Children*, Bakhtin notes the genre's combination of

> the free fantastic, the symbolic, at times even a mystical-religious element with an extreme and (from our point of view) crude *slum naturalism*. [...] The idea here fears no

> slum, is not afraid of any of life's filth. [...] The menippea loves to play with abrupt transitions and shifts, ups and downs, rises and falls [snakes and ladders?], unexpected comings together of distant and disunited things, mésalliances of all sorts. (Bakhtin, *Problems* 115, 118).

Bakhtin also identifies abnormal psychological states—including split personality, unusual dreams, and strange passions—as characteristic of Menippean satire (Bakhtin, *Problems* 116). Saleem's dream of the Widow, his telepathy, his amnesiac "man-dog" phase, and his obsession with Jamila Singer are just a few of Rushdie's many uses of "abnormal states." The novel also features the "scandal scenes," "eccentric behaviour" and violations of norms and customs noted by Bakhtin (Bakhtin, *Problems* 117), and displays the "passion for spatial and temporal expanses" characteristic of the genre (Stam 134).

But if Menippean principles attain a normative value by their congruence with central features of *Midnight's Children*'s style, plot, characterization, and thematic concerns, as well as with statements of authorial philosophy, Rushdie also shows those valorized principles under siege by tyrannical forces of monologic authority. The darkening of tone that so many readers experience in Book Three marks a defeat—in India's political realm as well as Saleem's personal realm—of optimism and joy by the very retrograde powers that the carnival-minded Menippean satirist would wish to subvert or relegate to the past. Overcome by a reality that no longer coheres with its principles, Menippean satire gives way to a more negative, attack-oriented satire. The Menippean vision remains implicit, however, as the normative basis from which the negative satiric attack is launched.

Book Three's general shift in tone from optimism to pessimism, from hope to its absence, is actually not as great or as sudden as some critics suggest. For one thing, there is plenty of incidental satire in Books One and Two. Targets include India's class- and caste-based prejudices (through the snobbery of M.C.C. participants), war propaganda, election-day thuggery, political corruption and inefficiency, Eurocentric history-writing (in which Europeans "discovered" India [*MC* 13]), and Indian mimicry (displayed by the inhabitants of Methwold's Estate, and metaphorically conveyed in the description of businessmen turning white). These satiric jabs are certainly subordinate to the predominant themes of Saleem's and India's early years, which cluster around Menippean concepts of hope, newness, becoming, and possibility. But they do help to show that such optimism is a construct, made from a deliberately selective vision. Indeed, it comes at a great cost: in order to stress the positive excitement of "the infant state's attempts at rushing towards full-sized adulthood" (*MC* 232), Rushdie must occlude the horrors of violence and displacement experienced by millions during the Partition riots. Books One and Two do contain many episodic portrayals of anti-Menippean energies—denial, oppression, monologism. But from the standoffs between Reverend Mother and Aadam Aziz to the careerist misrepresentations of Jamila Singer, these episodes do not inspire Saleem's anger because, like the Partition riots, they do not directly harm him. They can be sent up with playful detachment, domesticated to the exuberant manipulations of Menippean satire. Until the loss of his hair tonsure and fingertip, the most significant act of direct, unasked-for imposition upon Saleem is Mary Pereira's baby-switch; this, of course, has the positive effect of giving him a family and moving him out of the slum. However, those later bodily mutilations mark the formal introduction, long before Book Three, of the darker, more negative satiric energies that will increasingly dominate the narrative. In fact, the body is a primary locus on which the novel's generic tensions are enacted.

Saleem's body functions as an extreme example of what Peter Brooks calls the discursive, textualized body. In *Body Work*, Brooks defines the body in modern literature as "a site of signification—the place for the inscription of stories—and itself a signifier, a prime agent in narrative plot and meaning" (Brooks 5-6). Saleem engages in what Brooks calls the semiotic retrieval of the body in order to make it signify, or represent, or mean (Brooks 8-22). But for Saleem as actor-protagonist *in* narrative, that body has already been "written upon," marked, scarred. To inscribe the body is to recognize the artistic dilemma inherent in the contradiction between generating meaning and discovering meaning—between writing (or speaking) the body oneself and reading (or listening to) a body already written-upon by others. Subsumed in that structural tension of writing/reading and speaking/listening are the dualities of subject/object, self/other, controller/controlled, creation/destruction, active/passive, "affirming" Menippean satire/"negative" debunking satire. The novel encourages us to evaluate all such pairings hierarchically: the first element is valorized, the second the endangering threat to it. Thus the objectifying inscription of "negative" historical events on Saleem's body (border disputes, wars, the Emergency) determines and largely limits his freedom to positively inscribe his body as a subject in history. His "buffetted" body affects the stories that can be told, as well as the manner of their telling: "faster than Scheherazade" (*MC* 11). Saleem, after all, is much more convincing as "the sort of person *to whom things have been done*" (*MC* 232) than as the central, determining influence on Indian history he sometimes claims to be, no matter how scandalously appealing the Menippean empowerments of the latter may be. Saleem's body in its grotesque aspect—an irregular body whose open apertures exist in a dynamic give-and-take with the world that increasingly favours "take" over "give"—becomes the primary site on which a normative Menippean ethos is overwhelmed by a bitter, angry satire of negation and despair.

The first step in tracing this process in detail—in explicating the complex and varying connections of grotesque body images and satiric ethos—requires the recognition of a central device in Rushdie's novel: the literalized metaphor. When the freezing of Muslim assets causes Ahmed Sinai's testicles to freeze and Sinai babies to cease issuing forth, or when Saleem as "mirror" of India literally comes to contain its multiplicity in his head, connections that in a realistic novel would remain metaphorical—enacted in language only-are turned into literal events by the freedom of magic realism, or what we might call the Menippean fantastic. Many critics have remarked on Rushdie's use of this device in the novel. Most useful for our purposes, however, is a general theory advanced by Geoffrey Galt Harpham in *On the Grotesque*. Harpham views the merging of metaphoric and literal as a property of "mythic narrative," which traverses normally separate categories such as animal and human, or animate and inanimate. "At the margin of figurative metaphor and literal myth," he writes, "lies the grotesque, both and neither, a mingling and a unity" (Harpham 53). This blending of realms has a levelling effect on modern Western hierarchies of meaning and Aristotelian logic (Harpham 54). It offers instead an infinitely inclusive field of significance that embraces contradiction—one in which "no realm of being, visible or invisible, past or present, is absolutely discontinuous with any other, but all equally accessible and mutually interdependent" (Harpham 51).

Under Harpham's rubric, the trope of the literalized metaphor can be contextualized within Rushdie's project in several ways. First, it expresses Rushdie's preference for contradiction and multiplicity instead of a totalizing, unitary truth. Second, it captures the mythic sensibility of a novel steeped in Hindu mythology, a novel that can be read as a creation myth of independent India. Third, it evokes a traditional Hindu cast of mind that makes no distinction between the divine and the human, or man and nature; all are interconnected, and all are equally real (Younger 15). As Wendy Doniger O'Flaherty notes, Hindus accept contradiction and pluralism, and reject attempts to eliminate alternative views (O'Flaherty 5-7). Fourth, if the literalized metaphor is compatible with Rushdie's worldview and with Hindu thought, it also agrees with the carnival spirit of Menippean satire, which favours contradictory conjoinings, juxtapositions, and the revolutionary interpenetration of "officially" bounded and stratified realms of human life and of literary representation. Fifth and finally, this trope translates abstract ideas into physiological conditions. Virtually all of Rushdie's literalized metaphors manifest themselves as bodily abnormalities, and thus participate in the multiplicitous indeterminacy of the grotesque. In the literalized metaphor, then, the valorized transgressive openness of Menippean satire joins forces with the valorized transgressive openness of Bakhtin's related notion of the "grotesque body."

The two concepts of Menippean satire and grotesque body are never linked in Bakhtin's work. But he clearly finds both Menippean satire and "grotesque realism" preferable to what he see as the deriding, oppositional type of satire. "The satirist whose laughter is negative," Bakhtin says, "places himself above the object of his mockery, he is opposed to it" (Bakhtin, *Rabelais* 12). Menippean satire and the grotesque are associated with a participatory, ambivalent laughter that enables both affirmation and critique (Bakhtin, *Rabelais* 11; Bakhtin, *Dialogic* 26). Both ideas are theorized in conjunction with the concepts of "carnival," "dialogism," and "ambivalence," and both involve top-to-bottom reversals of hierarchy, crude naturalism, and bodily imagery suggestive of incompleteness and becoming, and a spirit of renewal and liberation from the status quo. Bakhtin's "Menippean satire" and his "grotesque body" have enough in common to warrant yoking together in what we might call the "Menippean grotesque."

As noted above, Bakhtin locates the origins of the modern Menippean spirit in a "carnival sense of the world" (Bakhtin, *Problems* 134) associated with medieval folk culture. Carnivalesque energy represents liberation from official orders, hierarchical fixities, and prevailing truths through a celebration of change, incompleteness, and renewal. In the work of Rabelais, through which Bakhtin's theory of carnival is largely developed, the primary symbol that makes concrete the transformative potential of the carnival spirit is the grotesque body: the ingesting, defecating, urinating, fornicating body of open apertures, where the physiological self flows into and out of the world. This conception of the unfinished body "blended with the world, with animals, with objects" turns it into a version of the "cosmic" realm, "the entire material bodily world in all its elements" (Bakhtin, *Rabelais* 27).

Bakhtin's ethical view of the grotesque body as a valorized semiotic medium challenges traditional alignments of grotesque images with satiric attack. Wolfgang Kayser, for instance, sees the grotesque as having origins in "a satiric world view" (Kayser 186-87) although he takes pains to distinguish the two concepts (Kayser 37). Theorizing the grotesque as "experienced only in the act of reception" (Kayser 181) Kayser identifies the feelings it evokes variously as estrangement, alienation, confusion, disparagement, and helplessness in the face of a disintegrating order. For him, the grotesque is a glimpse of "a chaos that is both horrible and ridiculous" (Kayser 53) and it reinforces "the discrepancy between world and Self" (Kayser 146-47). Bakhtin, for whom a disintegrating order is cause for joy, explicitly challenges Kayser for stressing the negative, the alien, and the terrifying at the expense of what Bakhtin sees as a positive counterpart:

> The existing world suddenly becomes alien (to use Kayser's terminology) precisely because there is the potentiality of a friendly world, of the golden age, of carnival truth. Man returns unto himself. The world is destroyed so that it may be regenerated and renewed. While dying it gives birth. (Bakhtin, *Rabelais* 48)

This rhapsodic view of the grotesque's liberating, revolutionary, democratizing potential is at the heart of Bakhtin's theory. That power and potential are a function of the carnivalesque and of the grotesque body's unfinished nature and unbounded interaction with the world. Images of what Bakhtin calls "the material bodily lower stratum"—with its open orifices producing urine, excrement, and reproductive fluids—may in one sense be associated with debasement: for Bakhtin "debasement is the fundamental artistic principle of grotesque realism; all that is sacred and exalted is rethought on the level of the material bodily stratum or else combined and mixed with its images" (Bakhtin, *Rabelais* 370-71). But these images are also ambivalent, associated in various ways with fertility, renewal, and regeneration. The grotesque can therefore serve traditional satiric purposes of attacking established pieties or stratifications of power. Bakhtin's emphasis, however, is on the constructive changes and "progress" (Bakhtin, *Rabelais* 406) that such an attack can inaugurate, rather than on the deconstructive, leveling effect of the attack itself. This orientation towards the optimistic over the pessimistic, the transformative over the critical, marks Bakhtin's greatest departure from other theorists.

Inscriptions of idea on the body in *Midnight's Children*—whether literalized or simply metaphoric—are normatively offered as positive, enabling events. Saleem's first self-description is as a "swallower of lives" who has "[c]onsumed multitudes" (*MC* 11); he says, "To understand just one life, you have to swallow the world" (*MC* 108). The individual gives way to the crowd, and for Rushdie this can be a good thing with enormous potential, just as Bakhtin's grotesque, unfinished body fulfills itself when it "swallows the world and is itself swallowed by the world" (Bakhtin, *Rabelais* 317). For Bakhtin, the important parts of the grotesque body are the open cavities, orifices, and apertures where "the confines between bodies and between the body and the world are overcome; there is an interchange and an interorientation" (Bakhtin, *Rabelais* 317). In *Midnight's Children* the most important apertures are the nose and the genitals. Aadam Aziz's nose, described in the novel as "the place where the outside world meets the world inside you" (*MC* 19), is said to have "dynasties waiting inside it" (*MC* 15), thus affiliating itself with the motifs of intermingling, fertility, and regeneration that Bakhtin associates with bodily orifices and protruberances. Saleem's "mighty cucumber of a nose" (*MC* 152) leaks into the world in the early years when he seems to have the greatest power and stature in his world; these are also the years when India as a new nation inspires the greatest optimism. But after the accident in the washing-chest, Saleem's nose becomes conduit for a greater form of access to and interaction with the world through his telepathic mind. It becomes a channel of communication, which Bakhtin also sees orifices and protuberances as representing (Stam 163). In this mode, the nose offers great hope and potential, but for the idealistic Saleem the results of his telepathic activities are as disappointing as the political events with which they overlap. When the nose is later surgically drained the effect is a disconnection from the multiple voices of community. The drainage is described through images of absence, isolation, and infertility: "A connection broken (for ever). Can't hear anything (nothing there to hear). [paragraph break] Silence, like a desert" (*MC* 295). The most important subsequent use to which his nose's interactive capacities are put is the aiding and abetting of death in the 1971 war. Increasingly over the length of the novel, the interaction between body and world through the nose is associated less with possibility and achievement and more with futility and ignoble deeds.

The nose is only one location for the novel's important imagery of leaking or dripping. In other instances, the images are also normatively positive. When Saleem says that "[t]hings—even people—have a way of leaking into each other [...] like flavours when you cook" (*MC* 39), he sees this as not merely inevitable but good. Leaking leads to transformation, creation, newness—to a productive impurity. And the fact that "the past has dripped into me" (*MC* 39) allows Saleem to perform the creative act of narration. But there are many negative, or at best ambivalent, uses of this imagery. The young Saleem's enormous dripping nose may be a metaphor of growth, potency, and potential, but "Toxy Catrack, of the outsize head and dribbling mouth" is an image of isolated imbecility (*MC* 129). And any positive associations attendant on baby Saleem's "heroic programme of self-enlargement" by draining successive women's breasts is qualified by corollary associations with greed, excess, unnaturalness, and the sterility of life-giving bodily organs rendered "dried-out as a desert after only a fortnight" (*MC* 124).

Examples abound. When the Rani of Cooch Naheen turns white, her disease leaks into history and infects businessmen after independence. Saleem's later speculation that his lust for meaning and centrality leaked into Indira Gandhi has clearly negative connotations: the leakage has produced the demagogic, multiplicity-denying slogan "India is Indira and Indira is India" for the post-Emergency election campaign (406). In a particularly negative use of the leak image, Saleem tells us that "children are the vessels into which adults pour their poison, and it was the poison of grown-ups which did for us" (*MC* 249). The M.C.C. fails because the children begin replicating the poison of their parents' prejudices, and can no longer collaborate. Saleem's cousin Zafar receives a heavy dose of adult poison after leaking urine into his bedclothes: his father hurls abuses ("Pimp! Woman! [...] Coward! Homosexual! Hindu!" [*MC* 281]). Later, Zafar's fiancée discovers his leakage and responds by willfully obstructing her own-the menstrual flow-so that she can put off becoming an adult and avoid marrying him. When Aunt Alia impregnates her cooking with negative emotions as a means of bitter revenge, the emotions leak into the members of Saleem's family who consume "the birianis of dissension and the nargisi koftas of discord" (*MC* 320). The effect is to drain the family of strength, sense, competence, coherence, love, and hope.

Saleem himself goes through a series of drainings, beginning with the loss of his finger. As noted above, this event marks the first step in the darkening, more pessimistic tone that finds its most intense expression in Book Three. The finger-mutilation is described by Saleem in apocalyptic terms that clearly challenge the Bakhtinian vision of the unbounded body as emblem of positive, regenerating flow between realms. In fact, Saleem takes pains to separate the non-material intermingling of *identities* from any material affront to the body's boundaries:

> O eternal opposition of inside and outside! Because a human being, inside himself, is anything but a whole, anything but homogeneous; all kinds of everywhichthing are jumbled up inside him, and he is one person one minute and another the next. The body, on the other hand, is homogeneous as anything. Indivisible, a one-piece suit, a sacred temple, if you will. It is important to preserve this wholeness. But the loss of my finger [...] has undone all that. Thus we enter into a state of affairs which is nothing short of revolutionary; and its effect on history is bound to be pretty damn startling. Uncork the body, and God knows what you permit to come tumbling out. Suddenly you are forever other than you were; and the

world becomes such that parents can cease to be parents, and love can turn to hate. (*MC* 230-31)

A finger, of course, is not one of Bakhtin's orifices of interaction between the body's internal and external spheres. The unnatural, externally imposed flowing of blood from a finger is a different order of event from a dripping nose or feeding breast; hence Saleem's dire tone. And the novel's instances of leaking and draining are in general increasingly imposed, increasingly the outcome of external assault on the body, distinct from the normal flow of orifices. At the end of his life Saleem's body, "buffeted by too much history," begins unnaturally to crack and crumble as a result of being "subjected to drainage above and drainage below" (*MC* 38). The drainages above (of Saleem's nose) and below (of his testicles) are both violent, inflicted processes that prevent further natural drainings (of snot and sperm). In some instances, then, "drainage" means the natural transgressions of the body's limits through the emissions of apertures associated in Bakhtin's system with abundant excess, new life, hope, and Menippean satire. In others, "drainage" means imposed transgressions of the bounded body and is associated with monologic tyranny and "negative" satire; the sterilization of the midnight children as "the draining-out of hope" during Emergency rule (*MC* 421) is the novel's central satiric moment.

Depending on contexts, then, images of the grotesque body draining into the world may have either positive or negative thematic value. In the first case they serve a Menippean vision of renewal and progress, referentially directed towards the qualities of Indian society that Rushdie valorizes: pluralism, democracy, hybridity, change. In the second case they serve an angry satiric attack on forces in modern India and Pakistan that deny those principles: fundamentalism, despotism, "purity," stasis. In both cases the satiric method and philosophy match the perceived primary qualities of the referents. The imagery is ambivalent, but not in Bakhtin's sense, which posits the positive associations (birth, community, renewal) as accompanying and ultimately triumphing over the negative associations (death, degeneration, alienation) embedded in the grotesque.

Some of these "negative," target-oriented satiric images of death by draining do in fact come with corollary suggestions of fertility, but it takes on an attenuated, parodic form. Saleem's surreal vision of a field of "crops" on a field near Dacca after the 1971 war turns out to be a pyramid of dead and dying soldiers—including three childhood friends—"leaking nourishing bone-marrow into the soil" (*MC* 360). This image of wasted youth supports Rushdie's satiric indictment of the agents behind a gruesome and unnecessary war far more powerfully and relevantly than it offers mitigating optimism through images of human crops and fertilizer; if anything, these images mock the very notion of fertility. Similarly, Saleem's alter ego Shiva is said to fulfill both aspects of his divine namesake (*MC* 425): he represents destruction by helping sterilize his fellow midnight children, and procreation by "[s]trewing bastards across the map of India" (*MC* 395). But if Saleem is unequivocal in aligning the removal of the midnight children's reproductive powers with a satiric denunciation of Emergency as "the draining-out of hope" for India's future, he seems hesitant to celebrate the next generation, Shiva's offspring, as a countervailing cause for optimism. Young Aadam Sinai and his peers will be a "tougher" generation, "not looking for their fate in prophecy or the stars, but forging it in the implacable furnaces of their wills" (*MC* 431). If this description suggests an agency and effectiveness never achieved by Saleem and *his* peers, it sounds closer to the selfish, bloody-minded, totalitarian agency of Shiva than the democratic idealism of Saleem. If these children of a darker era can challenge the current tyrannical powers of negation, it will be to replace them with something equally monologic and just as scary. A sense of apprehensive awe inheres in Saleem's description of this group as "fearsomely potent kiddies, growing waiting listening, rehearsing the moment when the world would become their plaything" (*MC* 431). This image of regeneration proves no more encouraging than the Emergency's other horrific contribution to reproduction imagery: the multiply cloned versions of Sanjay Gandhi that parody and discredit the very idea of regeneration.

A number of Western literary and sociological traditions are evoked by Rushdie's satiric imagery of tyrannic bodily abuse. English satirists from Swift to Huxley have championed the rights of the individual body against state interference. In Michel Foucault's pessimistic vision, the body is always institutionally coerced and ideologically conditioned to meet the utilitarian demands of "discipline" and "power," which see a docile and subjected body as socially, politically, and economically productive (Foucault, "Body" 179-87). For Foucault, moreover, the body "manifests the stigmata of past experience"; as "the inscribed surface of events," it is necessarily "a volume in perpetual disintegration" because a body imprinted by history is a body destroyed by history (Foucault, "Nietzsche" 148). The chief targets of Rushdie's "negative" satiric anger in *Midnight's Children* are institutionalized policies and procedures of a post-independence Indian state whose short history is written upon Saleem's body, ultimately destroying it.

But for Rushdie the body is not always necessarily the controlled, acted-upon body of Foucault. His novel is equally interpretable through a more traditional view espoused by the Enlightenment thinkers Adam Smith and David Hume, who in Catherine Gallagher's words "maintained a two-millenia-old tradition of seeing the individual body as sign—both as metaphor and as source—of the health or infirmity of the larger social body" (Gallagher 83). The healthy baby Saleem reflects a generally healthy young Indian state, while the bodily deterioration of the older Saleem is both a metaphor and a literal effect of ill health in the realms of the state and the body politic. Again, as a process these changing connections accommodate both Menippean-optimistic and critical-pessimistic forms of satiric energy. Interestingly, Rushdie's novel is also compatible with the major eighteenth-century challenger to Smith's and Hume's traditional alignments of bodily and social health. Thomas Malthus argued that healthy individual bodies may reflect a healthy social body in the present, but could cause its enfeeblement in the future by proliferating themselves and causing overpopulation. The healthy body is "a profoundly ambivalent phenomenon" for Malthus because of its capacity to "destroy the very prosperity that made it fecund, replacing health and innocence with misery and vice" (Gallagher 83). Malthus's pessimism resonates strongly in the context of India's burgeoning population and the various state campaigns of suasion aimed at curbing the social body's growth through birth control. It resonates too with the uncertain promise attributed to the second generation of midnight children sired by Shiva.

Indian concepts of the body are equally ambivalent, equally multiple and contradictory, and resonate in equally complex ways with Rushdie's satiric intents. As Gavin Flood shows in a survey of views among different Indian philosophical-religious groups, the body is thought of variously as the only criterion of personal identity, as an inseparable part of unitary reality, as a place of bondage and suffering, or as a locus of liberation (Flood 47). Saleem's body is all of these at different points. And if both Saleem and Rushdie value certain kinds of impurity and intermingling, the novel also invokes and gains satiric power from a significant strain in Indian thought that privileges bodily "perfection" and purity. In orthodox Brahminism, the body is seen as "polluted through its effluents"; passion and spontaneity must be suppressed to keep it safe from possession by malevolent forces (Flood 49). Indian art typically takes the perfect yogic body as a standard of perfection; discipline and penance make the body "etherealized so that it may become a fit vehicle for the realization of moksa [release from earthly bondage]" (Mukerjee 129).

A fascinating example of bodily discipline and perfection is documented in Joseph Alter's study of Indian wrestling, *The Wrestler's Body: Identity and Ideology in North India.* Alter describes the wrestler as embodying an ideology of social duty and nationalist reform through somatic disciplines of diet, exercise, and abstinence. Wrestling bouts disregard caste strictures of touchability; by positing the body as sole criteria of identity, such bouts critique the hierarchical construction of "the

Hindu body [as] the docile subject of a pervasive political anatomy" (Alter 24, 167-97). Because Hindu philosophy sees mind and body as "intrinsically linked," not separable into a "simple duality," the wrestler's physical exercise and mental meditation are seen as one indivisible activity (Alter 92). Wrestlers take from the world a customized diet with special emphasis on milk, almonds, and ghee, and they voluntarily block what their bodies might leak into the world by abstaining from sex and masturbation. Semen is seen to contain the essence of the body and of life. It is the quintessential fluid that distills all other fluids, including blood and marrow, and becomes for wrestlers "the locus of a person's moral character and physical prowess" (Alter 129, 137). Wrestlers extend their somatic enterprise into a self-congratulatory nationalist ideology in which the wrestler represents "the perfect citizen" standing against the hedonistic bodily indulgences of the modern body politic. Reforming the body is valorized by wrestlers as civic duty and patriotic act through which individuals, one by one, can counteract social degeneration. Alter undercuts the utopian idealism of the wrestlers' ideology with gentle irony: "Eventually, it is thought, the whole country will exercise and eat its way toward a civic utopia of propriety and public service" (Alter 247); celibacy will curb population growth and "poverty will fall before an inspired work ethic fueled by the natural energy of the wrestler's good health" (Alter 248).

Saleem's individualization of national destiny is no less preposterous, and if his experience is ultimately of the mutual failure of the body and of history, then a primary sign of the bodily and societal collapse that he narrates—for him as for the wrestlers—is the draining out of semen. Enormous symbolic and satiric values are attributed to this event; "the draining-out of hope" is also the beginning of Saleem's death. In her discussion of ancient (Vedic and Post-Vedic) beliefs about bodily fluids, O'Flaherty notes that while women's loss of blood (menstruation) and milk (nursing) were symbols of creation and fertility, the male's loss of blood and semen (his equivalent of female milk) were associated with death (O'Flaherty 40-44). The flow of male fluids was to be strictly controlled; a belief that semen was stored in the head made castration a form of symbolic beheading, resulting in a loss of more general powers including the powers of the imagination (O'Flaherty 81-7). As they are for Alter's modern-day wrestlers, women were seen as potential threats to men's precious fluids (O'Flaherty 56); a particularly dominant woman could drain a man of his life (O'Flaherty 77). When Saleem is drained of semen by a dominant Widow, he begins to die and India irrevocably enters a period of darkness. Saleem musters his remaining powers to narrate his story, although even the powers of imagination that serve him so well throughout begin to fail him as his disintegration becomes acute. The draining of fluids from his body is the final literalization of the intermingling of realms and transgression of boundaries that as metaphor—as idea—proves enabling, but that as material bodily fact manifests itself increasingly as failure or destruction.

Rushdie's novel thus navigates a complicated course between the metaphoric and the literal, between inclusive Menippean optimism and exclusive "negative" satiric pessimism, and between an orthodox Indian valorizing of purity and a secular migrant preference for impurity. Any simple conclusion about his vision of the nation is therefore hard to come by. However, if we let genre be our guide—and for Bakhtin genre always has sociopolitical implications—we can see Rushdie's vision of India residing in the "pessoptimistic" divide between these countervailing forces. As his controlling image of the leak proves life-enhancingly dialogic in principle but damagingly hostile to dialogue in practice, and as Menippean energies are overwhelmed by satiric, so Rushdie celebrates the Nehruvian vision with which independent India was "born"—as a secular, pluralistic democracy—but scourges the historical assaults on that vision that culminate in virtual "death" during Indira Gandhi's Emergency.

But if the novel seems to end with the gloom and despair of the satirist in his conventional role as defeated victim, there is a sense in which the defeat is not total. Graham Pechey writes of Bakhtin that

> His theory of social hegemony is written almost exclusively from the standpoint of a perennial counter-hegemony always in the making—always having the last laugh as it were on the monoglot powers-that-be but never *winning* in any properly political sense. In other words, the true priority of heteroglossia is never realised as decisive victory: the forms of its militant self-assertion constantly imply that priority which the monoglot and centralising forces have constantly to posit themselves against. (Pechey 52)

At the end of *Midnight's Children,* if we are to locate such a counter-hegemonic challenge anywhere it must be in the novel itself. Rushdie's most Bakhtinian essay, "Is Nothing Sacred?," is a paean to the novel as a "'privileged arena' of conflicting discourses" where "we can hear *voices talking about everything in every possible way*" (Rushdie, "Is Nothing 426, 429). The novel is a privileged genre for Rushdie for the same reasons it is for Bakhtin: insofar as literary genres have the power to "transform our awareness and conceptualization of external reality" (Gardiner 22), the dialogic world of the novel involves a "decentering of the ideological world" (Bakhtin, *Dialogic* 367). Rushdie's novel, so often seen as "teeming" with India's diversity, bursting forth "the *fecundity* of the repressed" (Sangari 166), exemplifies not only these aspects of Bakhtinian "novelness" but especially of its hyper-inclusive sub-species, the Menippean satire. The cracking-up of Saleem's body, which in one sense figures the destructive assaults of ignoble history, in another sense, as Mujeebuddin Syed has shown (Syed 103), draws on a Vedic tradition to figure creation—the pouring—out in narrative of the multitudes that Saleem has swallowed over his life. Saleem's pouring-out is Rushdie's pouring-in: together they create a polyphonic novel that can claim to include a wide spectrum of the nation's diversity. By contrast with the narrower scope of the nation's rulers, and as the normative ideal on which satire is based, the Menippean novel provides a subversive alternative to official state ideology. It asks its readers to return from the final moment of imminent death to the initial moment of exuberant birth, of first principles. It is in this India, the visionary secular democracy that has always fallen short in practice, that Rushdie wants to put his faith.

Notes

1. Much of the research for this article was conducted at the University of Toronto in connection with my doctoral thesis on postcolonial satire. I am grateful for the generous support of a SSHRC doctoral fellowship, and for the helpful comments of W.J. Howard, J. Edward Chamberlin, Chelva Kanaganayakam, Randall Martin, and the *ESC* readers.
2. Elliott's account of satire's origins in death-dealing magical curses traced through various ancient cultures does not draw on specifically Indian examples, although he asserts the universality of the belief "among people of every stage of civilization" (Elliott 285). The prevalence of magic and superstition in ancient India is well documented, and belief in the power of the words contained in curses and black-magic spells is discussed in Banerji and Chakraborty and Gupta (177-202).
3. For example, Rao proposes that "irony and bitter satire become the mainstay of Rushdie's worldview" (Rao 163); most of the Indian critics collected in Taneja and Dhawan invoke satire in discussing matters of tone, vision, or literary style. The trajectories and targets of Rushdie's satire are discussed incidentally or at length by numerous critics, including Harrison (36-48), Brennan (109, 164), Booker (990), Kanaganayakam (95), Bhaya Nair (1000), and Fletcher (99-111).
4. Bakhtin is not, of course, the only twentieth-century critic to theorize Menippean satire. Northrop Frye devotes several pages of *Anatomy of Criticism* to the genre (Frye 308-12), and while his ideas have been influential, it is hard not to agree with Dustin Griffin when he describes Frye's theory as "sketchy," "cryptic," and of limited use. Moreover, Griffin says, when Frye's theory is set beside the more elaborate and very different formulation of Bakhtin, "it almost seems as if Frye and Bakhtin are describing different forms" (Griffin 32-3).
5. Payne, in a book on Chaucer's debt to classical Menippean satire, uses Bakhtin's definition and adds seven of her own, all of which apply to *Midnight's Children*. These include: paired and opposed characters in dialogue (Saleem and Shiva, up to a point); a virtually endless quest assisted by a "helping" and commenting character (Saleem's search for meaning aided by Padma); non-pornographic obscenity; a sense of "unquenchable hope and a titanic energy"; the absence of unquestioned theological authority or abstract certainty (Payne 9-11). Indeed, when Payne says Menippean satire "requires that we accept as necessary the presentation of simultaneous unresolved points of view," and that it questions "the possibility of ideal standards" by showing that "the world is largely what we make it" (Payne 4-6), the genre can be seen not only to be compatible with Rushdie's views (in his essay "Is Nothing

Sacred," for instance) but also to predate certain "contemporary" theories commonly used to explain his work; Hutcheon describes the postmodern world view in virtually identical terms (Hutcheon x, 43).

6. These include ten Kortenaar, Durix (61) and Sangari (164).
7. Bakhtin's theories of the grotesque body are outlined in *Rabelais and His World* (esp. 303-436), whereas his views on Menippean satire are contained in *Problems of Dostoevsky's Poetics* (esp. 112-22), and in the essay "Epic and Novel" (esp. 21-28) in *The Dialogic Imagination: Four Essays*. Tzvetan Todorov remarks on the difficulty of making links among Bakhtin's theoretical texts, including *Rabelais* and *Problems*; it is hard to reconstruct a coherent "general system," since the texts are not cross-referenced (Todorov, Mikhail xii).

Works Cited

Ali, Tariq. Rev. of *Midnight's Children*, by Salman Rushdie. *New Left Review* 136 (1982): 87-95.

Alter, Joseph. *The Wrestler's Body: Identity and Ideology in North India.* Berkeley: U California P, 1992.

Aravamudan, Srinivas. "'Being God's Postman is No Fun, Yaar': Salman Rushdie's *The Satanic Verses.*" *diacritics* 19.2 (1989): 3-20.

Bakhtin, M.M [Mikhail]. *The Dialogic Imagination: Four Essays.* Ed. Michael Holquist. Trans. Caryl Emerson and Michael Holquist. Austin: U Texas P, 1981.

____. *Problems of Dostoevsky's Poetics.* Ed. and trans. Caryl Emerson. Minneapolis: U Minnesota P, 1984.

____. *Rabelais and His World.* Trans. Helene Iswolsky. Bloomington: Indiana UP, 1984.

Banerji, Sures Chandra and Chhanda Chakraborty. *Folklore in Ancient and Medieval India.* Calcutta: Punthi Pustak, 1991.

Bhaya Nair, Rukmini. "Text and Pre-Text: History as Gossip in Rushdie's Novels." *Economic and Political Weekly* 6 May 1989: 994-1000.

Booker, M. Keith. "Beauty and the Beast: Dualism as Despotism in the Fiction of Salman Rushdie." *ELH* 57 (1990): 977-97.

Brennan, Timothy. *Salman Rushdie and the Third World: Myths of the Nation.* New York: St. Martin's, 1989.

Brooks, Peter. *Body Work: Objects of Desire in Modern Narrative.* Cambridge: Harvard UP, 1993.

Durix, Jean-Pierre. "Magic Realism in *Midnight's Children.*" *Commonwealth: Essays and Studies* 8.1 (1985): 57-63.

Elliott, Robert C. *The Power of Satire: Magic, Ritual, Art.* Princeton: Princeton UP, 1960.

Fletcher, M.D. *Contemporary Political Satire: Narrative Strategies in the Post-Modern Context.* Lanham: UP America, 1987.

Flood, Gavin D. "Techniques of Body and Desire in Kashmir Saivism." *Religion* 22 (1992): 47-62.

Foucault, Michel. "The Body of the Condemned" and "Docile Bodies." *The Foucault Reader.* Ed. Paul Rabinow. New York: Pantheon, 1984. 170-87.

____. "Nietzsche, Genealogy, History." *Language, Counter-Memory, Practice: Selected Essays and Interviews.* Ed. Donald F. Bouchard. Trans. Donald F. Bouchard and Sherry Simon. Ithaca: Cornell UP, 1977. 139-64.

Frye, Northrop. *Anatomy of Criticism: Four Essays.* Princeton: Princeton UP, 1957.

Gallagher, Catherine. "The Body Versus the Social Body in the Works of Thomas Malthus and Henry Mayhew." *Representations* 14 (1986): 83-106.

Griffin, Dustin. *Satire: A Critical Reintroduction.* Lexington: UP Kentucky, 1994.

Gupta, Beni. *Magical Beliefs and Superstitions.* Delhi: Sundeep Prakashan, 1979.

Harpham, Geoffrey Galt. *On the Grotesque: Strategies of Contradiction in Art and Literature.* Princeton: Princeton UP, 1982.

Harrison, James. *Salman Rushdie.* New York: Twayne, 1992.

Hutcheon, Linda. *A Poetics of Postmodernism: History, Theory, Fiction.* New York: Routledge, 1988.

Kanaganayakam, Chelvanayakam. "Myth and Fabulosity in *Midnight's Children.*" *Dalhousie Review* 67 (1987): 86-98.

Kayser, Wolfgang. *The Grotesque in Art and Literature.* Trans. Ulrich Weisstein. 1963. New York: McGraw, 1966.

ten Kortenaar, Neil. "*Midnight's Children* and the Allegory of History." *ARIEL* 26.2 (1995): 41-62.

Mukerjee, Radhakamal. *The Cosmic Art of India: Symbol (Murti), Sentiment (Rasa) and Silence (Yoga).* Bombay: Allied, 1965.

O'Flaherty, Wendy Doniger. *Women, Androgynes, and Other Mythical Beasts.* Chicago: U Chicago P, 1980.

Payne, F. Anne. *Chaucer and Menippean Satire.* Madison: U Wisconsin P, 1981.

Pechey, Graham. "On the Borders of Bakhtin: Dialogisation, Decolonisation." *Bakhtin and Cultural Theory.* Ed. Ken Hirschkop and David Shepherd. Manchester: Manchester UP, 1989. 39-67.

Rao, M. Madhusudhana. *Salman Rushdie's Fiction: A Study* (*Satanic Verses Excluded*). New Delhi: Sterling, 1992.

Rushdie, Salman. "Imaginary Homelands." *Imaginary Homelands: Essays and Criticism 1981-1991.* London: Granta, 1991. 9-21.

____. "In Good Faith." *Imaginary Homelands: Essays and Criticism 1981-1991.* London: Granta, 1991. 393-414.

____. "Is Nothing Sacred?" *Imaginary Homelands: Essays and Criticism 1981-1991.* London: Granta, 1991. 415-29.

____. "On Palestinian Identity: a Conversation with Edward Said." *Imaginary Homelands: Essays and Criticism 1981-1991.* London: Granta, 1991. 166-84.

____. *Midnight's Children.* New York: Knopf, 1981.

____. "*Midnight's Children* and *Shame.*" *Kunapipi* 7.1 (1985): 1-19.

____. "Outside the Whale." Rushdie, *Imaginary Homelands: Essays and Criticism 1981-1991.* London: Granta, 1991. 87-101.

____. Remarks as participant in "Conservative Fictions: A Panel Discussion." Mod. Alberto Manguel. Wang International Festival of Authors. Toronto. 17 Oct. 1988.

____. *The Satanic Verses.* London: Viking, 1988.

Said, Edward W. *After the Last Sky: Palestinian Lives.* New York: Pantheon, 1986. 166-84.

Sangari, Kumkum. "The Politics of the Possible." *Cultural Critique* 7 (1987): 157-86.

Stam, Robert. *Subversive Pleasures: Bakhtin, Cultural Criticism, and Film.* 1989. Baltimore: Johns Hopkins UP, 1992.

Taneja, G.R. and R.K. Dhawan, eds. *The Novels of Salman Rushdie.* New Delhi: Indian Society for Commonwealth Studies/Prestige, 1992.

Todorov, Tzvetan. *The Fantastic: A Structural Approach to a Literary Genre.* Trans. Richard Howard. Cleveland: Case Western Reserve UP, 1973.

____. *Mikhail Bakhtin: The Dialogical Principle.* Trans. Wlad Godzich. Minneapolis: U Minnesota P, 1984.

Younger, Paul. *Introduction to Indian Religious Thought.* Philadelphia: Westminster, 1972.

Originally published in *English Studies in Canada* 24.1 (Mar. 1998): 61-81. Reprinted with permission.

5

THE (HI)STORY OF PADMA'S 1001 DIFFERENT FACES

PIER PAOLO PICIUCCO

> I usually resist the idea of allegory. In India there is too much of it, allegory is a kind of disease. People try to decode everything, every story or text allegorically, and although clearly there are elements that you could call allegorical in *Midnight's Children* and *Shame*, the books are not allegories in the way that *The Pilgrim's Progress* is, where everything stands for something and the real story is a story that is not told. Allegory asks readers to make a translation, to uncover a secret that has not actually been told. In that sense I don't think my books operate as allegories.

Salman Rushdie is a fictional character created by the ingenious mind of Saleem Sinai, who made him a very unreliable narrator and speaker. Although his idea quoted above can in fact be easily understood if the parallel with *The Pilgrim's Progress* is implied, the core of the message, his reluctance to explain the fundamental tenets in *Midnight's Children* (*MC*) in terms of an allegorical code, is surprising, to say the least. Many of the critical debates on his novels over the years would lose their substance and *MC* itself, in my opinion, could hardly have achieved the international resonance it has enjoyed since publication, should we read the book without reference to a symbolic convention. In the present paper I aim at illustrating a theory on a new reading of the novel, focussing on the character of Padma, "an ambivalent figure within the novel", but taking for granted that allegories work as a main agent informing various characters, events and perspectives with significant meanings and/or interpretations. While I attempt at analising the multifacedness of this very peculiar character and therefore propose a series of different readings, I discourage the reader from taking the individual interpretations as neatly distinguished one from the other, but rather to perceive the assortment and amalgamation-or should we say the chutnification?-of these patterns to be the crux of the issue.

As has been often underlined, *MC* is a container of stories and my reading has simply followed the one featuring Padma as the main character. While other stories are much shorter, Rushdie has chosen this particular one to stretch for the whole length of the novel, although obviously interrupted by various stops and continuous digressions. What seemed interesting to me was that, although she remains the same character from the beginning, Padma undergoes a significant change in the eyes of the reader towards the end of the book. *MC* is the acrobatic unfolding of tales and anecdotes by a talented narrator who writes/tells these stories from his desk. Since his task is all-absorbing, he needs another figure to materially take care of him while he completely devotes himself to narrating anecdotes. Hence the creation of Padma, "nurse and cook," whose nature and function soon appear ambivalent: she is not the real author of the stories but, say, the author's "vital collaborator." Considering the intimacy between these two figures, ("I must go to bed. Padma is waiting; and I need a little warmth,") that her brief parting from him is to be viewed as an exceptional case and due to her hot temper, and that she is totally dedicated to her man, the reader may reasonably presume that they are husband and wife. This is never stated but, since no different solution is suggested, it would not be a completely wild guess on the reader's part: a further element justifying such a hypothesis is that together Saleem and Padma seem a very traditional couple, spouses who have lived together for a very long time and whose union is now governed by inertia. It is not before the end of the novel that the reader is informed of the whole truth: they are simply partners, allegedly not even very long-standing ones at that. She tries to convince him to marry her, but he seems to resist. It is in the very last pages of the novel that Saleem meets again his ayah, Mary Pereira, and through their dialogue the reader is made aware that Saleem has finally decided to surrender: "'Why you getting married so sudden sudden?' Because Padma wants. No she is not in trouble" (*MC* 459). In the fashion of many Rushdie's stories, this one, too, has an open ending and the reader does not witness Padma's much awaited celebration. To complicate matters, the finale's gloomy atmosphere leaves more than a simple doubt about such a romantic evolution.

Much has been said about both the similar representation of female characters in the fiction of Rushdie and the symbolic role of Padma in the novel, at various levels. It is my opinion that the role she plays could be seen in relation to that of the other women described in *MC*; more in detail, I suggest that she be seen as a surrogate of femininity. Likewise, Saleem would be representative of masculinity. Needless to say, Rushdie's approach to this canon is considerably altered by a distortion lens and sarcasm. Elsewhere I have dealt with the stereotypical representations of female and masculine characters, indicating that Indian writers are very inclined to apply a peculiar cultural code to fictional discourse when referring to similar prototypes: *MC* would be another example reinforcing that theory. Without entering into details, I will simply say that an Indian philosophical and aesthetic principle directly inherited from a traditional view, but still in keeping with the modern times, the Sankhya concept, views the whole universe as the creation of two complementary agents: *purusha* and *prakrti*. The former is generally associated with spirits; it is a concept implying plurality, inaction, thought, air and manliness. The latter is nature, activity, earth, femininity. They are to be considered as two equally important forms of energy whose final union leads to the creation of the universe. Whether or not Rushdie intentionally alluded to this philosophical bipolarism while sketching the figures of Saleem and Padma is hard to say (I would be more inclined not to believe so), but the number of parallels linking Padma to prakrti and Saleem to purusha is striking. Each perspective will illustrate them as perfectly complementary agents, following a canon which, if not directly relating to the Sankhya concept, is only slightly different from it. What is relevant here, though, is not a philosophical explanation of the events described but an interpretation of these two figures as the primordial man and woman. Their union (or should we say simply their relationship, considering the final pessimistic tone of the novel?) would lead to the creation of the novel. This perspective would provide a key of interpretation to various behaviours and characteristics of these two characters I will discuss later: suffice it to say now that it may explain Saleem's powerful verbosity countered by Padma's more evident sexual urge, a cliché much contested by a feminist reading (see Verma 1991: 158).

Both the characters in fact appear extremely well endowed with particular features, totally lacking other attributes at the same time. Whereas Saleem is in fact a fertile story-teller, he is emasculated: while Padma is illiterate, she seems driven by very intense physical urges. In this context, *MC* can also be seen as the challenge between wordiness and desire. The ironical allusion to his sexual organ, called "my 'other pencil'" (*MC* 121) by Saleem, would find further implications here. Incidentally, we may remember that psychoanalysis verged on very similar results. Sigmund Freud in fact explained the mechanisms leading the artist to the creative process as the effect of instinctive unsatisfied longings, which he deemed very akin to the libido. In this perspective, the desire to tell and the sexual impulse would prefigure as the two parallel forces which we would find personified as Saleem and Padma in *MC*. In a particular instance his act of writing appears explicitly as a surrogate of a sexual intercourse:

> Is it possible to be jealous of written words? To resent nocturnal scribblings as though they were the very flesh and blood of a sexual rival? I can think of no other

> reason for Padma's bizarre behaviour; and this explanation at least has the merit of being as outlandish as the rage into which she fell when, tonight, I made the error of writing (and reading aloud) a word which should not have been spoken [...] ever since the episode of the quack doctor's visit, I have sniffed out a strange discontent in Padma, exuding its enigmatic spoor for her eccrine (or apocrine) glands. (*MC* 121)

This is exactly in keeping with the structure of *Arabian Nights*. Sheherazade, in fact, uses the nights at her disposal in order to entertain her king with tales rather than with sexual pleasure.

Debates on the relevance of intertextual strategies in the fiction of Salman Rushdie have always been a central topic. Contaminations by Marquez's *One Hundred Years of Solitude*, Grass's *The Tin Drum*, Sterne's *Tristram Shandy* and *Arabian Nights*, among various others, are either highlighted in the course of narration or have been acknowledged by the writer in various interviews. Although they sooner or later emerge in the plot adding more spice to Saleem's "chutney," they do not share the same weight in the general plan of the book. Of the texts listed above, the only one which candidly appears in *MC* is *Arabian Nights* and its importance has already been stressed in the work of other scholars. However, I would stretch the analogies between the two texts a bit further than this, by suggesting an interpretation of *Arabian Nights* functioning as a macrotext to *MC*. This fact is crucial to our debate in that in the process of appropriation of the medieval collection of stories, Rushdie adopts a sex-switching strategy. Saleem, the archetypal man, is reproposed as the young virgin Sheherazade, while Padma, the feminine principle, is turned into the terrifying king Shahriyar. Structurally, in fact, both *Arabian Nights* and *MC* are love-stories. Implausible, paradoxical, allegorical, exaggerated, but nonetheless love-stories. As far as *MC* is concerned, it is a strange relationship which develops between the two characters, a relationship which illustrates a tragi-comic dichotomy. As Hutcheon rightly argues, "instead of satisfaction, he offers her sublimation."

And, as we know, sublimation of desire is also the strategy employed by Sheherazade with king Shahriyar to win his thirst for blood and become his wife. Of course, Rushdie makes use of irony to represent the dramatic destiny of Saleem-Sheherazade: Saleem can keep Padma at a safe distance and control her till he tells her stories. And what longer is there to narrate than the (hi)story of the Indian republic? Padma's victory, on the other hand, lies in her patience: she lets Saleem unfold all his stories and exhaust his power. When he is about to finish, he is weak and abruptly capitulates: he accepts the marriage proposal. This reading may provide an explanation to Padma and Saleem's different discursive strategies: his digressive penchant juxtaposed to her "what-happened-nextism" (*MC* 39). In the strange challenge between the two, it is always Saleem who feels threatened by some danger or another. Padma-Shahriyar is in fact safe whatever happens to her, at least in comparison to him. This is why Saleem, beyond adopting a digressive discursive strategy, tries, significantly towards the very end of his narration, to dissuade her with various motivations that their union is impossible: it is then that he tactically reveals his emasculation to her and it is again only towards the end that he warns her against the tragic end she would meet, should she marry him. Women are in fact dogged by a perverse doom with him. Yet, Padma easily overcomes all these fears and wins him in the end.

The slightly pessimistic part of this strange love-relationship is the unbalanced emotional commitment for each other. Padma in fact is deeply in love with Saleem: "Padma fell for me from the first, seeing in me an outlet for her vast reservoir of pent-up solicitude." (*MC* 460) On the other hand, he, who is surely affected to her, does not necessarily share her same feelings. Rather than love, he seems regulated by a kind of a habit, a part of a ritual, a sort of a self-centred disposition at times; Saleem's moves are therefore governed by a fair amount of coldness. Discussing the whole fictional corpus of Rushdie, Ahmad rightly points out: "for all its marvellous humour, Rushdie's imagined world is, in its lovelessness, almost Orwellian."

I understand at this point that my reading is quite original as it disputes various other commonly accepted theories. Firstly, it emphasises that the architecture of *MC* is structured on the myth of *Arabian Nights*. Scholars, on the other hand, have often missed such a clue, maybe because searching for mythical references in the Hindu or Muslim pantheon:

> In *Midnight's Children*, myth functions as a kind of a shorthand to convey concepts though it is rarely fully and elaborately worked out, unlike in Joyce's *Ulysses* and Eliot's *The Waste Land* which use myth as a framework.

Secondly, it opposes the commonplace that Padma

> is not part of the story proper but occupies selected "asides" in which she participates with Saleem in composing the novel we are reading. Her relationship is not with Saleem the character, but with Saleem the narrator and author

Finally, it contradicts the opinion that Rushdie's treatment of female characters always denotes implied strategies of male dominance (Ahmed 1992: 142-52). My theory would in fact propose the reading of the plot as a sort of an open challenge between Padma and Saleem within a strange love relationship. Padma's final victory, or at least Saleem's surrender considering that the story is deliberately left open-ended, would eschew such a conclusion. That is far more significant in that, if Rushdie firstly adopts a sex switching code when applying *Arabian Nights*' model to his novel, he later comes back to the original situation when establishing who is the winner. In both the texts, in fact, it is the woman who prevails in the end. What is more important in this context, is that Padma's victory is not so much associated with a personal victory, but rather with that of a gender:

> most of the male characters are weak (it is not only Saleem who has to say: "women have made me: and also unmade") whereas most of the women are strong and independent. They invariably get what they want because they have the strength or willpower.

If we then refer to the allegorical meaning of such a peculiar construction, these interpretations of the two protagonists may appear to be the most important. Actually, this is not exactly what happens in *MC*. Rushdie in fact subverts the priorities generally assumed in *Arabian Nights*; his act of appropriation implies that the private (love-)story of the two heroes be relegated to a secondary role by their telling of the stories. What substantially distinguishes *MC* from *Arabian Nights* in terms of structural approach, is that Sheherazade's tales, although extremely entertaining, remain a set of discursive agents isolated from her personal predicament, while Saleem's story is deeply amalgamated with his present development with Padma and, more relevantly still, the choice of the subject discussed makes it the focal point of the book. Whereas, say, a reader of *Arabian Nights* could equally do without some of Sheherazade's fabulous stories, a reader of *MC* is totally absorbed by Rushdie's rewriting of Indian history and can partially ignore Saleem and Padma's liaison. That is why the structural corpus of *MC* and the mythological frame end up being a section of lesser weight, in comparison to the central tale. The following interpretations of Padma are to be placed outside her emotional commitment for Saleem and, more importantly, outside the structural frame referring to *Arabian Nights*; they are those which more consistently fuelled the theoretical debates around the reception of *MC*.

A Marxist reading of *MC* has emphasised Padma's symbolical value as a plebeian commentator next to Saleem, illustrative of the local elitism (Brennan 1989: 100-09). This interpretation has therefore focussed on the hegemonic prevalence of the central/bourgeois/male agents over the liminal/plebeian/female identity. What is particularly engaging and original about this reading is that this theory avoids acknowledging in Saleem alone the emblem of India, but it demonstrates that a complete national identification is to be searched for in the combination of Saleem and Padma. Yet, in *MC* we can detect that Rushdie deliberately focuses his attention on Saleem's story only, totally overlooking Padma's background. The reader's conclusions about Padma plebeian lineage, although manifest, cannot be supported by the evidence of her story in the text because that is totally abrogated.

Gender criticism has not generally been extremely soft with Rushdie, to use a delicate euphemism. Outside the code of reference to *Arabian Nights*, and the parallel with king Shahriyar-Sheherazade, Padma seems to be modelled on the traditional Indian wife. Her world is the domestic sphere, she is totally dedicated to her husband and it is assumed that patience is her most characterising trait. She is supposed to live in the shadow of her husband and, as Parnell argues, "like most of Rushdie's women she is not a shaper of events but an adjunct to her male" (Moore-Gilbert 1996: 250). Furthermore, the huge gap between his high-level education and her illiteracy, which induces Saleem to tag her as "my one disciple" (*MC* 149), have become an unhappy caricature of a sad social reality. What has justifiably most irritated gender criticism is that Padma has been clearly sketched out as a stereotype, as a character representative of a whole gender. This is the context in which I would place the criticism to Rushdie's alleged misogyny. The fact that this interpretation of Padma's figure may radically contrast with the one illustrated at the beginning of this paper should not surprise us too much, because they pertain to two different registers of discourse. Apart from evaluating such contradictions within the set of norms generally accepted by the post-modern cliché, I am much inclined to view paradoxical ideological ambiguity as a trademark of Rushdie's writing.

An analysis of Padma's role in terms of narratological discourse is not likely to lead us towards a more straightforward result. This is doubtless one of the fields in which Rushdie revealed himself as a master of shuffling cards. Other scholars have treated the subject with significant insight and I cannot hope to solve the matter briefly. I will just point at some strategies enabling Rushdie to create such an anarchic construction.

To begin with, the evident dichotomy between the implied orality of Saleem's speech and his being sat at his table writing his tales, a strategy perceptively discussed by Brennan as "written orality" (Brennan 1989: 139), consequently introduces the first ambiguity of role for Padma. Is she a listener or a reader? Apparently, she must paradoxically cover both the functions at the same time, implying in such a contradiction in terms also that she is a "primitively illiterate" "reader's surrogate." We may then explain the strident haziness about her role in two different ways: firstly, since Rushdie imagines a reader completely different from her, Padma's function as a narratee is simply allegorical, as Wilson argues (Fletcher 1994: 65-66). Secondly, her role is limited to that of the listener only in that the implied reader is a figure different from her. Saleem's narration, in fact, is not necessarily directed at her only, but to a (much) more educated kind of readership, if not to other subjects still.

Padma, in addition, is strategic to Rushdie's deconstruction of a narration responding to a set of pre-established norms. Once more, contradiction is the favourite medium of resistance to conventional narration. Padma's widely acknowledged passivity as a traditional Indian wife turns out to be extremely productive to the text, in that her presence is essential to the economy of the novel. The reader is explicitly made aware that Saleem has only a short-lived independence in the brief interval when she is missing. Various theories credit her with different strategic roles which are always of primary importance and, significantly, at odds with her status of an illiterate: Batty maintains that "Padma's role as Saleem's 'necessary ear' (149) should not obscure her status as co-creator of the narrative," Cundy affirms that "Padma is a vital spur and judge of Saleem's autobiography," while Brennan argues that "Padma is not only a passive receptor, or disembodied voice of the national conscience, but a literary *critic*" (Brennan 1989: 101). However we choose to classify her, her identity is almost to be defined in terms of opposition to Saleem's.

A variety of different interpretations have divided critics on Padma's alleged identifications within the Hindu pantheon, too. Whereas Saleem is quite clearly associated with the figure of Ganesha for a number of reasons, Padma's reference to the Hindu mythology seems more flexible. Her traditional role of patient Indian wife, "just one step behind her husband," would indicate in Sita a possible prototype for her character: this parallel would then probably apply to those engaged in gender criticism, being the figure of Sita among the chosen banners for women emancipation in India today. Significantly, Uma Parameswaran, who is more inclined to favour her prevailing identity on Saleem, prefers to associate her to Durga, the archetypal Mother Earth. Goonetilleke, on the other hand, considers Padma a sort of Saleem's Muse and he equates her to Saraswathi, the goddess of creative arts (Goonetilleke 1998: 41). The mythical association of Padma with a deity, anyway, is much more the effect of Saleem's jokes with the significance of her name:

> her mother told her, when she was only small, that she had been named after the lotus goddess, whose most common appellation amongst village folk is 'The One Who Possesses Dung' (*MC* 24)

The Lotus-Goddess in Hindu mythology is Lakshmi, the goddess of Beauty and the equivalent of Aphrodites in Greek mythology. She is commonly associated with desire and fertility, attributes which Rushdie would deform into a grotesque. In addition, Lakshmi's famous appellative of Shri suggests general well being, material prosperity and ruling majesty, all features which are completely reversed in Padma. This may further prove how pertinent is Brennan's Marxist interpretation of the character.

Since *MC* is a novel which constantly implies cross-references with other literary texts, we may evaluate Padma's allusions in that perspective, too. Fortunately, the possible parallels to similar characters in other novels drastically limit the wide range of connections to other literary works originally entailed by *MC*. Significantly, there seems to be no association with the traditional Sanskrit epics-at least with the most important ones-although the practice of oral story-telling is quite common in that context. Alter convincingly stresses that "Saleem's Padma plays a role analogous to Tristram's Jenny, though she is more a dramatised naive reader of the narrative than is Jenny." A proclivity for triviality and gossip, as well as the narrator's titanic amount of self-centredness, in fact, assert undeniable links with Sterne's masterpiece. Merivale, on the other hand, analyses *MC* in reference with Grass's *The Tin Drum* and she draws a parallel between Bruno and Padma, establishing a correspondence on the narratological ground:

> Saleem and Oskar are writing, telling, or reading out their stories with a frame narrative, to a clearly delineated listener, a "narratee," who is a stand-in for the implied reader and a perpetual reminder of the present tense of narrating time. Bruno [...] and Padma [...] are both permitted to interrupt and even to contribute short sections of their own.

Last but not least, a psychological analysis may reveal further interesting aspects of Padma's character. Contrary to what her traditional role of Indian wife may suggest at first, she is quite unusual if compared to other characters in *MC* and not necessarily subject to its internal code. The fragmented experience-Saleem resisting his own fragmentation and the perforated sheet are the most evident metaphors of this process-seems to be one of the constants which regulate the aesthetic principles at the base of *MC*'s creative thrust. Significantly, Padma escapes this norm. Similarly, she evades the principle assigning various names to each character as the plot unfolds; in that respect, her identity remains undisturbed by the events. This notwithstanding, as much of the previous discussion has shown, her identity and/or function is to be defined only in strict relationship to that of Saleem. Since she is involved as an opponent/accomplice in all his tasks, she becomes a sort of "alter ego" for him in the whole course of narration. Regardless of the critical perspective employed to analyse her connection with Saleem, it remains undisputable that her relationship with him is founded on a strictly complementary code. Substantially, *MC* is the final result of the sum: Saleem + Padma. It is their union, rather than their being associated as different identities, which leads to a fruitful and fertile combination. As also Banerjee appropriately underscores, "together they make history" (Dhawan and Taneja 1992: 25). Considering the vast amount of cross-references to autobiographical elements that spice the pages of *MC*, and the discounted association Rushdie/Saleem, one should not be surprised to discover that Padma bares significant symbolical similarities to a real woman, although I would hasten to add that this may hardly be a flattering parallel. After all, Shandy's "dear, dear Jenny"-one of Padma's prototypes-was the fictional personification of a real maiden, Catherine de Fourmentelle.

As also the present study is likely to illustrate, Salman Rushdie elegantly shows a mastery of two different cultural codes and implies the creation of a third cultural pole, eschewing the polarization of the postcolonial era. *MC*, as well as the other novels he has written, is therefore an authentic reservoir of intertextual allusions and a rich and complex system of symbols. This is why, I suppose, it is more fun writing a paper on his fiction than reading his novels.

Notes

1. W.J. Weatherby, *Salman Rushdie: Sentenced to Death* (New York: Carroll and Graf, 1990) 18.
2. Tim Parnell, "Salman Rushdie: from Colonial Politics to Post-modern Poetics," *Writing India 1757-1990*, ed. Bart Moore-Gilbert (Manchester and New York: Manchester UP, 1996) 250.
3. Ashutosh Banerjee, "Narrative Technique in *Midnight's Children*," *The Novels of Salman Rushdie*, ed. G.R. Taneja and R.K. Dhawan (New Delhi, Indian Society for Commonwealth Studies, 1992) 25.
4. Salman Rushdie, *Midnight's Children* (1995; London: Vintage, 1991) 37.
5. Pier Paolo Piciucco, "Woman in the Fiction of Arun Joshi," *Cross-Cultural Voices*, ed. Claudio Gorlier and Isabella Maria Zoppi (Roma: Bulzoni, 1997) and "Femininity in the Fiction of R.K. Narayan: a Study," *Indian Writings In English*, vol. 7, ed. Manmohan K. Bhatnagar and M. Rajeshwar (Delhi: Atlantic, 2000) for instance.
6. See Freud, Sigmund, *Freud Library 14: Art and Literature* (London: Penguin, 1990.
7. See for instance, Wendy B Fabris, "Sherehazade's Children: Magical Realism and Postcolonial Fiction," *Magical Realism. Theory, History,*

Community, ed. Zamora and Fabris (Durham and London: Duke UP, 1995.

8. Linda Hutcheon, *A Poetics of Postmodernism* (London and New York: Routledge, 1988) 162.
9. Aijaz hmed, *In Theory: Classes, Nations, Literatures* (London and New York: Verso, 1992) 151.
10. D.C.R.A. Goonetilleke, *Salman Rushdie* (New York: St. Martin's Press, 1998) 19.
11. Timothy Brennan, *Salman Rushdie and the Third World* (London: Macmillan, 1989) 100. See also Charu Verma, "Padma's Tragedy: a Feminist Deconstruction of Rushdie's *Midnight's Children*," *Feminism and Recent Fiction in English*, ed. Sushila Singh (New Delhi: Prestige, 1991) 154.
12. Uma Parameswaran, *The Perforated Sheet: Essays on Salman Rushdie's Art* (Delhi: Affiliated East-West, 1988) 20.
13. Harish Trivedi, "Salman the Funtoosh: Magic Bilingualism in *Midnight's Children*," *Rushdie's* Midnight's Children*: a Book of Readings*, ed. Meenakshi Mukherjee (New Delhi: Pencraft, 1999) 82.
14. Keith Wilson, "*Midnight's Children* and Reader Responsibility," *Reading Rushdie: Perspectives on the Fiction of Salman Rushdie*, ed. M.D. Fletcher (Amsterdam and Atlanta: Rodopi, 1994) 64.
15. To the *Midnight's Children* at p. 480, for instance.
16. Nancy Batty, "The Art of Suspense: Rushdie 1001 (Mid-)Nights," *Rushdie's* Midnight's Children*: a Book of Readings*, ed. Meenakshi Mukherjee (New Delhi: Pencraft, 1999) 100.
17. Catherine Cundy, *Salman Rushdie* (Manchester and New York: Manchester UP, 1996) 30.
18. See David Kinsley, *Hindu Goddesses: Visions of the Divine Feminine in the Hindu Religious Tradition* (Delhi: Motilal Banarsidass, 1987) 19-29.
19. Robert Alter, "*Midnight's Children* and *Tristram Shandy*," *Rushdie's* Midnight's Children*: a Book of Readings*, ed. Meenakshi Mukherjee (New Delhi: Pencraft, 1999) 113.
20. Patricia Merival, "Saleem Fathered by Oskar: Intertextual Strategies in *Midnight's Children* and *The Tin Drum*," *Rushdie's* Midnight's Children*: a Book of Readings*, ed. Meenakshi Mukherjee (New Delhi: Pencraft, 1999) 124.
21. See Goonetilleke 1-5.

Works Cited

Ahmed, Aijaz. *In Theory: Classes, Nations, Literatures*. London and New York: Verso, 1992.

Alter, Robert. "*Midnight's Children* and *Tristram Shandy*." *Rushdie's* Midnight's Children*: a Book of Readings*. Ed. Meenakshi Mukherjee. New Delhi: Pencraft, 1999.

Banerjee, Ashutosh. "Narrative Technique in *Midnight's Children*." *The Novels of Salman Rushdie*. Ed. G.R. Taneja and R.K. Dhawan. New Delhi: Indian Society for Commonwealth Studies, 1992.

Batty, Nancy. "The Art of Suspense: Rushdie 1001 (Mid-)Nights." *Rushdie's* Midnight's Children*: a Book of Readings*. Ed. Meenakshi Mukherjee. New Delhi: Pencraft, 1999.

Brennan, Timothy. *Salman Rushdie and the Third World*. London: Macmillan, 1989.

Cundy, Catherine. *Salman Rushdie*. Manchester and New York: Manchester UP, 1996.

Fabris, Wendy B. "Sherehazade's Children: Magical Realism and Postcolonial Fiction." *Magical Realism. Theory, History, Community*. Ed. Zamora and Fabris. Durham and London: Duke UP, 1995.

Freud, Sigmund. *Freud Library 14: Art and Literature*. London: Penguin, 1990.

Goonetilleke, D.C.R.A.. *Salman Rushdie*. New York, St. Martin's Press, 1998.

Hutcheon, Linda. *A Poetics of Postmodernism*. London and New York: Routledge, 1988.

Kinsley, David. *Hindu Goddesses: Visions of the Divine Feminine in the Hindu Religious Tradition*. Delhi: Motilal Banarsidass, 1987.

Merival, Patricia. "Saleem Fathered by Oskar: Intertextual Strategies in *Midnight's Children* and *The Tin Drum*." *Rushdie's Midnight's* Children*: a Book of Readings*. Ed. Meenakshi Mukherjee. New Delhi, Pencraft, 1999.

Parameswaran, Uma. *The Perforated Sheet. Essays on Salman Rushdie's Art*. Delhi : Affiliated East-West, 1988.

Parnell, Tim. "Salman Rushdie: from Colonial Politics to Post-modern Poetics." *Writing India 1757-1990*. Ed. Bart Moore-Gilbert. Manchester and New York: Manchester UP, 1996.

Piciucco, Pier Paolo. "Femininity in the Fiction of R.K. Narayan: a Study." *Indian Writings In English* Vol. 7. Ed. Manmohan K. Bhatnagar and M. Rajeshwar. Delhi: Atlantic, 2000.

Piciucco, Pier Paolo. "Woman in the Fiction of Arun Joshi." *Cross-Cultural Voices*. Ed. Claudio Gorlier and Isabella Maria Zoppi. Roma: Bulzoni, 1997.

Rushdie, Salman. *Midnight's Children*. 1991. London: intage, 1995.

Trivedi, Harish. "Salman the Funtoosh: Magic Bilingualism in *Midnight's Children*." *Rushdie's* Midnight's Children*: a Book of Readings*. Ed. Meenakshi Mukherjee. New Delhi: Pencraft, 1999.

Verma, Charu. "Padma's Tragedy: a Feminist Deconstruction of Rushdie's *Midnight's Children.*" *Feminism and Recent Fiction in English.* Ed. Sushila Singh. New Delhi: Prestige, 1991.

Weatherby, W.J. *Salman Rushdie: Sentenced to Death.* New York: Carroll and Graf, 1990.

Wilson, Keith. "*Midnight's Children* and Reader Responsibility." *Reading Rushdie: Perspectives on the Fiction of Salman Rushdie.* Ed. M.D. Fletcher. Amsterdam and Atlanta: Rodopi, 1994.

6

CENTRES AND MARGINS: SHAME'S 'OTHER' NATION

SYED MUJEEBUDDIN

> The language of critique is effective [...] to the extent which it overcomes the grounds of opposition and opens up a space of 'translation': a place of hybridity [...] neither the one nor the other [...] and changes, as it must, the very forms of our recognition of the moment of politics.
>
> — Homi Bhabha

Salman Rushdie's third novel, Shame,[2] like its predecessor *MC,* again addresses itself to a centre other than the metropolitan one: authoritarian regimes that seek validity in doctrinaire Islam. If *MC* draws a stark, uncharitable picture of India, its parodic concerns, its subversion of the Indo-Anglian novel's conventions of national authenticity, even its severe indictment of the political leadership in India, are all yet marked by a frazzled hope. *Shame* on the other hand draws a bleak, harsh portrait of Pakistan.

Speaking about the contrast between *MC* and *Shame,* Rushdie has pointed out that the "moods" of the two books pertained to "a shift in my own mood": "I had the feeling, with Pakistan, of claustrophobia, and in India of wide open landscapes, and in simple terms the two books reflect those two views. The compass of *Shame* is more confined. *Shame* is not a portrait of a nation, it's a portrait of a ruliSng class, and *Midnight's Children* tries to be a bit broader than that [...]."[3] Thus India "if it means anything means plurality," while on the other hand Pakistan "although it has different races [...] feels more like a singularity, because there is just the one religion and there's a much greater homogeneity both of language and faith, especially since the loss of the east and required a different treatment."[4] "The different treatment" that Rushdie metes out Pakistan results in its portrait as a desolate, despondent, oppressive and oppressing landscape. Bounded by a noose-like frontier that strangles its inhabitants, *Shame's* Pakistan is a dystopia, an absolute "area of darkness," that is incapable of generating ideas that liberate.

Unlike the "teeming," crowded, quality of the plurality of Indian life that Saleem in *MC* symbolises—the multitudes that jostle inside him and eventually break him up—*Shame* is riddled with images of empty, labyrinthine houses in remote places and frontiers surrounded by nothingness. Thus the house in 'Nishapur,' Omar Khayyam's "mother-country" is a "reclusive mansion" a "third world" that is "neither material nor spiritual" a "sweltering, entropical zone" where "nothing new seemed capable of growth," a "hideously indeterminate frontier universe," an "infertile and time-eroded labyrinth" and a "thing-infested jungle" (30-31), while Rani Harappa's house is located in the "backyard of the universe" (94). Mohenjo, (Mohenjo-Daro means "the mound of the dead"[5]), the Harrappa country estate, is also a closed universe that stretches "from horizon to horizon," and is "afflicted by a chronic water shortage, (and) populated by laughing scornful monsters [...]" (94). The house itself is described as a small labyrinth—"Verandahs run along all four walls; a long covered mosquito-netted walkway joins the kitchen bungalow,"—and is opulent—"And oil paintings and chandeliers and high ceilings and a flat tar-macadamed roof [...]" (95). The frontier too is an empty place that sets off Omar's fear of the "Edge" and makes him a victim of vertigo forever afterwards. After *MC*'s crowdedness, the terrifying emptiness of *Shame's* landscape seems to symbolise a veritable trap, figured through the different kinds of solitary confinements that Iskander and Rani Harrappa experience. As Mary-Anne Paton rightly points out this emptiness and its accompanying solitude is Rushdie's image of hell—"one person miles away from another person."[6]

The narrative focuses on the "careers, corruptions, ribaldries and rivalries"[7] of its two main protagonists Iskander Harrappa and Raza Hyder, the former modelled on the personality of Zulfikhar Ali Bhutto and the latter on Gen. Zia Ul Haq, both powerful political figures in Pakistan until their violent deaths. In superb parody and burlesque Rushdie recreates the major strands of the contemporary history of Pakistan, and tells the story of a very small group of people who are "responsible for the *making of history* and for the controlling of power" and for whom "politics is a kind of family quarrel."[8] As Aijaz Ahmed points out this plot device is a brilliant "technical resolution" and successfully reflects "the monopolistic structure of dictatorial power and the very narrow social spectrum within which this power in Pakistan circulates."[9]

This centre of power is posited against the peripheral figures of the protagonist Omar Khayyam Shakil and the women, mainly Sufiya Zinobia the heroine of the novel who embodies in quite a literal way Pakistan itself. However there is another figure, the narrator himself, who emphasises his own marginal status and in aligning himself with the other peripheral figures of the novel[10] inaugurates an imaginative coalition between himself and them. In a passage couched in exquisite irony, the narrator conflates himself, his 'hero' Omar Khayyam Shakil, and the translatedly popular, 'Oriental' figure of Omar Khayyam, who the narrator points out in the text, was never very popular in his native Persia but existed in the West "in a translation that really is a complete reworking of his verses" (29), very different both in spirit and content. "I too am a translated man," says the narrator, "I have been borne across. It is generally believed that something is always lost in translation; I cling to the notion—and use in evidence the success of Fitzgerald-Khayyam—that something can also be gained" (29). Yet like Saleem in *MC,* the narrator being omnipresent, is also at the same time the centre of all things and makes claims of authority to speak about Pakistan. The narrator's articulation of Pakistan's calamity-ridden history is marked by an acute consciousness of his own intrusion into indigenous affairs and his virtual appropriation of the native voice as is evident in the defensive claims that the narrator makes to authority through an anticipation of the allegations of intrusiveness.

> *Outsider! Trespasser! You have no right to this subject*! [...] I know nobody ever arrested me. Nor are they ever likely to.

> Poacher! Pirate! We reject your authority. *We know you, with your foreign language wrapped around you like a flag: speaking about us in your forked tongue, what can you tell but lies*? I reply with more questions: is history to be considered the property of the participants solely? In what courts are such claims staked, what boundary commissions map out the territories?
>
> Can only the dead speak? (28)

The elliptical question hints at Rushdie's own awareness of the powerlessness of the peripheralised native and more importantly the chosen or enforced silence of the indigenous intellectual when confronted by the wrath of a totalitarian state: the imprisoned poet, who was hung upside-down by his ankles and beaten, "as if a new born baby whose lungs had to be coerced into action so that he could squeal" (28). The image of an infant hanging upside-down also equates the 'voiceless' poet with Omar Khayyam Shakil who despite his name is devoid of any poetry and even a voice: "[...] you will note that my hero has already been ankle-hung, and that his name is the name of a famous poet; but no quatrains ever issued or will issue from his pen" (28).

The poet's and Shakil's inability to "squeal" is Rushdie's cue to take up the mantle, "So here I am instead, inventing what never happened to me" (28). Yet this "artistic journey," as Jean-Pierre Durix calls it,[11] is marked by an awareness that to produce a mythic Pakistan is to traverse the imaginative topography of Orientalist studies that produced and represented the East as the 'Other' and thus commit a further act of epistemic violence.

But he points out, as in the case of the Fitzgerald-Khayyam persona "something can also be gained" and offers the plurality manifest in his fabulous story of a fictional "Peccavistan." Thus what he actually posits against the monodic centre of Pakistan's singular discourse of religious and political power is the polyglot narrative of *Shame* itself:[12] parodies of holy texts,[13] ironic legends (the stories of Iskander Harrappa and Raza Hyder), cinematic motifs (movement back and forth in a mixture of flash-backs and montage), and a babel of voices that not only bespeak the narrator's own migrancy but also the marginal status of the women.

II

Rushdie's *Shame*, like its predecessor, *MC*, is again concerned with presenting an alternative view of history. If Saleem's 'authority' to speak in *MC* is derived from his being a sibling of the newly independent nation, the narrator in *Shame* conflates his migrant status with the status of Pakistan and his telling of its tale to the creation of the "*insufficiently imagined*" (87) nation itself:

> When individuals come unstuck from their native land, they are called migrants. When nations do the same (Bangladesh), that act is called secession [...].
>
> I may be such a person. Pakistan may be such a country. (86-87)

Moreover, the term Pakistan itself is an acronym that was "born in exile which then went east, was borne-across or translated, and imposed itself on history; a returning migrant, settling down on partitioned land, forming a palimpsest on the past" (87). The narrator comments on how Pakistan was built: Pakistan is a "palimpsest" that "obscures what lies beneath," in order to build which, "it was necessary to cover up Indian history, to deny that Indian centuries lay just beneath the surface of Pakistani Standard Time. The past was rewritten; there was nothing else to be done" (87).

The fact that the "job of rewriting history" was commandeered by the "immigrants, the *mohajirs*" (87), implicitly lends the narrator, an immigrant himself, the authority to expropriate "the job of rewriting" that history once again. For, as he says, "I, too, like all migrants, am a fantasist" and

> build imaginary countries and try to impose them on the ones that exist. I, too, face the problem of history: what to retain, what to dump, how to hold on to what memory insists on relinquishing, how to deal with change [...] (87-88).

Yet unlike the making of Pakistan, the narrator's tale is one that insists on "excavating what lies beneath"[14]—the histories that Pakistan's intellectual and political leadership suppresses or excludes. If his "modern fairy tale" (70) distorts the officially established truth it only does so in order to draw "better maps of reality."[15] Rushdie regards that the act of redescribing a world is itself a "political act" and a "necessary first step towards changing it," specially when the "State takes reality into its own hands, and sets about distorting it, altering the past to fit its present needs."[16] He sees politicians and writers as "natural rivals" for,

> Both groups try to make the world in their own image; they fight for the same territory. And the novel is one way of denying the official, politicians' version of truth.[17]

Rushdie pits his truth against the "politicians' " version and his fabulous tale quite competently gives the lie to official truth. Rushdie's strategy is to blur the boundaries between fiction and truth, story and history. Rushdie himself has spoken about the need to see the connection between history and story in his work as an important one:

> [...] I have always used a kind of historical method in the completely unmethodical way that is the luxury of fiction. I do think this connection of history and story important to remember. The Italian word *storia* means both things; the Urdu word *qissa* means a tale and it means history.[18]

Thus it is not surprising that the imposition of the fabulous "Peccavistan," with its sense of inequity, purity and conquest fused together,[19] over the 'actually existing' Pakistan, 'accurately' renders the socio-political life of Pakistan even as it records its 'exclusions':

> [...] the issue of *Time* magazine (or was it *Newsweek*?) which never got into the country because it carried an article about President Ayub Khan's alleged Swiss bank account; or about the bandits on the trunk roads who are condemned for doing, as private enterprise, what the government does as public policy; or about genocide in Baluchistan; [...] or about the attempt to declare the sari an obscene garment; or about the extra hangings—the first for

> twenty years—that were ordered purely to legitimise the execution of Mr. Zulfikar Ali Bhutto; or about why Bhutto's hangman has vanished into thin air [...] or about smuggling, the boom in heroin exports, military dictators, venal civilians, corrupt civil servants, bought judges, newspapers of whose stories the only thing that can confidently be said is that they are lies [...] (70)

Shame revels in the paradox that its "military dictators, venal civilians, corrupt civil servants, bought judges," are pallid, phantom images of these 'exclusions,' caricatures of 'real' personalities. In positing the real with the fantastic and story with history Rushdie is actually presenting the reader with an 'anti-history': for unlike conventional histories that describe golden ages and glorious conquests, his tale about Pakistan is one where "clowns and goons play(ing) out the plots of high tragedies."[20] The novel is cluttered with 'great names,' and yet everyone of the characters bearing a great name shows his or her petty and paltry sides through his or her actions:[21] Haroun (named after the great caliph Haroun Rashid) is just a pretty boy and an insecure son of a great father; Babar Shakil (named after the founder of the Moghul dynasty in India) is a dissolute person who copulates with wooly sheep; Rani Harappa, very unlike her maiden name (Rani Humayun means Queen Humayun—Emperor Humayun was Babar's son, and father of Akbar, the great Moghul emperor) lacks authority even in her own house, where ayahs and old servants rule; Bilquis's father Mahmoud the Woman and his Empire Talkies ironically recall Mahmud of Ghazni (971-1030), known as the "Sword of Islam,"[22] one of the earliest Muslim conquerors of India and hence held among historians as one of the pioneers who established a Muslim presence and "Empire" in India; and last but not least Omar Khayyam Shakil, the peripheral hero with the great poet's name, very unlike the sense that his last name bears ("Shakil" means "well-formed," "comely" or "handsome"), is gross in his corpulence and intemperate in his habits and personifies shamelessness itself in the novel.

But above all *Shame's* 'anti-history' is about Raza Hyder and Iskander Harrappa. Again the names that Rushdie gives his protagonists serve his purpose of 'setting' them up. Thus in *Shame's* appellation for Gen. Zia Ul Haq, Raza Hyder, Rushdie deliberately uses the name Raza,[23] to suggest the sense of the Hindi word for 'King,' "Raja,"[24] while borrowing the name Hyder itself from the name of the eighteenth century Muslim army commander from Mysore, Hyder Ali. Significantly, like Raza Hyder in *Shame*, Hyder Ali (1722-1782) started off from being a *naik*, a corporal, in the Raja of Mysore's army and "rose by ability to command the army."[25] However, he displaced the Prime Minister, and "retired" the Raja, making him "a prisoner in his own palace,"[26] to take effective control of the kingdom.

Yet unlike Hyder Ali's illustrious son Tippu Sultan (1749-53?), who became famous as the "Tiger of Mysore" and whose ability to strike terror in British hearts has attained folkloric status, Raza Hyder's progency, an idiot daughter, becomes a living testimony of his own shame and ultimately the cause of apocalyptic destruction.

Similarly, Zulfikar Ali Bhutto gets the Persianised name of Alexander the Great,[27] Iskander, while his surname Harappa is used to playfully suggest Iskander's lineage as dating to even before Alexander—the pre-historic Harappan civilisation itself. Both allegorical *personae*—Bhutto-Iskander and Haq-Raza—are grotesque caricatures of their great names, while at the same time being "pale shadows"[28] of their real-life counter-parts. What is significant, though, is that their 'anti-history' is presented as women's tales. The women who marched in from the peripheries to demand the inclusion of their "tragedies, histories and comedies" (173) also get a chance to present their own version of the truth. The repertoire of "juicy-gory" gossip in Bariamma's house-hold underlines the strategy, again, of using 'story' to present a "sub-version" of history and forms the core of *Shame's* strategy. For as Rukmini Bhaya Nair puts it, in *Shame* narrative is "shaped as gossip" and is "creatively empowered to reclaim the metaphors of an elite history."[29] Thus if these gossipy tales are "the glue that held the clan together, binding the generations in webs of whispered secrets" (76), it is through the repeated recounting, exemplified in Bilquis's story, that they acquire the sanctity of truth, of history:

> Her story altered, at first, in the retellings, but finally it settled down, and after that nobody, neither teller nor listener, would tolerate any deviation from the hallowed sacred text. (76)

Raza Hyder's remark to Bilquis after her 'initiation' marks this passage of story into history, "The recounting of histories is for us a rite of blood" (77).

This telling of family tales, as pointed out earlier, actually constitutes creating an alternative, 'anti-history,' for unlike the epic heroisms and magnificent epochs that 'elite' histories speak of, these stories are,

> lurid affairs, featuring divorces, bankruptcies, droughts, cheating friends, child mortality, diseases of the breast, men cut down in their prime, failed hopes, lost beauty, women who grew obscenely fat, smuggling deals, opium-taking poets, pining virgins, curses, typhoid, bandits, homosexuality, sterility, frigidity, rape, the high price of food, gamblers, drunks, murders, suicides and God. (76)

Bariamma's sardonic telling of Raza Hyder's tale, her story of the "strong-man of the nation," who is also a melodramatic "type who cried too easily" (78), is one such example. The tale of the conquest of the "valley of tears" is delectably ironical:

> [...] He returned a hero, having seized for our new holy land a mountain valley so high and inaccessible that even goats had difficulty in breathing up there; so intrepid he was, so tremendous, that all true patriots has to gasp—and you must not believe that propaganda which says that the enemy did not bother to defend the place [...] (79).

This 'mock-hero' is further rendered pathetic when the tale of the birth of his "re-incarnated son" is told. In a deliciously wicked scene Rushdie and Bariamma poke fun at the General's refusal to accept "defeat" and his 'fighting' qualities, when his frenzied longing for a boy is shattered and Sufiya Zenobia, instead of the expected boy, is born. The terminology of the battle-ground used here, only sets off Raza Hyder's ludicrous attempt "to affect biology by a superhuman act of will" (90).

> Defeat? But this was Old Razor Guts himself, conqueror of

> glaciers, vanquisher of frosty meadows and ice-fleeced mountain sheep! Was the future strong-man of the nation so easily crushed? Not a bit of it. Did the midwife's bombshell lead to unconditional surrender? Certainly not. Raza began to argue; and the words came in rushes, inexorable as tanks. The walls of the hospital shook and retreated; horses shied, unseating riders, on the nearby polo fields.
>
> [...]
>
> And blasted from his lips like cannonballs: 'Genitalia! Can! Be! Obscured!' (89)

This grotesquely comic tale, says the narrator, may have been "a little embellished during its many tellings and retellings," but he refuses to question "the veracity of oral tradition." (90) Remarkably, the narrator's own tale complements and mirrors this "oral" tradition and if he too "embellishes" his story a little, it only serves to highlight the grotesqueness that lies hidden behind the normal and the perturbing corruption that official truth seeks to obscure.

The the "pukka Peter sellers Indian" of Raza Hyder[30] is used to highlight the cruel, sadist ways of the General. The theatricality of his actions—praying on television and taking oaths on the Quran—actually set off his lies, so that his motto, "Stability in the name of God" (249) is taken to be a joke, apparent in the Chief Martial Law Administrator's initials CMLA, which we are told, actually stand for *Cancel My Last Announcement.* The ruthlessness of the comic Raza is reflected in his readiness to murder his own daughter when he realises that she could be a danger to him.

The narrator similarly lampoons the democratic pretensions of the late Zulfikar Ali Bhutto through his fictional portrait of Iskander Harappa. Again like in Raza Hyder's case the severest indictment comes from the women's version of the truth—Rani Harappa's eighteen embroidered shawls that depict Iskander Harappa's 'anti-history.'

The embroidered shawls exemplify the ingenious, if tenous, inter-textuality of Rushdie's conceits. For here, unlike

Bariamma's 'folk-tale' of Raza Hyder's great conquests, Rani Harappa's shawls, as a motif, seem to be based on an actual source of history, albeit the history of England—the Bayeux Tapestry depicting William the Conqueror's conquest of England.[31]

Traditionally attributed to Queen Matilda, wife of William the Conqueror, and her hand-maidens,[32] the so-called "Tapestry," like Rani's "epitaph of wool" for Iskander (191), "is in fact an embroidery in coloured wools on a linen base."[33] Rani's "eighteen shawls of memory" (191) also bear similarity to the Bayeax Tapestry in so far as both testimonies are largely silent and pictorial, interspersed with captioned inscriptions and legends.

However, in the context of Rani's exilic condition and near-abandoned status, more important is the ironic evocation of a devoted Queen's proud tribute to her 'Lord and Master's' glorious conquest. For what is depicted in Rani's embroidered testimony is not the grandeur of a majestic personality but the 'truth' of Iskander's lust for power that masquerades as love for his people, and his insatiable pleasure-seeking ways hidden behind his "servant of Duty" (192) facade. Appropriately given the title, "The Shamelessness of Iskander the Great" (191), the embroidered shawls stand witness to everything that Arjumand, blinded by her love for her father, refuses to see—a saga of lust, revenge and terror, replete with blood and gore. Thus Rani's account of the 'life and times' of Iskander Harappa constitutes, unlike the Bayeaux Tapestry, an alternative version of official and elite history. It is a defiant act of subversion as well, for Rani not only sets the record straight but by signing her maiden-name, *Humayun,* she also seeks to retrieve her own self from "the mothballs of the past" (191), and "the fine mist of oblivion" (194) that Iskander had consigned her life into.

What is also significant about the embroidered shawls is the fact that they bear an inter-textual debt to Faiz Ahmed Faiz's famous *ghazal,* "Do Not Ask of Me, My Love"[34] a poem that Rushdie himself quotes in *SV* (334-35).[35] Though the poem's context is a different one, the startling conceit in the lines quotes below, demonstrates that *Shame* is acquainted with not only

Faiz's ideas on elitist history but also the actual figuring of those ideas:

An-ginat sadyon ke tarik bahemana tilism
Resham o atlas o kamkhab men bunwa'e hu'e
Ja-ba-ja bikte hue kucha o bazar men jism
Khak men lithare hue, khun men nahlae hue
Jism nikale hu'e amraz ke tannuron se
Pip bahti hu'i galte hu'e nasuron se-[36]

In Victor Kiernan's translation these lines read:

The dark beastly spell of countless centuries,
Woven into silk and satin and brocade,—
Bodies sold everywhere in alley and market,
Smeared with dust, washed in blood,
Bodies that have emerged from the ovens of
diseases, Pus flowing from rotten ulcers—[37]

Elitist history woven as it is in "silk, satin, and brocade" hides the misery that countless people have suffered through times immemorial. If Faiz's unconventional juxtaposition of velvety luxuriousness with images of physical decay and corruption of the human body poignantly highlights the limitations of conventional history, Rani Harappa's shawls focus precisely on what is conveniently excluded in the recording of so-called great men's lives. Thus for each projected virtue of Iskander, Rani offers us an alternative view. Lasciviousness, egotism, revenge, torture, terror, election rigging, and death [...] the bodies sprawled across the shawl, the men without genitals, the sundered legs, the intestines in place of faces, the alien legion of the dead [...] *twenty, fifty, a hundred thousand dead, who knows, and not enough scarlet thread on earth to show the blood*, the people hanging upside down with dogs at their open guts, the people grinning lifelessly with bullet-holes for second mouths, the people united in the worm-feast of that shawl of flesh and death [...] (195).

—everything about the "dark beastly spell" of Iskander's reign is woven into the brocade of Rani's shawls.

One notes that in Rani Harappa's shawls, Rushdie fuses together historical and literary motifs. *Shame's* metaphors and images—conceits, rather—function as palimpsests and signify a dynamic hybridity that is brazen and polemic in its politics, as against the "palimpsest" of Pakistan itself that expressly obscures "what lies beneath" (87). Thus it is significant that in the palimpsest of the shawl, the West as history and the East as literature[38] are pressed into service to severely indict the corrupt power politics of ruling-class Pakistan.

If Rani Harappa's eighteen shawls constitute an "act of accusation on the grandest conceivable scale" (193), the severest indictment of the insularity of Pakistani society is emblematised in Sufiya Zinobia. The puny idiot girl, "the wrong miracle," who blushed right from the moment she was born, is a personification of shame itself, her blushes signifying the shame of the world she is born into. A "saint" who endures the shamelessness of others (141), Sufiya suffers until the latent violence, intrinsic to a marriage between shame and shamelessness (as *Shame's* logic goes) erupts and the mild, idiot girl becomes a ferocious, marauding beast. In the "bi-polar"[39] world of shame and shamelessness, the narrative of *Shame* suggests, the only solution lies in violence: "Between shame and shamelessness lies the axis upon which we turn; meteorological conditions at both these poles are of the most extreme, ferocious type. Shamelessness, shame: the roots of violence" (115-16).

Discussing this aspect of *Shame,* of the violence that Rushdie suggests is inherent in the dialectics of shame and shamelessness, Aijaz Ahmad observes that "violence is not in itself capable of regeneration, and it is doubtful, Fanon notwithstanding, that violence is intrinsically even a cleansing virtue." He thus finds the very dialectic—"of shame and shamelessness and their condensation in eruptions of violence"—governing the "conceptual framework of the novel" fundamentally flawed.[40]

Ahmad, in his otherwise astute assessment of *Shame*, here

misperceives the violence in the novel as something that is there for its own sake—"violence [...] in itself"—and overlooks the fact that its *raison d'etre* is derived from its manifesto which is, as Peter Craven puts it, one of "political and historical action."[41] Thus if the novel itself, in its outspoken criticism and in its brutal satire of Pakistan's ruling class constitutes a political action, the narrator's attempts at retrieving the past that lies obscured beneath the palimpsest of the present reflects again an individual, even heroic action, much like the action that Saleem in *MC* takes in retrieving and 'chutnifying' his version of history."

However, more significant is the way that *Shame* shows its preference for women who are dynamic and aggressive and rejects the passive roles that women are reduced to playing and sometimes, under the pervasive influence of patriarchal values, even will this subjection upon themselves. Accordingly, almost all the 'normal' women in *Shame* are shown as passive or complicit with patriarchal values and are consequently rejected and are shown in the most negative light: thus Arjumand Harappa who is so blinded by her love for her father that she refuses to see even his most glaring omissions is condemned, like her mother to a life without love; the author's contempt for Naveed Hyder, and her propensity towards 'sitting on her hair,' is evident when he summarily dismisses the story of her rebellion as not worthy of comparison with Anna Muhammad's; Bilquis's disappointment in her own inability to produce a son marks her as complicit with patriarchal values; even Bariamma, embalmed in the fixity of her gossipy tales is subjected to the author's contempt and ridicule. It is only Rani and Omar Khayyam's three mothers, apart from Sufiya Zinobia that receive sympathy and understanding from the author.

Rushdie's thrust towards action is manifested in the name he gives his heroine—Sufiya Zinobia. Apart from the obvious reference to Sufism in 'Sufiya,' the name evokes the personalities of some of the women involved with the Prophet during his lifetime. Thus in 'Sufiya' we also find the name of Safiyah, the Prophet's Jewish wife, and in Zinobia, the three women named Zainab integral in many ways to the Prophet's life — two of them his wives and one a daughter. However, more importantly

'Zenobia' is also the name of the third century Queen of Palmyra, famous for her "beauty and intelligence" and yet one whose "name has also been a symbol of ruthless arrogance."[42]

These revenant presences in the elaborate pun in Sufiya's name are indicative of the crucial point that Rushdie makes in the novel—of the beast that lurks in the beauty. Rushdie's use of the name is deliberately oxymoronic so that the pure and innocent but inactive and cloistered women of the Prophet's family are sharply contrasted with the ambitious and ruthless Zenobia.

This juxtaposition of the dynamic and the placid, the active and the passive in Sufiya Zinobia's name also becomes apparent in Rushdie's discussion of the other "ghosts" that "haunt" Sufiya's story: the British Pakistani girl, who was killed by her father because she had shamed him by making love to an English boy, the unnamed 'Asian' girl, who was beaten up on the underground by a gang of white teenaged boys, and the boy who had, impossibly, "ignited of his own accord" (117) and burned himself to death. The narrator here delineates the predicament of people caught in situations where they are either the victims of other people's shame, as exemplified by the story of the Pakistani girl, or, are themselves mortified by their situations, as typified by the case of the unnamed girl. Reflecting on the latter's reluctance to talk about this incidence, the narrator points out that "it is a typical reaction, and the girl is not one girl but many" (117).

The "burning" boy's case connects the humiliation suffered by coloured people in a metropolitan society with the sense of shame inflicted on women in "traditional" societies. The narrator ruminating on the televised images of racial riots in England, feels that the young people whose "shame burning on their brows" not only set "fire to the shops, police shields, cars" (117) but also to the humiliation that they have suffered in a racist society:

> Humiliate people for long enough and a wildness bursts out of them. Afterwards, surveying the wreckage of their rage, they look bewildered, uncomprehending, young. Did we do such things? Us? But we are just ordinary kids, nice

> people, we didn't know we could [...] then, slowly, pride dawns on them, pride in their power, in having learned to hit back. (117)

The narrator fantasizes a similar fury unleashed in the girl against the thugs who beat her up in the underground train:

> how she would have thrashed the white kids within an inch of their lives, breaking arms legs noses balls, without knowing whence the violence came, without seeing how she, so slight a figure, could command such awesome strength [...].I feel gleeful about this notion: it's a seductive, silky thing, this violence, yes it is. (117)

The "seductive, silky [...] violence," however, as pointed out earlier is not a wanton phenomena. As the narrator points out, one has to find the energy and the fire in our own selves: "We are energy; we are fire; we are light" but what is important is "Finding the key, stepping through that truth [...]." In short, it is 'action' that engenders the "pride in [...] power" and leads to violence, which in its turn leads to change.

However, the fact that Sufiya Zinobia is the only one who can act renders Rushdie's perception of action problematic. Firstly the repeated "connections" that Rushdie makes while trying to show Sufiya Zinobia's plight as a universal predicament, robs her of the existential pathos that could render her action meaningful. Sufiya exists so much in the mind and fantasy of the narrator and the "ghosts" that he rigs up to contextualise her character, that the reader inevitably feels distanced from her. Secondly, the fact that the crucial act of "Finding the key, stepping through that truth [...]" occurs in the fantasy of the narrator and the madness of Sufiya Zinobia, turns the notion itself, of action, into an abstraction devoid of any pragmatic value.

Moreover, as Ahmad rightly points out, Rushdie constantly elides his political fable with a civil society "that is declared to be co-terminal with this state structure, equally deformed and irretrievably marked by its purported civilisation (Islam) and its generic origin (the partition)."[43] Also in emphasising action Rushdie exaggerates the role of individuals and ignores the role of constructive, group activism; as Inderpal Grewal points out the only time the organised effort of the women's movement in Pakistan is mentioned it is dismissed within the space of a paragraph.[44]

Nevertheless in *Shame* Rushdie has made a crucial move towards a consideration of social praxis as action and his next novel, despite its more controversial nature would have a maturer and more positive consideration of action.

Notes

1. Bhabha quoted in Anne Maxwell's "Current Debates in Theories of Colonial Discourse," *Kunapipi* 13.3: 72.

   See also Homi Bhabha, "The Commitment of Theory," *New Formations* 5 (1988): 10-11.
2. Salman Rushdie, *Shame* (1983; London: Picador, 1984). All quotations are from this edition, with page numbers cited in parenthesis.
3. "Salman Rushdie," Interview conducted by David Brooks and Marie-Anne Paton, *Helix* 19/20 (1984): 64-65.
4. Brooks, "Salman Rushdie" 65.
5. Timothy Brennan, *Salman Rushdie and the Third World: Myths of the Nation* (London: Macmillan, 1989) 119.
6. Brooks, "Salman Rushdie" 68.
7. Aijaz Ahmad, "Rushdie's *Shame*: Postmodernism, Migrancy and Representation of Women," *Economic and Political Weekly* 15 June 1991: 1466.
8. Salman Rushdie, "Lecture/Interview," *Kunapipi* 8.1 (1985): 18.
9. Ahmad 1466.
10. Whether this narrator figure is Rushdie himself is a moot point; however Aijaz Ahmad's insistence on viewing the narrator's voice as Rushdie's own cannot be dismissed easily especially since Rushdie himself has admitted as much.

    See (1) "A Dangerous Art Form," interview with Salman Rushdie in *Third World Book Review* 1.1 (2) "Lecture/Interview" in *Kunapipi* 13 (3) The *Helix* interview 58.
11. Jean-Pierre Durix, "The Artistic Journey in Salman Rushdie's Shame," *World Literature Written in English* 23.2 (Spring 1984): 451-63.
12. Brennan points out that the many sub-plots of *MC* give way, in *Shame* to a mosaic of a chain of "juxtaposed and basically self-contained parables" so that the earlier novel's strong and "dominant" centre is replaced by several individual points of view. But Brennan here

overlooks the narrator himself who is as central to *Shame*'s narrative as Saleem was in *MC*.

See Timothy Brennan, *Salman Rushdie and the Third World: Myths of the Nation* 122-23.

13. See Brennan's excellent "*Shame*'s Holy Book" in his *Salman Rushdie and the Third World: Myths of the Nation* 124-35.
14. Anuradha Dingwaney, "Authorizing *Midnight's Children* and *Shame*: Salman Rushdie's Constructions of Authority," *Reworlding: The Literature of the Indian Diaspora*, ed. Emmanuel S. Nelson (Westport CT: Greenwood, 1992) 162.
15. Salman Rushdie, "Outside the Whale," *Imaginary Homelands: Essays and Criticism 1981-1991* (London: Granta, 1991) 100.
16. Rushdie, "Imaginary Homelands," *Imaginary Homelands* 13-14.
17. Rushdie, "Imaginary Homelands" 14.
18. Brooks, "Salman Rushdie" 58.
19. *Peccavi*, "I have sinned," and Napier's famous coded telegraph, conveying his victory over Sind, jostles here with the meaning of the word "Pakistan," "the country of the pure."
20. Rushdie, "Lecture/Interview" 15.
21. Incidentally, a majority of these 'names' are traditionally associated with 'Indian' history, even though a large part of this history also happened in what is now Pakistan. It is worthwhile recording that not only has Pakistan been always a part of the Moghal empire, but also the traditional route for the Turko-Afghan marauders and Mongolian conquerors. Iskander's surname, Harappa, and the name of his country estate Mohenjo, are the names of the famous prehistoric sites, located in Pakistan but considered signs indicative of the earliest *Indian* civilisation. Rushdie is making sure that his readers wouldn't forget that "Indian centuries 1(i.e.) just beneath the surface of Pakistani Standard Time" (87).
22. Stanley Wolpert, *A New History of India* (New York: OUP, 1989) 106-07.
23. "Raza" (Persian/Urdu) literally means "agree"; as a man's name it can mean one who agrees with the "will of God," or even the "will of God," itself.
24. See also Brennan 120.
25. Percival Spear, *India: A Modern History* (Ann Arbor: Michigan UP, 1961) 218.
26. *Encyclopedia Britannica*, vol. 6, 15th ed. 1992.
27. A personality that finds mention even in the Quran—Zul Qurnain whose story is recounted in the chapter entitled *al-Kahf* (The Cave).

    See Abdullah Yusuf Ali, trans. *The Holy Quran* (Beirut: Dar Al Arabia, 1968) 760-65.
28. Brooks, "Salman Rushdie" 59.

29. Rukmini Bhaya Nair, "Text and Pretext: History as Gossip in Rushdie's Novels," *Economic and Political Weekly* 6 May 1989: 995.

30. Peter Craven, "Salman Rushdie's Rough Magic," *Scripsi* 3.2-3 (1985): 144.

31. Rushdie actually cites the landing of William the Conqueror and the Battle of Hastings in *SV*. Significantly, the immigrant-conquerors Chamcha and Farista, like William also "land" in Hastings.

32. *New Columbia Encyclopedia,* 4th ed. 1975.

33. Still popularly known as "la Tapisserie de la Reine Mathilde" in France, the Bayeax Tapestry is in fact now, correctly, attributed to Odo, Bishop of Bayeaux and William's brother who commissioned it. Interestingly though, like Rushdie's Pakistan which was born in the West and "which then went East" (87) the Tapestry is regarded as being made in England, (more specifically, in St. Augustine's Abbey in Canterbury!), which was then taken to France.

    See R. Allen Brown, *The Norman Conquest,* "Documents of Medieval History Series," ed.. G.W.S. Barrowa and Edward Miller (London: Edward Arnold, 1984) 172-73 and *New Columbia Encyclopedia,* 4th ed. 1975.

34. Victor Kiernan translates Faiz's *Mujh se Pehle si Mohabbat Mere Mahboob na Maang* as "Love, Do No Ask." See *Poems by Faiz* (Unesco: Vanguard Books, 1971, 65.

35. Rushdie in *SV* uses, what he calls a "variant" of Mahmood Jamal's translation of Faiz's poem. Neither does he quote the poem in full. The lines quotes here by me form the second stanza of Faiz's poem, which is incidentally also the part that Rushdie does *not* quote. (*See* "Acknowledgements" at the end of *SV*.)

36. The romanization (or transliteration) of Faiz's Urdu *ghazal* is borrowed from Victor Kiernan's book, *Poems from Faiz* 65-67. It has not been possible to reproduce Kiernan's usage of signs and symbols, and consequently his superb delienation of the nuances of Urdu, due to technical reasons.

37. Kiernan, *Poems by Faiz* 65-67.

38. Rushdie has often remarked that his work is read as "fantasy" in the West and as "history" in the East.

    See, for instance his interview in *Scripsi* 3.2-3 (1985): 113.

39. Rudolf Bader, "On Blood and Blushing: Bipolarity in Salman Rushdie's Shame," *International Fiction Review* 15.1 (Winter 1988): 30-33.

40. Ahmad, "Rushdie's *Shame*" 1467.

41. Craven 141.

42. *Columbia Encyclopedia* 1975.

43. Ahmad 1466.

44. Inderpal Grewal, "Salman Rushdie: Marginality, Women, and Shame," *Genders* 3.38 (Nov. 1988): 24-42.

7

THE POLITICS OF REPRESSION AND RESISTANCE IN SALMAN RUSHDIE'S *SHAME*

NELUKA SILVA

> [...] I really wanted to get the low-down on things, and at length I brought up the stuff that was on my mind, beginning with a question about the execution of Zulfikar Ali Bhutto. But only half the question got past my lips; the other half joined the ranks of the area's many unasked queries, because I felt an extremely painful kick land on my shins and, without crying out, switched in mid-sentence back to sporting topics.

In Salman Rushdie's *Shame*, for the 'I' narrator, the pain of not speaking is very real. A kick in the shins physically prevents him from asking a question. To him, it is a harmless question, but is clearly within the realms of the unspeakable. This encounter with censorship produces a profound sense of perplexity as the 'I' narrator discovers what people can and cannot do or say in the cause of the Pakistan nation-state. So like everyone else, he has to confine himself to what is regarded as the innocuous, in order that (to borrow Rushdie's term) 'civility' is maintained (*S* 27). As the 'I' narrator sets about elucidating the forms of decorum and propriety that pervade his social milieu, his own precarious position as an 'outsider, trespasser,' as well as the rationale behind maintaining this tight-lipped facade, is established in the description of Pakistan.

After the Partition of the Indian subcontinent in 1947, Pakistan's insecurity as a new nation has emerged as an overriding concern for intellectuals and the international community. The force of the military, the breakdown of democracy and structures of good governance, as well as the unstable state of civil society, have been critiqued in *Shame*. The source of instability is foregrounded in the novel through the metaphors of translation and palimpsest: So it was a word born in exile which then went East, was borne across or translated, and imposed itself on history; a returning migrant, settling down on partitioned land, forming a palimpsest on the past. A palimpsest obscures what lies beneath. To build Pakistan it was necessary to cover up Indian history, to deny that Indian centuries lay just beneath the surface of Pakistani Standard Time. The past was rewritten; there was nothing else to be done (*S* 87).

In his use of the word translation, the 'I' narrator exposes the suppressive strategies of nation-building. Like the word Pakistan, the dominant ideology of the nation-state involves covering up, and here an appraisal of the effects of 'palimpsest' is crucial to Rushdie's vision of the political culture of his novel. 'Palimpsest' suggests that there is always the possibility of subversion because, despite attempts to completely 'erase' what is written, traces of the original remain visible. Erasure also implies censorship. Rushdie's view of censorship in Pakistan is that it is 'ubiquitous,' and its effects are 'the absence of information and the presence of lies.' In the light of Pakistan's politics, censorship also entails rewriting the past, and forging a distinct, new national identity. The anxiety to create 'purity' or 'newness' necessitates erasure but, as corroborated by the breakaway of East Pakistan, this process has a heavy price attached to it.

Who is responsible for making decisions about how the nation should be constructed? And does the obsession to rewrite history originate from insecurity and shame or from shamelessness? As Rushdie strives to answer these questions, the intersection of religion, politics, and the linkages with violence and repression are closely and uneasily interwoven in his narrative. Three groups of highly-ranked men, the politicians—represented by Iskander Harappa and Raza Hyder-the military, and the religious leaders, control the fate of Pakistan. They promulgate decisive and coercive steps on the masses, such as decreeing Urdu to be the official language, formulating the administrative patterns of the East wing, prohibiting alcohol, and imposing diverse forms of oppression. Pakistan's priests/religious leaders (the mullahs) and the military are mutually dependent on each other. Together they install the overwhelming atmosphere of repression in the nation-state. Yet, as the authors of the social and cultural codes, they are exempt from following these codes.

Significantly, the patriarchal and masculinist character of religious institutions and the military allow their chief actors to make value-judgements on particular actions and utterances. There are things which cannot be said: to do so is, in the eyes of the military, to commit a crime, in the eyes of the mullahs, a sin. Indeed, the soldiers and priests/religious leaders adopt these measures to protect the nation from the instability that comes from what they regard as, liberalism, radical ideas and subversion. Recognising the emotional force of religion, they enlist support from the mullahs and invoke the Quran (*S* 203-04) which, as Timothy Brennan argues, "[...] is the text that gives Pakistan its authority as a nation."

The 'sacred language' of religion, the top-layer of the palimpsest in Pakistan, is made public in Hyder's manipulation of the television interview. When the interviewer challenges the 'barbarism' of Islamic punishments, Hyder's retort is: "These are the holy words of God, as revealed in sacred texts. Now if they are holy words of God, they cannot also be barbaric. It is not possible. They must be some other thing" (*S* 245).

There is an implicit criticism of Raza Hyder's manipulations of the discourses of religion. In addition to the Quran, the incessant 'whinings' of Maulana Dawood (Hyder's religious authority), are appropriated as the normative discourse of the Nation (*S* 247).

Under Dawood's instigation, repression in any form—whether it is 'banning booze,' altering television schedules or dismantling the legal system—is sanctioned on the premise that 'God was in charge' (*S* 247, 248). Religion, like power, is enforced from the top.

> So-called Islamic 'fundamentalism' does not spring, in Pakistan, from the people. It is imposed on them from above. [...] This is how religions shore up dictators; by encircling them with words of power, words which the people are reluctant to see discredited, disenfranchised, mocked (*S* 251).

However, the characters and 'I' narrator in *Shame* are not just censored by the military and the mullahs. Another form of censorship, to explain it another way, *takallouf* also controls their utterances. It is an extensive area of the unsayeable. Takallouf applies to notions of social decorum and propriety between the sexes, and ensures that strict gender distinctions are maintained. Takallouf saturates the text creating an intense sense of claustrophobia. From the outset, the three Shakil sisters are first 'caged' by their father. They then inflict self-imprisonment during their simultaneous pregnancy and continue to be entrapped in their 'cage.' The cage-effect is so powerful that, in the final dénouement, even dictators cannot escape from it. The cage metaphor underlines the chapter entitled "A Necklace of Shoes" in which, amidst the presence of the military, dictatorships, torture and jail resides the 'caged' ambience of social elegance and etiquette, and which brings us back to the 'I' narrator's predicament. An 'absence of information,' an inability to speak and an overbearing sense of entrapment (identified with the censorship process) are part of the fabric of the protagonists' world. In order to 'speak' the 'I' narrator has to devise ingenious and elusive ways, precluding any signs of suspicion. His position is analogous to the fates of the female characters, for whom it is not merely speaking that is a traumatic process.

Female Stories—Tales of the Repressed

If between the male figures a range of 'repressions' is unearthed, then their effects are most visible on those who are repressed: the female characters. The narrator is extremely conscious of how repression works and describes it as: Repression is a seamless garment; a society which is authoritarian in its social and sexual codes, which crushes its women beneath the intolerable burdens of honour and propriety, breeds repressions of other kinds as well (*S* 173). This position is reaffirmed in another moment of authorial intervention. The implied author comments that his narrative is originally intended as a 'masculine tale,' but: "They [women] marched in from the peripheries of the story to demand the inclusion of their own tragedies, histories and comedies" (*S* 173).

This comment is followed by the assertion that "it is commonly and, I believe, accurately said of Pakistan that her women are much more impressive than her men [...] their chains, nevertheless, are no fictions. They exist. They are getting heavier" (*S* 173). It suggests an awareness of women's exclusion and marginality, and signals the attempt to include their voices.

The portrayal of the principal female characters in the novel, their relationships with the men and their strategies of resistance occupy a significant part of the 'domestic' narrative. Although there is potential for assigning a symbolic value to their roles, the women are individualised and some of the most moving episodes in the novel are drawn through them. From the outset the women characters are entrapped within interlocking systems of power relations.

Their tribulations, vulnerability and resignation are forcefully mapped. They are the victims of the male ego, whether it is of the father or the husband, and the construction of the other female characters are replete with images concerning repression. The three Shakil sisters, for instance, are imprisoned by their father "inside that labyrinthine mansion until his dying day; virtually uneducated" (*S* 13). Similarly, Bilquìs Hyder, Raza's wife who is forced to migrate (from India) during Partition when her father's cinema empire is set ablaze, is so conditioned by her father's will that she is left with nothing except her shame and a "dupatta of modesty" (*S* 63). The arranged marriage between Rani Humayun and

Iskander Harappa also exemplifies these codified gender relations. The marriage ceremony, complete with its debauchery (the lecherous great-uncle pinching the bottoms of the women) and opulence (signified by the weight of Rani's jewellery), sets the tone for their relationship (*S* 79-81).

This repression leads to sexual and psychological frustrations, the effects of which are visible later and impinge on subsequent relationships. Tenuous marital relationships produce another generation of women who are equally incapacitated by male repression. Each one negotiates her familial and social tensions differently, but whatever method they choose—resistance or resignation—they are forced to contend with cultural expectations, which include marriage and the capacity to produce male children (since a female child is a sign of personal and familial ignominy). The pathos is evoked by the representation of a climate where a woman derives consolation from another woman's 'inability' to produce a son (*S* 84). Furthermore, a woman is also not allowed to enjoy sex, and if she is widowed she is even "less than a wife, worthless" (*S* 84, 88, 158).

Even when their experiences form a vital composite of the political narrative, female experiences, as portrayed in *Shame*, are often subsumed or elided by a religio-patriarchal discourse and removed from the public realm. Thus, to 'include' their stories is to include their modes of resistance and these forms are informed by the specific circumstances of oppression. I will chart the subversion of patriarchal dominance by exploring the constitution of takallouf and the image of the chowdar (also called the chadur) which is sometimes used in conjunction with, or in place of, the purda and its encroachment into the lives of the protagonists.

In the novel, purda is defined as a "garment of womanly honour" (*S* 64). It can encompass a range of meanings and is chiefly associated with Islamic societies. To be veiled provides a woman with a place in society. The garment defines a woman's modesty and restrictions on her interactions with men in society. Santi Rozairo quotes Maulana Maududi, a Pakistani Muslim theologian who sees purda as operating to guard against the 'dangerously uncontrolled' human sexual urge. Purda embraces signification of honour and shame and is directly concerned with the status of women.

While purda may denote restriction, in *Shame* it also functions as parody and is manipulated within the narrative to embody a transgressive value. When Bilquìs Hyder ventures outside her home for the first time, her only 'protection' is the veil. When her clothes are torn from her body by the explosion, she is secure in the knowledge that it secures her modesty. The irony of course is that this is not the case. Once she recognises its inadequacy the veil becomes a source of shame (*S* 64). I read this moment as a parody of the so-called 'garment of womanly honour' since it is directly linked, not to modesty, but to nakedness. In this instance, even though it is redundant, it still weighs heavy on her, giving her a 'false' sense of modesty. This episode exhibits the psychological implications of wearing a purda.

Ironically, in *Shame,* the veil is denied the kind of fixed meaning found in religio-political discourses. The mobility of the veil, literally as the material 'flapping' in the wind, leads to an understanding of Bilquìs Hyder's subsequent obsession with "the disease of fixity" (*S* 68). Yet, it is also exploited because purda allows her to conceal herself from society. She sets about shrouding herself in black veils, a device of making herself 'invisible' and escaping from the personal anguish of her life (*S* 208). The anxiety to elude visibility is concomitant with the breakdown of language. Prolonged exposure to repression denudes her of coherent expression, and language is inadequate to pronounce her despair against society. Therefore, she takes refuge in solipsism and obliquity, which become screening devices. Like the purda, solipsism and obliquity 'clothes' language, meaning and intention.

Another way of 'speaking the unspeakable' is enacted by Rani Harappa. Throughout the years of Iskander's philandering and maltreatment she does not undertake a clamorous protest. Her single but powerful act of defiance finds expression in the eighteen shawls she embroiders when she is sequestered on her rural estate; each shawl intricately captures the debaucherous, violent and inhuman acts of her husband's career. Among them are the shawls of terror. In the 'torture shawl,' she depicts the 'blindfolded prisoners tied to chairs while jailers hurled buckets of water, now boiling hot (the thread-steam rose), now freezing cold, until the bodies of the victims grew confused and cold water raised hot burns upon their skins: weals of red embroidery rose scarlike' (*S* 193). The remaining shawls, especially those concerning the handling of dissent in East Pakistan, are equally explicit in their portrayal of physical violence. Rani's role does not merely expose the infractions of the freedom of an individual, but the terrors of leadership. The performativity of transmitting 'her country's past and future in the eternity of the unspoken word' is achieved through a 'domestic,' traditionally 'feminine' activity. Her revelations in the shawls explode the 'macho' images of patriarchy, of politicians' sycophantic and murderous acts. The shawls also incorporate a critique of nationalist politics, which sanctions the violation of human rights when they are committed 'in the name of the nation' (*S* 193, 195). Even if one is inclined to dismiss the descriptions of relentless terror in the shawls as the imagination of a 'neurotic' woman, it is corroborated by other evidence, such as the references to the atrocities perpetrated during the election campaigns. Rani's graphic representation of the atrocities perpetrated in the East wing can be set against the backdrop of the events in Kabara. The shawls expose the artificiality of the nation-state, official historiography and its rhetorical strategies. The controlled terror in the shawls—objects of beauty after all—emerge from the fact that fantasy is a close approximation of reality.

Why does Rani find recourse to embroider the shawls? One factor that must be considered in 'The Shamelessness of Iskander the Great' is the issue of authorship (*S* 191). She signs them under the name of Rani Humayun. Even if Rani cannot publicly renounce the marital bond, in reverting to her maiden-name she symbolically disassociates herself from her husband. It is a disavowal of a large part of her history and provokes a violent response from her daughter. Yet the shawls are also Rani's legacy to her daughter through which she hopes to dispel

Arjumand's delusions about her father. Her daughter, however, refuses to acknowledge the putative claims of Iskander's corruption. She responds by placing her mother under house arrest (*S* 277). Even though Rani does not succeed in convincing her daughter of Iskander's misdemeanours, they allow her to foreground how the permanence of the patriarchal nation-state is predicated on the oppression of women. The shawls also metaphorically link with takallouf and the chowdar but, paradoxically, in the novel the shawls 'speak' even as the veil silences. Significantly, Rani chooses to 'tell her story' by adopting an article of female clothing. Since she is constrained by the 'unspeakable,' a wife's unquestioning loyalty to her husband, she must confine herself to what is perceived as an 'innocuous,' familiar device, overtly identified with the 'feminine' and the domestic, but tacitly enabling her to transgress patriarchal codes of conduct.

Her daughter, Arjumand, on the other hand, devises her own form of resistance. She is psychologically conditioned by her father's words: "It's a man's world. Rise above your gender as you grow" (*S* 126). Arjumand bandages her breasts and strenuously endeavours to efface her sexuality and disavow the institutions of marriage and motherhood. Her eagerness to look and act like a man is blatant, yet this is undercut by the overriding display of 'open hatred' towards any man but her father (*S* 210). For example, she derives immense satisfaction from teasing the naive captain of the guard when she is under house arrest. It has been argued that the unconscious misogyny of Rushdie is unveiled in Arjumand: in the uneasy equation between the asexual woman who repudiates marriage and the man-hater. Arjumand, who shuns any semblance of femininity emerges as a 'frigid and desexualised' woman. Superficially, there seems little comparison between mother and daughter. Yet Arjumand also reacts against patriarchy, albeit in her case protest is strident and extreme. It stems from contempt towards what she perceives as the weakness of women and the belief that, in order to acquire power, it is necessary to enlist its patriarchal structures. Her approach raises questions about the validity and appropriateness of such a mode of resistance. In a social system where the practice of 'veiling' defines a woman's self-worth and identity, Arjumand's repudiation of it, and the social institutions it represents, seems to cripple her just as much as her mother's compliance with these systems circumscribes the latter.

The daughters of Bilquìs and Raza subvert the system in their own ways. Sufiya and Naveed are seen as the embodiments of shame and good news. Initially, Naveed performs the role of the ideal woman by producing an endless stream of children (mostly sons). However, as her reproductive capacity increases her name becomes an ironic signification of her fecundity. In her lies the burden of mothering because she functions solely as a 'baby-machine.' Her husband is completely oblivious to her physical and psychological condition and his only objective is to ensure the fulfilment of reproduction. Finally, after producing twenty-seven children, she realises that she can no longer maintain her social value. Her reproductive capacity is pushed to the level of the grotesque and within the narrative mode of *Shame* this excess of reproduction becomes a political statement.

In Naveed's case purda operates in a different way. Her incessant 'production' of children enforces seclusion because pregnancy, childbirth and the aftercare of the infant occur in the domestic space. If purda, as Shaheed and Mumtaz recognise, is a method of keeping the woman dependant on her husband, constant pregnancy then is also a form of purda which ensures Naveed's dependence on her husband. However, she opts-out of this system by resorting to suicide. The episode where she hangs herself is particularly poignant. She fills the room with the fragrance of 'Joy by Jean Patou' (the most expensive perfume in the world) and she is found with 'jasmine in her hair' (*S* 228). The use of flowers recalls Ophelia's death in Hamlet and, as in Shakespeare's play, pathos is heightened by excessive 'feminine' touches.

Female oppression, as visible in the depiction of Naveed, is both gendered and classed. As an upper-class woman she has a set of expectations placed upon her. In addition to the procreative aspect, Naveed's suicide enacts the tensions of wearing the 'right' perfume, constantly looking groomed and beautiful and producing babies while doing so. Defining woman solely in these terms culminates in the most powerful and terrifying form of self-expression. The overstress on 'femininity' in the suicide can be read as feminist because the excess inscribed in the representation of the suicide disrupts and unsettles expectations of gender identity. The extreme signification of femininity, the perfume and flowers associated with Naveed's death is a form of parody of both gender and class norms and expectations. The 'gender meanings' encoded within the 'parodic styles' is, as Butler identifies, a "part of hegemonic, misogynist culture" which are "denaturalised and mobilised through their parodic recontextualisation." The parodic repetition of gender becomes subversive because it "exposes the illusion of gender identity as an intractable depth and inner substance."

Furthermore, suicide, as a practice and as a metaphor signifies "the refusal to be conscripted." Suicide can be productive in opening a dialogue about sexual difference. It is a tragic indicator of the level of powerlessness and desperation of women, and bears profound witness to the patriarchal authority and general atmosphere of socio-political suffocation. Suicide, therefore, cannot be written off as nihilistic, but is an individual's vehement protest against the multiple forms of oppression she endures.

If suicide is one way of contending with daily reality, then Sufiya, Naveed's sister represents another. From the moment of her birth Sufiya assumes the social stigma of being a daughter, and is referred to as "the wrong miracle" (*S* 89). Her blush at birth is transfigured into the sign for the collective shame of the community. She is the product of multiple, 'silenced' voices (the kind of intertextual modes of narrative in *Shame* that I will be dealing with below), growing 'out of the corpse' of the narrative of the young Pakistani girl living in England who is murdered by her father (*S* 116). Her husband, Omar Khayyam, the embodiment of shamelessness, is counterpoised against Sufiya, who is the epitome of shame, both in name and personality. She links the title with the multiple nuances of shame/sharam. At each stage of the narrative the escalation of her shame is matched by a similarly accruing violence, thus establishing the textual nexus between shame and violence (*S* 138, 214-16).

It is, however, possible to read another form of insurgency into the development of Sufiya's character. If she is a repository for her society's shame, then she does not merely absorb it and remain passive but transforms it into a form of revolutionary hysteria. Through her narrative the escalating violences can be read from a feminist perspective. Her modus operandi of wrenching off her victim's heads and her omnipresence embody some elements of the destructive dimension of Kali, the goddess (*S* 216). The (male) human targets reveal an agglomeration of female revenge. The Beauty and the Beast metaphor hovers within her characterisation. The traditional associations of passivity incorporated within the Beauty myth is shunned and replaced instead by the bestial fighter who initially destroys animals and fields. After her marriage, when Sufiya finds that her husband does not sleep with her but has sexual intercourse with the servant, she questions the state of her life and marriage and responds with a concomitant rise in violence. The self-blame and imputing of guilt upon herself is especially tragic (*S* 215). It resonates with the kind of 'female' guilt acquired from seizing agency that Cixous alludes to in "The Laugh of the Medusa." Cixous poses the question, 'who, feeling a funny desire stirring inside her (to sing, to write, to dare to speak, in short, to bring out something new) hasn't thought she was sick?" Aijaz Ahmad finds Sufiya's appraisal of the constraints placed upon her implausible because she has 'the brain of a six-year old' or, alternatively, she can be written off as 'hysterical.' It must be acknowledged that the Beauty and the Beast myth feeds into notions of hysteria, and Elaine Showalter effectively unpacks the patriarchal underpinnings of hysteria. It is considered 'elusive and enigmatic and resistant to masculine rationality and the symptoms and cultural meanings have changed' from era to era and culture to culture.

Still regarded as 'the quintessential female malady,' hysteria continues to be explained as emanating from sexual frustration. This stance fails to consider the cultural argument that locates hysteria within patriarchal society as the expression of unsatisfied and thwarted aspects of women's lives, intellectual frustrations, lack of mobility and/or the need for control and autonomy. On one level, Sufiya's violence may be seen to encode undertones of the sexually frustrated woman. However, her character is more complex than that, she is inscribed by the discourses of the state and its endemic corruption. She manifests an internalisation of guilt not only for what she perceives as her complicity in the events of the narrative, but for Pakistan as a whole. Even if she is incapable of grasping the more intricate repressive systems defining her reality, the extremes of gender socialisation are entrenched in her psyche so that her revenge is directed at all man-kind. The narrative energy devoted to the depiction of Sufiya is of excessive passion and aggression (which are traditionally valorised as masculine traits). Her actions destabilise and demand the attention of the male establishment and open up possibilities of agency that are, as Butler argues, 'insidiously foreclosed by positions that take identity categories as foundational and fixed,' for instance, mother, daughter or wife.

Polyphonous Voices that Subvert the Narrative of the Nation

In coding the narrative of Sufiya's exploits, the intermixing of genres, and the collapse between the 'real,' the grotesque and the fantastical occur. This establishes a close link with the romance of fairytale. The narrative strategy employed to express Sufiya's story is a useful starting point to consider the question of how one can tell the story of repression in a repressive climate. It is for this reason perhaps, that Rushdie's narrator is anxious to reiterate the fairy-tale quality of his narrative (*S* 70, 257), and the Beauty and the Beast metaphor (*S* 139, 215).

The novel is also an enactment of the predicament of the 'I' narrator. In denying any realistic intention, the narrator heightens the reader's sensitivity to the atmosphere of extreme censorship and signals that, like his women protagonists, he too is circumscribed by takallouf. Here the narrator is placed in an analogous position to the women who inhabit the fictional world of the text. In order to tell his subversive tales, Rushdie's narrator/implied author has to occupy the position of 'woman.' The closure is also reinforced through other factors like his status as a migrant. His perception of being constituted as 'borne across' or translated, is thematically bound up with the fate of his fictional territory, which is 'borne across' from the combination of Indian and British history and culture. The 'other' ways of telling the tale empower him because when the only other alternative in the novel is the masculinist historiography of the Nation, he traverses beyond the realms of 'realism' to unearth the marginal voices. A fusion of genres, whether it is journalese, grotesque, fantasy, documentary or fairy-tale allows the 'I' narrator to present the untidy details of his territory more sharply.

In claiming to write a fairy-tale there is an endeavour to circumvent these exigencies. The choice of the genre is not innocent because, according to Timothy Brennan, the fairy-tale is 'the genres of the subversives—the covert satirist operating under conditions of intense repression." Its appropriateness is the capacity of being rooted in a partially material referential world, located outside the political in an ostensibly innocent space, while disrupting illusions invested in 'official' narratives of the Nation. Fantasy and parody inform his 'fairy-tale' throughout but despite their appearance as 'satiric' manifestations, the chief male actors record the machinations of Pakistan's patriarchs. *Shame* transforms Pakistan into the fantasy of fairy-tale while incorporating the 'factual.' Part of the 'polyphonous collage' is the narrator's admission that his title, character and theme originate from a news item and the story is assembled from newspaper clippings and anecdotes. Brennan relates the narrative strategies as designed towards a parodying of sacred texts, especially the Quran. The digressive technique, recurrent leitmotifs (such as the cage), elliptical utterances and an elaborate number symbolism—of the number three (Omar's three mothers, the three families: Shakil, Hyder and Harappa)—support Brennan's hypothesis. In modelling his work on the 'sacred texts,' an assault is made on the collusion between religion and politics. It disrupts Pakistan's claim to nationhood through its legitimating meta-narrative.

Fairy-tale is not Rushdie's only generic mode because *Shame*'s eclecticism is evident in the mixture of parody, ridicule, fantasy, grotesque, tragedy and realism, all of which draw attention to themselves as narrative as well as to the interstices of the narration of the nation. *Shame*'s multi-layered narratives and plural voices are designed to destabilise the logic of the palimpsest which, while attempting to conceal the original, also holds together traces of writing below the topmost layer. The history of the subcontinent is a palimpsest comprising many 'layers' of time and events. It is an image intended to subvert the linear, chronological narrative of Pakistan. This linearity is jettisoned in favour of thickness and collage, and the frequent slippages of genres provide a space for the utterances of the muted, the dispossessed and the marginalised. These multi-layered voices and intermingling of genres may explain the uncertainties in the novel. For instance, Ahmad argues that, 'the fictional equivalents of the literal facts of recent Pakistani history tend too much towards parody while many of the other parts tend too much towards burlesque' and 'Rushdie has given us a Laughter which laughs, unfortunately, much too often." Despite the fantastic elements, from the reports we read of the lives of the elite in gossip columns, there is a note of plausibility in the descriptions of the machinations of these characters.

The kind of 'reality' represented by Rushdie's characters, and the violences they execute, lie along a continuum of the grotesque. They carry overtones of the Jacobean revenge tragedy, which make a statement about the transhistorical linkages of revenge and violence. The methods of decimation adopted by Sufiya, and the political manoeuvres in *Shame*, uneasily resemble each other, recalling the impact of the revenge tragedy which often unveils links between personal and political savagery. Thus through Sufiya, the personal and political nexus is forged.

Ahmad finds that, for the most part, the women characters are limited by ineffectual actions which nullify any liberating potential and are maladjusted by madness, sexual frenzy, fevers of the brain or hatred. In trying to 'break out' of the 'cage' of patriarchy they destroy themselves. Ahmad contends that although women seem to embody a large part of the narrative, they do not control the structure, and neither are they endowed with an empowering voice. Rather, he feels that a male narrator dictates the narrative and the women's voices are refracted through his perspective. This interpretation would be valid if the novel privileged the point-of-view of the male characters. I feel that Ahmad does not adequately engage with Rushdie's subversion of patriarchy and religion, nor does he address how the male characters' transgressions are not exonerated. The men are clearly the agents of repression and blame is imputed to them. As for the liberatory potential of the women, to anticipate total emancipation from the entrapment of patriarchy is idealistic. On the other hand, Ahmad's reading of the brief portrayal of the women's activism in *Shame* is insightful. The narrator's intervention defuses the viability of positive change because when he is confronted with the women's march against the Hudood Ordinance in February 1983, it is registered as an act 'against God' and dismissed as the work of a group of 'irreligious' women. The 'sacred language' is inscribed to proscribe political protest (*S* 249). By recording the women's behaviour as 'irreligious'—official history denies, once again, the possibility of insurgency resulting from the 'subaltern's' will, initiation or agency. The mobilisation of force against the demonstrators is similarly justified by religion. Both Inderpal Grewal and Aijaz Ahmad select this episode as Rushdie's failure to acknowledge the powerful practices of opposition that have been part of the history of women in Pakistan. They also feel that Rushdie repeats the recuperative gestures of the official discourse of the nation.

However, while agreeing that these points are troublesome, and the description of the women's march is limiting, the novel represents the workings of a certain postcolonial climate, which may not necessarily coincide with the author's perspective of events. Throughout the novel self-conscious efforts to throw into question the reliability of his narrator suggests that Rushdie may not want to be identified with/as the narrator. It is primarily the elite characters who find a voice in the novel, and although Rushdie is from this class, his eagerness to distance himself from them, displays his awareness of the extreme power and repression they wield. The novel is not merely an allegory of the political vicissitudes of Pakistan during the Bhutto and Zia administrations, but a vigorous critique of the ruling class. It opens up an oppositional space to debate the practices of a particular form of hegemony. The narrator's assertion that 'The justifying myth of the nation has been unmade' can be read in the light of the political culture represented in the novel (*S* 251).

Rushdie sets about demystifying the sacrosanct nature of 'national' myths, enshrined as the 'bedrock' of the nation, revealing that they are neither natural nor fixed thus exposing their points of crisis (they are the layer of the palimpsest which is foisted upon the nation). In Rushdie's novel, shame is foregrounded as a principal locus of instability in the foundation of the nation. The fictional nation is precariously held together by the promotion and manipulation of a formulation of shame based on and deriving from the sacred language. The quest for 'stability in the name of God' enlists shame as a regulating principle. However, the restraining effects of shame are ultimately counter-productive because: "shamelessness, shame: the roots of violence" and, "in the end, [...] it all blows up in your face" (*S* 115-16, 173). Shame or sharanı acquires a range of meanings, from embarrassment to the lack of a 'fixed' place in the world, and the novel's multiple voices and generic strains provoke formal links with the title (*S* 39). To make a character feel shame is to control him/her. Duniyazad Begum insults Biquìs' 'barrenness,' and its effect on the family inscribes the social content of shame (*S* 84). Later on in her life, at her daughter Naveed's funeral, Biquìs forges her own form of control by making her husband feel ashamed for the consequences of his repression: "Feel bad for the life that has been lost. I blame you for this. Shame, shame" (*S* 228). The linkages between personal shame and collective shame are crucial to the consolidation of the Pakistan nation-state and the absence of a fixed meaning of shame undermines the authoritative discourses of the nation. The novel gestures towards the possibility of political emancipation within a dictatorship. However, Rushdie is only able to articulate this possibility through the ostensibly apolitical genre of the fairy tale. Yet the return to the aesthetics of the grotesque and the fantastic, where the dictator "will be toppled by goblinish, faery means," highlights Rushdie's inscription of the fairy tale genre with political significance (*S* 257).

In the light of the repressive political culture and the atmosphere of censorship, Rushdie's refusal to write a 'realistic' novel is not an aesthetic but a political decision and the reader is persistently warned against a 'realistic' reading. In maintaining this vigilance, Rushdie carves out a space within which he can criticise the repressive practices of the nation-state without being overtly political, and thereby eschewing the risk of his book being 'banned' or 'burned.' *Shame* enacts the problematising of narrative in a socio-political context where 'speaking' is the privilege of the elite (often male) agent which is not to say that the subaltern cannot speak, nor mean that she cannot talk, even through unconventional forms, such as the shawls. Just as in the palimpsest where the imprint underneath can never be completely erased so the dissident voices of women cannot be completely suppressed either.

Notes

1. Salman Rushdie, *Shame* (London: Picador, 1983) 27. Further references are given parenthetically, preceded by *S*.
2. Palimpsest is defined as 'a parchment etc. which has been written upon twice, the original writing having been rubbed out' *The Shorter Oxford English Dictionary* (Third Edition). I am grateful to John MacLeod for his insightful discussion on this issue.
3. Salman Rushdie, "Censorship," *Imaginary Homelands* (1983; London: Granta, 1991) 38, 39.
4. The main antagonists in *Shame* are Iskander Harappa, who is modelled on Pakistan's former Prime Minister, Bhutto; Raza Hyder, a fictional representation of Zia Ul-Haq; Omar Khayyam Shakil and their respective families. The interactions between the Harappa family and the Hyder family are given plausibility through intermarriage. At the age of forty Iskander becomes the civilian Prime Minister. He is then replaced in a

military coup by Hyder. Rani Harappa, Isky's wife and Raza's cousin, as well as their daughter, Arjumand (Virgin Ironpants) who hero-worships her father, also take on active roles in the landscape of the novel. The link between Raza Hyder and Iskander is forged through Omar Shakil. He attaches himself initially to Iskander as a companion and subsequently to Raza after his marriage to Sufiya Zinobia (Raza's daughter).

5. Brennan (1989: 125).
6. In *Shame*, takallouf, an 'untranslatable word' refers to "a form of tongue-tying formality, a social restraint so extreme as to make it impossible for the victim to express what he or she really means" (*S* 104).
7. Ahmad (1992: 139).
8. Ahmad (1992: 143).
9. Strictly speaking, the chadur refers to the veil worn by Muslim women to cover the head and upper part of the body, while purda is the black gown, along with the head and face veil, worn by women in the Middle East (Rozairo, 1992: 95). Often, both are used as metaphors for the constraining effects of religion and culture on women. In common parlance there is a collapse between the distinctions, so that purda, chadur and duppata are interchangeable. Farida Shaheed and Khawar Mumtaz define purda as 'literally a curtain, used both for the physical veiling of women and the institution of segregating the sexes and secluding women, but it also applies to define codes of behaviour (1987: xi).
10. There is evidence to suggest that other religious groups, for instance, high caste Hindus in North India, have also adopted the purda. It is also regarded as a product of Judaism (Rozairo, 1992: 88).
11. Rozairo (1992: 89).
12. On her return to Pakistan, Benazir Bhutto's deliberate choice of wearing the veil in public may be explained in the light of this psychological bind and has been remarked upon by Rukhsana Ahmad (1991: 17).
13. Moss (1992: 29).
14. Ahmad (1992: 144).
15. Shaheed and Mumtaz (1987: 30).
16. Butler (1990: 138).
17. Butler (1990: 146). While acknowledging the immense significance of Butler's theories of performance and gender, my main contention with Butler's work is that performance and gender need to be located within its spatio-temporal specificities. Anne McClintock has voiced similar concerns about the erasure of race, history, culture and power configurations in Butler's work (1997).
18. Bauer (1991: 673).

19. See Ajit Mookerjee (1988) for a detailed exploration of the Kali myth.
20. Cixous (1991: 335).
21. Ahmad (1992: 147).
22. Showalter (1987: 129-30).
23. Showalter (1987: 129).
24. Showalter (1987: 131-32).
25. Butler (1990: 147).
26. Brennan (1989: 135).
27. Fletcher (1986); Ahmad (1992); Moss (1992).
28. Watson-Williams (1984: 38).
29. Brennan (1989: 124, 127).
30. Ahmad (1992: 141).
31. Ahmad (1992: 145).
32. Grewal (1988: 38) and Ahmad (1992: 150).
33. Ahmad (1992: 151).
34. Ahmad (1992: 139).
35. If the 'I' narrator's fears of having his book banned seems exaggerated, it is because, in Pakistan, once censorship is imposed, like a fatwa, it is permanent and cannot be removed (Kishwar Naheed in interview with Neluka Silva, Bradford, UK, 17 Sept. 1997).

Works Cited

Ahmad, Aijaz. *In Theory: Classes, Nations, Literatures*. London and New York: Verso, 1992.

Ahmad, R. *We Sinful Women: Contemporary Urdu Feminist Poetry*. London: The Women's Press, 1991.

Batty, Nancy E. "The Art of Suspense." *Reading Rushdie: Perspectives on the Fiction of Salman Rushdie*. Ed. M.D. Fletcher. Amsterdam and Atlanta: Rodopi, 1994. 69-81.

Bauer, D. "Gender in Bakhtin's Carnival." *Feminisms: An Anthology of Literary Theory and Criticism*. Ed. R. Warhol and D. Price Herndl. New Brunswick and New Jersey: Rutgers UP, 1991. 671-84.

Brennan, Timothy. *Salman Rushdie and the Third World*. London: Macmillan, 1989.

Butler, Judith. *Gender Trouble*. London: Routledge, 1990.

Cixous, Hélèn. "The Laugh of Medusa." *Feminisms, An Anthology of Literary Theory and Criticism*. Ed. R.R. Warhol and D.P. Herndl. 1975. New Jersey: Rutgers UP, 1991. 334-49.

Cundy, Catharine. *Salman Rushdie*. Manchester: Manchester UP, 1996.

Fletcher, M.D. "Rushdie's *Shame* as Apologue." *The Journal of Commonwealth Literature* 21.1 (1986): 120-32.

Grewal, Inderpal. "Salman Rushdie: Marginality, Women and *Shame*." *Genders* 3 (1988): 24-42.

Harrison, James. *Salman Rushdie*. New York: Twayne Publishers, 1992.

McClintock, Anne. "Transexions: Race, Queer and Cyber Crossings." Conference paper at "Transformations: Thinking through Feminism." University of Lancaster. 19 July 1997.

Mookerjee, A. *Kali, the Feminine Force*. London: Thames and Hudson, 1988.

Moss, Stephanie. "The Cream of the Crop: Female Characters in Salman Rushdie's *Shame*." *International Fiction Review* 19.1 (1992): 28-30

Parameswaran, Uma. 1983. "'Handcuffed to History': Salman Rushdie's Art." *ARIEL* 14.4 (1983): 34-45.

____. "Salman Rushdie's *Shame*: An Overview of a Labyrinth." *The New Indian Novel in English: A Study of the 1980's*. Ed. V. Kirpal. New Delhi: Allied Publishers, 1990. 109-20.

Rozairo, S. *Purity and Communal Boundaries: Women and Social Change in a Bangladeshi Village*. London and New Jersey: Zed Books, 1992.

Rushdie, Salman. *Shame*. London: Picador, 1983.

____. "Censorship." *Imaginary Homelands*. 1983. London, Granta, 1991. 37-40.

Shaheed F. and K. Mumtaz. *Women of Pakistan: Two Steps Forward, One Step Back?* London and New Jersey: Zed Books, 1987.

Showalter, Elaine. *The Female Malady: Women, Madness and English Culture, 1830-1980*. London: Virago, 1987.

Watson-Williams, Helen. "An Antique Land, Salman Rushdie's *Shame*." *Westerly* 4 (1984): 37-45.

8

RUSHDIE AND HIS WORLD: THE CARNIVALESQUE, MASQUERADE, AND GROTESQUE REALISM IN HIS FICTION

BLAIR MAHONEY

> In its multivalent oppositional play, carnival refuses to surrender the critical and cultural tools of the dominant class, and in this sense, carnival can be seen above all as a site of insurgency, and not merely withdrawal.
>
> —Mary Russo (218).

The novels of Salman Rushdie, especially *The Satanic Verses*, display a number of recurring elements: shifting and hybrid identities, the dislocation of the migrant, the dangers of essentialism and fixity, and the subversive carnivalesque elements of migrant subcultures. Mikhail Bakhtin's work on the transgressive nature of carnival and masquerade provides the tools to best explain the picture of postcolonial hybrid subjectivity that Rushdie depicts in his novels.

In his novels, Rushdie constructs versions of postcolonial subjectivity and the nation which break free of essentialist and monolithic thinking and which are based instead on ideas of hybridity and multiplicity. He does this by depicting characters whose identities are shifting and multiple, who don a variety of masks without necessarily using them to conceal essential identities. The migrant is the perfect figure to illustrate this conception of multiple, shifting identity, for the migrant belongs in one sense everywhere and in another sense nowhere. Rushdie shows that a nation such as Great Britain is not as homogeneous as some of its inhabitants might like to think. The British Empire has come home, has imploded, bringing with it diverse, heterogeneous elements as migrants from the so-called "margins" converge on the so-called "centre." Some of these elements can be assimilated into the mainstream, but there always remains something unassimilable, an unreconcilable part that resists all efforts to suppress difference and contributes to the multiplicity of self and nation.

In contrast to the prevailing view that the postmodern fragmented subject is inimical to the prospect of political agency, Rushdie's novels demonstrate that a fixed and unitary identity is not necessary for the postcolonial subject to achieve agency and bring about political change. Indeed, Rushdie's hybrid and multiple characters are in many ways able to bring about more political change than are unchanging and static characters. It is through hybridity that newness and change enter the political world.

Postcolonial Carnival

> Carnival is presented by Bakhtin as a world of topsy-turvy, of heteroglot exuberance, of ceaseless overrunning and excess where all is mixed, hybrid, ritually degraded and defiled.
>
> —Stallybrass and White (8).

In the opening pages of *Rabelais and his World*, Bakhtin draws a distinction between two different types of worlds that existed in medieval Europe: one public and official, the other based on unofficial forms and outside the sphere of influence of Church and State. This latter world engaged in rituals of inversion that parodied and ridiculed those of the official world:

> All these forms of protocol and ritual based on laughter and consecrated by tradition existed in all the countries of medieval Europe; they were sharply distinct from the serious official, ecclesiastical, feudal, and political cult forms and ceremonials. They offered a completely different, nonofficial, extraecclesiastical and extrapolitical aspect of the world, of man, and of human relations; they built a second world and a second life outside officialdom (Bakhtin 5-6).

When Saladin Chamcha, in *The Satanic Verses*, returns to England after surviving the explosion of the plane by which he was travelling, it is a very different England to the one he left. He discovers a split between official and nonofficial worlds very similar to that described by Bakhtin.

In *The Satanic Verses*, the characters of Saladin Chamcha and Gibreel Farishta explore the range of carnivalesque options. The novel shows the split between official and nonofficial in the scenes of the riots that originate in the vicinity of Club Hot Wax. These riots express a popular uprising of those immigrant underclasses that feel they are being victimised by the police and the official authorities. Indeed, Saladin himself is the recipient of police brutality. The vicious beating he receives at the hand of the policemen could not have occurred in the official England that he once believed in; the official England is more like "that Sussex of rewards and fairies which every schoolboy knew" (*SV* 158). The police are very much a part of the official world, however, acting as the representatives of those who wield power.

This official role of the police is evident in the riot scenes which Rushdie describes using the terminology of television. The camera is often perceived as a neutral medium that merely presents the facts, but Rushdie shows that it is able to be manipulated and is a component of the official world, the world of order:

> —Cut.—A man lit by a sun-gun speaks rapidly into a microphone. Behind him there is a disorderment of shadows. But between the reporter and the disordered shadow-lands there stands a wall: men in riot helmets, carrying shields [...]. A camera is a thing easily broken or purloined; its fragility makes it fastidious. A camera requires law, order, the thin blue line. Seeking to preserve itself, it remains behind the shielding wall, observing the shadow-lands from afar, and of course from above: that is, it chooses sides (*SV* 454-55).

The camera looks down from above, that is, from the official world, onto the nonofficial world of the rioters. It is shielded from the nonofficial world by the line of policemen, and is representative of order, presenting the nonofficial world as a place of shadows and disorder. The positioning of the camera and reporter in the light of the sun guns associates Europeans (the media and the police) with light and reason and Africans and Asians (the rioters) with disorder and lawlessness. *The Satanic Verses* has introduced a racial element into the official and nonofficial worlds described by Bakhtin.

In *The Satanic Verses* the existing hierarchy mercilessly discriminates against the nonofficial immigrant culture which exists in London. Those immigrants, with their different religions and beliefs, are not compatible with "the existing religious, political, and moral values" of the official world (*SV* 9). They must turn instead to the nonofficial world of the carnivalesque, which Bakhtin describes as celebrating

> temporary liberation from the prevailing truth and from the established order; it marked the suspension of all hierarchical rank, privileges, norms, and prohibitions. Carnival was the true feast of time, the feast of becoming, change, and renewal. It was hostile to all that was immortalized and completed (Bakhtin 10).

The carnivalesque, then, is concerned with what Rushdie calls bringing newness into the world, with bringing about change in the existing order. Bakhtin also points out, however, that this liberation is only temporary.

One of the major criticisms of the carnival as a theoretical construct is that its transgressive power is licensed by the authorities, making it an outlet for radical urges to be harmlessly expelled. Peter Stallybrass and Allon White, for example, state that "[m]ost politically thoughtful commentators wonder, like Eagleton, whether the 'licensed release' of carnival is not simply a form of social control of the low by the high and therefore serves the interests of that very official culture which it apparently opposes" (Stallybrass & White 13).[1] Stallybrass and White go on, however, to claim that carnival is not completely ineffective in bringing about political and social change. When combined with a strong political agenda and a high level of friction in the community, it can bring about real change. They write, "for long periods carnival may be a stable and cyclical ritual with no noticeable politically transformative effects but that, given the presence of sharpened political antagonism, it may often act as *catalyst* and *site of actual and symbolic struggle*" (Stallybrass & White 14), and they observe that "it is in fact striking how frequently violent social clashes apparently 'coincided' with carnival" (Stallybrass & White 14). This coincidence between carnival and violent social clash occurs in *The Satanic Verses* when the riots, which bear many features of Bakhtin's carnival, erupt as a reaction against the racism of the English police. The regular rituals of inversion which take place in Club Hot Wax are relatively harmless expressions of displeasure towards the establishment, and as such are allowed to continue, but when these same sentiments meet with the catalyst of police brutality and the death in custody of a prominent figure in the community, they result in riots that have real potential to cause damage to the establishment. Action is taken, therefore, by those in power to try to prevent this more serious outpouring of carnivalesque practices.[2]

In one of the prominent carnivalesque scenes in *The Satanic Verses*, at Club Hot Wax, the crowd, predominantly immigrants, call out the name of the authority figure whose wax effigy they wish to see melted in a gigantic microwave oven:

> Attendants move toward the tableau of hate-figures, pounce upon the night's sacrificial offering, the one most often selected, if truth be told; at least three times a week. Her permawaved coiffure, her pearls, her suit of blue. *Maggie-maggie-maggie*, bays the crowd. *Burn-burn-burn*. The doll,—the *guy*,—is strapped into the Hot Seat. Pinkwalla throws the switch. And O how prettily she melts, from the inside out, crumpling into formlessness. Then she is a puddle, and the crowd sighs its ecstasy: *done*. "The fire this time," Pinkwalla tells them. Music regains the night (*SV* 293).

Here we see Bakhtin's ritual of transgression taking place in the unofficial underground world of the immigrants, who have suffered more than most due to the policies of the Conservative British government.[3] They select the figure of the Prime Minister to perform a comic uncrowning and humiliation of the supreme authority figure in the country. The events at Club Hot Wax are an inversion of the official ritual that takes place on November 5, when an effigy of Guy Fawkes, one of the rebels who tried to blow up the English parliament, is burnt. Rushdie alludes to this in the above passage when he refers to the effigy of Thatcher as a guy. In the official celebration a person who attempted to transgress the authority of the State is humiliated, but in the Hot Wax ritual it is the authority figure that is subjected to the melting that corresponds to Bakhtin's comic uncrowning.

The melting of the effigy is a carnivalesque celebration, and as such provides a "temporary liberation from the prevailing truth and from the established order," and a "suspension of all hierarchical rank, privileges, norms, and prohibitions" (Bakhtin 10). In Club Hot Wax, the patrons are temporarily out of the reach of racist taunts, police harassment and oppressive government policies. There all rank is suspended and they can invert the power relations between the Prime Minister and themselves, exercising their power over her image and exacting their symbolic revenge. The Club Hot Wax ritual corresponds closely to Bakhtin's description of medieval carnival and its rituals and symbols:

> We find here a characteristic logic, the peculiar logic of the "inside out" (*à l'envers*), of the "turnabout," of a continual shifting from top to bottom, from front to rear, of numerous parodies and travesties, humiliations, profanations, comic crownings and uncrownings. A second life, a second world of folk culture is thus constructed; it is to a certain extent a parody of the extracarnival life, a "world inside out" (Bakhtin 11).

The wax effigies are parodic representations of authority figures made to undergo a ritual humiliation. The comic uncrowning takes place in a microwave oven which melts them from the "inside out," exemplifying the logic of the inside out, whereby hierarchies are inverted and power relations altered for a temporary period. Such an inversion requires, of course, an acceptance of the existing categories, and a recognition that hierarchies of power exist between them. The carnival aims for social change of some sort, however, for, as Bakhtin says, it "was the true feast of time, the feast of becoming, change, and renewal" (Bakhtin 10).

Rushdie, in *The Satanic Verses*, tries to answer the question, "How does newness come into the world?" (*SV* 8), and the opening pages of the novel are replete with images of rebirth and change. The change that the novel is working towards is not simply an inversion of existing hierarchies such as we see occurring in Club Hot Wax; it involves moving through these binary oppositions to a new and hybrid conception of identity and culture. Rushdie provides an example of simplistic and destructive carnivalesque inversion in the novel when Gibreel Farishta imagines himself to be (and perhaps really is, by the novel's uncertain logic) the Archangel Gibreel, come to wreak vengeance on the godless English. In a scene that reverses the traditional relationship between coloniser and colonised, he imagines himself to be the one in the position of power, and even quotes Frantz Fanon on the desire of the colonised subject to invert the hierarchy in which he or she is trapped:

> He would show them—yes!—his *power*.—These powerless English!—Did they not think their history would return to haunt them?—"The native is an oppressed person whose permanent dream is to become the persecutor" (Fanon). English women no longer bound him; the conspiracy stood exposed!—Then away with all fogs. He would make this land anew. He was the Archangel, Gibreel.—*And I'm back!* (*SV* 353)

Gibreel here espouses a kind of philosophical absolutism in which he stands for absolute good and the English for absolute evil. He has reversed the hierarchy of colonialism and claims to see the true nature of the world: a world which does not allow for shades of meaning.

The theme of the destructive nature of such absolutism recurs throughout *The Satanic Verses* and closely ties in with the inversion of hierarchies. Such inversions reinscribe terms such as coloniser and colonised, confirming them as fixed categories. The only change that results is the perception of which term is superior. Such purity of ideals, and the taking up of the position of absolute adversary to some other absolute is shown to be ultimately ruinous in the cases of Tavleen the hijacker and Hind of Jahilia, as well as in Gibreel's case. Homi Bhabha's reading of Fanon emphasises the need to move beyond the absolutism that is required in the process of inverting the hierarchy and celebrating that which was formerly derided:

> Fanon recognises the crucial importance, for subordinated peoples, of asserting their indigenous cultural traditions and retrieving their repressed histories. But he is far too aware of the dangers of the fixity and fetishism of identities within the calcification of colonial cultures to recommend that "roots" be struck in the celebratory romance of the past or by homogenising the history of the present (Bhabha 1994: 9).

The passage sheds light on the fragment of Fanon that is quoted by Gibreel, for it shows that although fixed origins and identity are to some extent understandable desires for the colonised subject they can also be dangerous, as can the uncritical reversal of the power relations between oppressor and oppressed. As Bhabha and Rushdie indicate, it is more productive to accept fragmentation and diversity and to move past the binary oppositions altogether, toward an ideal that is predicated upon compromise and alliances that bridge difference.

The Satanic Verses and the Grotesque

> In shattering the mirror of representation, and its range of western bourgeois social and psychic "identifications," the spectacle of colonial fantasy sets itself up as an uncanny "double." Its terrifying figures—savages, grotesques, mimic men—reveal things so profoundly familiar to the West that it cannot bear to remember them.
>
> —Homi Bhabha, "Representation and the Colonial Text" (119-20).

One of the principle features of the carnival is what Bakhtin labels "grotesque realism." He describes the grotesque body as an image for the larger community, a community that continuously expands and is bound up in cycles of birth and rebirth, change and renewal: "The material bodily principle is contained not in the biological individual, not in the bourgeois ego, but in the people, a people who are continually growing and renewed. This is why all that is bodily becomes grandiose, exaggerated, immeasurable" (Bakhtin 19). As Bakhtin explains it, the image of the grotesque body is an unsettled one, continually in process and, due to the metamorphoses it experiences, connected with the multiple and hybrid identities written about by Rushdie. It thus has an uncertain relation to time, refusing to remain static and consistent for any significant period. Bakhtin also points out the ambivalence of the image: "The grotesque image," he writes,

> reflects a phenomenon in transformation, an as yet unfinished metamorphosis, of death and birth, growth and becoming. The relation to time is one determining trait of the grotesque image. The other indispensable trait is ambivalence. For in this image we find both poles of transformation, the old and the new, the dying and the procreating, the beginning and the end of the metamorphosis (Bakhtin 24).

The ambivalence Bakhtin describes here is an important feature of grotesque realism and carnivalesque images in general. This ambivalence indicates that the images are not in themselves transgressive; they may be transgressive images but they carry no political force unless there is some motivation behind them—unless, as Stallybrass and White point out, the carnival is combined with concrete grievances and antagonism (Stallybrass & White 14). The ambivalence of grotesque realism and masquerade is due to their invocation of certain practices and institutions in order to undercut them; in order to arrive at the new they must first invoke the old. These invocations of the old mean operating within the existing system and being implicated in the very things that are being subverted.

The extent to which Bakhtin's description of the elements of grotesque realism coincides with the discourses of racism is quite remarkable, and illuminates in particular the incident in *The Satanic Verses* in which Saladin is transformed into a grotesque devil figure. Bakhtin considers the elements of grotesque realism, connected as they are with processes of change and renewal, to be positive, and this is how I have been treating them thus far: as positive ways to subvert the status quo and bring about change. The specific elements of grotesque realism which Bakhtin enumerates, though, are often used in negative racist stereotypes. For example, Bakhtin writes:

> The body discloses its essence as a principle of growth which exceeds its own limits only in copulation, pregnancy, childbirth, the throes of death, eating, drinking, or defecation. This is the ever unfinished, ever creating body, the link in the chain of genetic development, or more correctly speaking, two links shown at the point where they enter into each other (Bakhtin 26).

In racist discourse, people of colour are frequently referred to as being grotesque in just this manner, as being primarily sexual, unclean, and forever reproducing. Bakhtin applies his analysis to the medieval poor in the novels of Rabelais, and such representations have also been applied to the underclasses, characterising them as a vast, squalid rabble. Bakhtin, nevertheless, sees these grotesque elements as positive forces for change instead of the degrading features of the downtrodden. In a similar fashion, Rushdie reclaims the negative images that have been applied to people of colour and uses them to mobilise resistance to the very racist discourses from which they come. The catalyst for the reclamation of negative images in *The Satanic Verses* is Saladin Chamcha, an Indian resident of England who becomes transformed into a grotesque, devilish creature.

Sometimes the differences between cultures can seem enormous, and Rushdie dramatises this perception of the gulf between cultures in his portrayal of the mutation of Saladin Chamcha into the horrific figure of racist fantasies and fears. Reflecting on his transformed, goatish, and Satanic form Saladin says to himself, "The grotesque has me, as before the quotidian had me, in its thrall" (260). The grotesque works in two main ways in *The Satanic Verses*: as a literalisation of racist images of people of colour, and as a symbol of change and becoming: a potent force that can be harnessed and used to overthrow oppression.

Firstly, the grotesque figure that Saladin has become is the perfect object for the fear and loathing with which the racist views the immigrant of colour in Britain. When Saladin is arrested for being an illegal immigrant and is thrown into a police van he notices the changes that he appears to have undergone:

> His thighs had grown uncommonly wide and powerful as well as hairy. Below the knee the hairiness came to a halt, and his legs narrowed into tough, bony, almost fleshless calves, terminating in a pair of shiny, cloven hoofs, such as one might find on any billy-goat. Saladin was also taken aback by the sight of his phallus, greatly enlarged and embarrassingly erect, an organ that he had the greatest difficulty in acknowledging as his own (*SV* 157).

Chamcha is puzzled that the policemen in the van take his bizarre transformation completely within their stride, but were he more aware of the racism of his adopted country he would not be so surprised at their acceptance of his Satanic appearance. His animal-like appearance and his visible strength and sexual potency literally reproduce their racist conceptions. He is a creature both to be feared and to be ridiculed. His difference is greatly exaggerated as he is completely transformed into the Other that bears no resemblance to "normal" human beings such as the white, middle-class, male policemen. These racist policemen also perceive people of colour as dirty and lacking in personal hygiene, and Saladin fulfils their expectations when he leaves goat pellets on the floor of the van, leading one of the policemen to remark, "You're all the same. Can't expect animals to observe civilized standards. Eh?" (*SV* 159).

Rushdie makes a number of points here, and the prominent one concerns racist stereotypes. The policeman makes the comment that "they" (immigrants) are all the same, and by so doing fixes a single identity onto a large and heterogeneous group of people. The problem is not so much that he is wrong to see all immigrants as dirty and ignorant of British standards of cleanliness, but more that he is wrong to both identify all immigrants as the same and to fix that identity onto them, precluding any possibility of diversity or of change. It is not that the policemen mistakenly see immigrants as unclean, strong, and virile, but rather that immigrants, like Britons of European heritage, are a diverse group of people who cannot be categorised in such a rigid and destructive manner. And to go even further, it would not matter even if the stereotypes were generally true, for each person deserves to be treated individually, not just as a member of a larger group defined by one attribute such as race or sex. Rushdie is not trying to say that racists are wrong in saying that all immigrants are bad because "in fact" all immigrants are good; he is, instead, portraying characters who are both good and bad at the same time.

The racist attitudes held by the policemen and others are responsible for the transformation of Saladin into a grotesque, satanic creature. When Saladin is taken to a prison hospital full of creatures similar to himself, and asks another inmate why they are like this, he gets the answer, "They describe us [...]. That's all. They have the power of description, and we succumb to the pictures they construct" (168). By describing him and other immigrants in this degrading manner, the policemen have turned them into precisely what it is that they fear and despise. Following the logic of the novel, in which ideas become reality, Saladin encounters a woman at the hospital who literalises the common racist idea that immigrants breed at a rapid rate and their aim is to take over the country:

> he heard a woman grunting and shrieking, at what sounded like the end of a painful labour; followed by the yowling of a new-born baby. However, the woman's cries did not subside when the baby's began; if anything, they redoubled in their intensity, and perhaps fifteen minutes later Chamcha distinctly heard a second infant's voice joining the first. Still the woman's birth-agony refused to end, and at intervals ranging from fifteen to thirty minutes for what seemed like an endless time she continued to add new babies to the already improbable numbers marching, like conquering armies, from her womb (*SV* 166).

Such literalisations as this undermine the racist ideas on which they are based by showing just how ludicrous they are. Rushdie has pushed the racist fear or fantasy to grotesque extremes here, and, while debilitating for the woman who must endure such constant agony, the fantasy also threatens the racists who conceived it, with the image of the conquering armies marching out of her womb. Those racists use grotesque realism as an oppressive construct in the form of racist stereotypes, but oppressed groups can reclaim the grotesque images as a site of resistance, turning the images against their creators.

Bakhtin has identified what he calls the "essential principle" of grotesque realism as degradation, "that is, the lowering of all that is high, spiritual, ideal, abstract; it is a transfer to the material level, to the sphere of earth and body in their indissoluble unity" (Bakhtin 19-20). Saladin's transformation into a goat-like creature involves precisely this physicalising of the abstract. He represents Satan, brought down to earth in physical form, and he embodies abstract racist conceptions of immigrants. Bakhtin does not, however, conceptualise degradation as the entirely negative process of racist oppression, but instead sees it as containing the potential for positive change and renewal. Like the images of rebirth which proliferate in the opening chapter of *The Satanic Verses,* he speaks of new beginnings and birth arising out of death:

> To degrade is to bury, to sow, and to kill simultaneously, in order to bring forth something more and better .... Degradation digs a bodily grave for a new birth; it has not only a destructive, negative aspect, but also a regenerating one. To degrade an object does not imply merely hurling it into the void of nonexistence, into absolute destruction, but to hurl it down to the reproductive lower stratum, the zone in which conception and a new birth take place. Grotesque realism knows no other lower level; it is the fruitful earth and womb. It is always conceiving (*SV* 21).

Bakhtin answers Rushdie's question "[h]ow does newness come into the world?" (Bakhtin 8) by suggesting that it emerges out of the processes of death and degradation. He sees the grotesque body as a symbol of change with its continual transformations and focus on the processes of life, such as birth, death, eating, drinking, and defecation. He takes those images which form a large part of racist constructions and looks for their positive and transformative elements. This reclamation of predominantly negative images plays an important part in *The Satanic Verses*.

The first instance of such a reclamation in the novel occurs when the prophet in the Jahilia section of the novel takes the name Mahound:

> Here he is neither Mahomet nor MoeHammered; has adopted, instead, the demon-tag the farangis hung around his neck. To turn insults into strengths, whigs, tories, Blacks all chose to wear with pride the names they were given in scorn; likewise, our mountain-climbing, prophet-motivated solitary is to be the medieval baby-frightener, the Devil's synonym: Mahound (*SV* 93).

Similarly, Jumpy Joshi reclaims, in a poem he has written, Enoch Powell's notorious racist "River of Blood" metaphor, hoping to turn it into something that can be used to oppose racism instead of support it (*SV* 186). And later in the novel Uhuru Simba reclaims the role of the "uppity nigger" who is out to cause trouble and promote change (*SV* 414). The most powerful image of reclamation in the novel, however, is of that very grotesque and racist image that Saladin has come to literally embody. The oppressed underclass start to mobilise around this image, seeing in the grotesque body, as did Bakhtin, a potent force for change and rebirth. Children begin wearing rubber devil-horns and Saladin's satanic form starts to appear on banners at political demonstrations. Once more, the language of reclamation is used as Mishal explains to Saladin the reasons for his popularity: "you're a hero. I mean, people can really identify with you. It's an image white society has rejected for so long that we can really take it, you know, occupy it, inhabit it, reclaim it and make it our own" (*SV* 286-87). There is an ambivalence here that harks back to my earlier mention of the way that the racist images of the grotesque are products of both fantasy and fear. As with the image of the woman continually giving birth to the "conquering armies," the grotesque creature that Saladin has become is both degrading and frightening. He is, as his fellow inmate in the prison hospital tells him, a product of racist conceptions and descriptions, yet those very descriptions have transformed him into a being that has the power to strike back against them. Mishal observes that the other immigrants can really identify with him, and they can unite under him in order to fight against the common experience of oppression of which he is a symbol. By refusing to observe the diversity and individual skills and attributes of the various ethnic minorities and instead lumping them all together, the racists have unwittingly also provided them with the unity that they require in order to strike back against oppression. The various groups have united on the issue of racial oppression, forging a common identity that has in some ways also been thrust upon them, and have worked together despite their many differences to try and achieve change in this one area.[4]

The Satanic Verses and Masquerade

> the notion that man has a body distinct from his soul, is to be expunged; this I shall do, by printing in the infernal method, by corrosives, which in Hell are salutary and medicinal, melting apparent surfaces away, and displaying the infinite which was hid.
>
> —William Blake, *The Marriage of Heaven and Hell*

Bakhtin has written of masquerade, another of the important elements of the carnival, that the mask is

> the most complex theme of folk culture. The mask is connected with the joy of change and reincarnation, with gay relativity and with the merry negation of uniformity and similarity; *it rejects conformity to oneself.* The mask is related to transition, metamorphoses, the violation of natural boundaries, to mockery and familiar nicknames. It contains the playful element of life; it is based on a peculiar interrelation of reality and image, characteristic of the most ancient rituals and spectacles (Bakhtin 39-40, my emphasis).

As with grotesque realism, and indeed all elements of carnival, Bakhtin perceives masquerade to be intricately bound up with notions of change and rebirth. This is because when one puts on a mask one is reborn as a new person, to an extent; one identity has been changed for another, or, to look at it another way, one identity has been hidden beneath another.[5] The above quotation, however, proposes a radical notion of difference. Bakhtin suggests that the masquerade emphasises difference not between self and other, but difference *within* the self; masquerade exposes the self as multiple rather than as a unified whole, because masquerading as a different self reveals the presence of more than one self in the same body. Like grotesque realism, masquerade embodies the act of transformation, indeed, Bakhtin says that "[i]t reveals the essence of the grotesque" (Bakhtin 40). More specifically, the use of masks results in "such manifestations as parodies, caricatures, grimaces, eccentric postures, and comic gestures" (Bakhtin 40). Just as the grotesque body is continually metamorphosing into different selves, so the masquerader changes masks and dons new selves. Bakhtin sees the use of masks as symbolic of reincarnation; they alter people's identities, allowing them to be "reborn" as new people. The masquerade contributes to the play of difference and the feeling of uncertainty that is a central feature of carnival in its unsettling of official certainties and fixity.

The principal participants in *The Satanic Verses* are, by their very professions, party to the practice of putting on masks, as both Gibreel and Saladin are actors. Gibreel is a superstar of Indian cinema, and specialises in portraying deities in movies that are known as "theologicals." James Harrison has pointed out that a particularly profound metamorphosis must take place when an actor portrays a deity, and at the start of his long career Gibreel often had to don masks in order to play Hanuman the monkey god or Ganesh the elephant-headed god (Harrison 91). Saladin, too, is no stranger to masks in his career as an actor in England. Mostly forced to do voice-overs due to his unfortunate handicap of having the wrong skin colour to appear on television (as his manager Hal Valance informs him, ads "research better" without people "of the tinted persuasion" in them), Saladin becomes the "man of a thousand voices," able to use his voice as a mask, changing voices to take on different identities while he remains unseen. Later, he lands a leading role on a television programme called "The Aliens Show," but he has to remain unseen, once more, hidden beneath a latex suit.[6]

The effect that masquerade has when bringing together apparently incompatible notions or selves can also be used to good effect by the migrant who wishes to subvert existing structures. The narrator of *The Satanic Verses*, for example, muses on the effectiveness of masquerade as a strategy of resistance for the migrant:

> A man who sets out to make himself up is taking on the Creator's role, according to one way of seeing things; he's unnatural, a blasphemer, an abomination of abominations. From another angle, you could see pathos in him, heroism in his struggle, in his willingness to risk: not all mutants survive. Or, consider him sociopolitically: most migrants learn, and can become disguises. Our own false descriptions to counter the falsehoods invented about us, concealing for reasons of security our secret selves (*SV* 49).

The narrator presents a number of views on masquerade here, all coming from different angles. The first comes from a religious perspective that is steeped in purity and the sovereignty of the whole and individual self. Such a perspective cannot allow either the blasphemy of usurping the role of the Creator or the heresy of the hybrid or multiple self. The second perspective considers masquerade to be a risky business, an heroic struggle against oppression. The last, and I think most interesting viewpoint, sees masquerade as a process of resistance against the racism that many migrants encounter. In order to counter the false and damaging descriptions of those such as the police officers who beat up Saladin, the migrant is forced to come up with alternative identities, identities which need not be any closer to an objective "truth" than those perpetuated by racists, but which protect the migrant from further abuse. Indeed, the suggestion is made that it may even be desirable to construct "false" identities in order to protect a self or selves that the migrant wishes to remain secret. In this way the young Saladin at boarding school learns to masquerade as a way of becoming accepted:

> he began to act, to find masks that these fellows would recognize, paleface masks, clown-masks, until he fooled

> them into thinking he was *okay*, he was *people-like-us*. He fooled them the way a sensitive human being can persuade gorillas to accept him into their family, to fondle and caress and stuff bananas in his mouth (*SV* 43).

His masquerade is a survival technique, and principally involves suppressing differences and imitating features of the group to which he wants to belong. Rushdie's description of Saladin's masquerade involves an ironic twist in that he likens the imitator to a human gaining acceptance from a group of gorillas, despite Saladin being the one who is doing the "aping."

Rushdie explores the existence of a secret, possibly essential and unchanging, self beneath the masks wsorn by the migrant in a number of ways in *The Satanic Verses*. Changez Chamchawala sees his son desperately trying to become an Englishman and does not approve of this rejection of an Indian self that he perceives as essential and unchanging. In a letter to Saladin he associates such a masquerade with Satan, who Saladin ironically comes to resemble in a transformation that is not of his willing:

> "A man untrue to himself becomes a two-legged lie, and such beasts are Shaitan's best work," he wrote, and also, in a more sentimental vein: "I have your soul kept safe, my son, here in this walnut-tree. The devil has only your body. When you are free of him, return and claim your immortal spirit. It flourishes in the garden" (*SV* 48).

This view, with its separation of body and soul, of depths and surfaces, echoes that of Zeeny Vakil, who urges Saladin to drop his masquerade and become Indian once more, something that he is not prepared to do, even though his body also seems to be trying to persuade him as his accent starts to slip, and he starts to speak once more in a "Bombay lilt." At other times, however, she sees not an essential Indian self beneath his masks, but a void, the "terrible vacuum" that Bakhtin associated with the Romantic mask: "when you aren't doing funny voices or acting grand, and when you forget people are watching, you look just like a blank. You know? An empty slate, nobody home"

(*SV* 61). Pamela, too, sees this absence at Saladin's core: "I could see the centre of you, that question so frightful that you had to protect it with all that posturing certainty. That empty space" (*SV* 183). Saladin himself reinforces this view of identity as a series of masks beneath which there is not an essential being but rather an absence of being when he reflects on the meaning of an oft-used cliché:

> *I'm not myself,* he thought as a faint fluttering feeling began in the vicinity of his heart. But what does that mean, anyway, he added bitterly. After all, "les acteurs ne sont pas des gens," as the great ham Frederick had explained in *Les Enfants du Paradis.* Masks beneath masks until suddenly the bare bloodless skull (*SV* 34).

By saying "I'm not myself," Saladin implicitly compares a certain outward self-image to an internal model from which it differs. When he says that, though, he suddenly realises the literal truth of this statement, as he has no essential self he can locate to which he can compare his outward mask. In his idea of himself he consists entirely of masks, which, when he removes them, expose the absence that Zeeny and Pamela have caught glimpses of. Rushdie suggests here that, by denying his Indian side, Saladin empties himself, becoming the absence perceived by Zeeny and Pamela. He becomes complete at the end of the novel only when he accepts his Indian selves as part of his multiple and hybrid construction.

The question of the nature of the self is addressed explicitly by Muhammad Sufyan, the proprietor of the Shaandaar Café, as he ponders the nature of Saladin's metamorphosis. He comments that the "Question of mutability of the essence of the self ... has long been subject of profound debate" (*SV* 276), and characterises the debate as being divided between the views of Lucretius and those of Ovid. According to Lucretius, "Whatever by its changing goes out of its frontiers ... that thing ... by doing so brings immediate death to its old self" (*SV* 276). This means that we have no essential being and that when one identity is replaced by another, the old one is irrevocably lost. Saladin, before his transformation, inclines toward this view when he considers that he has put his old self behind him and replaced it with his new, English identity. Working against this, however, his voice starts to slip on his return to India, and his old self seems to be struggling out from behind his mask. Muhammad Sufyan himself subscribes to the Ovidian conception of identity which allows for an immortal essence: "As yielding wax ... is stamped with new designs and changes shape and seems not still the same, Yet is indeed the same, even so our souls ... are still the same forever, but adopt In their migrations ever-varying forms" (*SV* 276-77).

While Saladin appears to fail in his quest to discard his Indian identity in favour of an English one, he decides to throw himself into his new Satanic identity, and become that totally, even as he sees he has no choice in the matter:

> He chose Lucretius over Ovid. The inconstant soul, the mutability of everything, das Ich, every last speck ... He would enter into his new self; *he would become what he had become*: loud, stenchy, hideous, outsize, grotesque, inhuman, powerful (*SV* 288-89).

Saladin therefore internalises his external condition, becoming the identity that has been thrust upon him. He embraces his grotesque new identity, and, although he detests his appearance, he still recognises the powerful possibilities it contains.

Overall, the novel, like Muhammad Sufyan, tends towards the Ovidian rather than the Lucretian conception of identity. In the bizarre opening scene of the novel, Gibreel, as he falls towards England out of an exploded plane, sings a song which aptly summarises Ovid's view of an eternal essence as the basis of identity:

> "O, my shoes are Japanese," Gibreel sang, translating the old song into English in semi-conscious deference to the uprushing host-nation, "These trousers English, if you please. On my head, red Russian hat; my heart's Indian for all that" (*SV* 5).

Underneath the multicultural exterior lies an essence, a heart, a soul, that retains his Indian identity. The clothes, and outward appearance and behaviour in general, may define a person in some way, but they cannot alter every part of the individual, something remains unaltered, just as wax melted and shaped into a different form is still wax. This is the message that we get from Saladin's trip back to India where he detects his old identity trying to creep back: "Watch out, Chamcha, look out for your shadow. That black fellow creeping up behind" (*SV* 53). His voice betrays him, slipping back to a 'Bombay lilt' he thought he had left behind, and after the plane crash he finds his face has also lost the rigidity that he has cultivated and returned to its old cherubic state. As much as he tries to rid himself of this self, the novel seems to suggest, it keeps on coming back. This reaches a climax when he visits his father on his deathbed and reaches a reconciliation with him. As he sat next to his father,

> Saladin felt hourly closer to many old, rejected selves, many alternative Saladins—or rather Salahuddins—which had split off from himself as he made his various life choices, but which had apparently continued to exist, perhaps in the parallel universes of quantum theory (*SV* 523).

Once more his old self, or, as is stated here, selves, are coming back to haunt him. Instead of continuing to reject these selves, however, he starts feeling closer to them, coming to terms with himself (himselves) at the same time he comes to terms with his father. These old selves he identifies with his old name, Salahuddin, a name he had rejected in his quest to become what he perceived as English, and a name which he now comes to embrace once more. Names are another outward indicator of possible identifications, and Saladin changed his to become more accepted in England. Now, however, he changes back to Salahuddin to identify once more as an Indian. The passage quoted suggests a continuing essence of some sort that has persisted despite the changes that Saladin has made in his life. That essence, however, grows and multiplies with him and does not remain fixed and unchanging. It is a hybrid rather than a pure essence, and consists of all the identities that he has previously adopted. Rushdie suggests in the conclusion of the novel that one can never leave behind one's past, and, at the same time, that one's past is not a solid and fixed object but a varied and multiple essence.

The conclusion of *The Satanic Verses* ties up the carnivalesque elements in the novel. Saladin has transcended the crude inversions of carnival exemplified by Gibreel and his adversarial attitude. He no longer rejects his Indian side and has reached a space of negotiation between his English and Indian elements where newness can emerge. That newness is a hybrid combination of all the selves, English and Indian, that he has constructed. He no longer has the physically grotesque features that were a result of racist conceptions, but he retains the spirit of grotesque realism described by Bakhtin. He remains a body in process, continually changing and evolving into something new, dying and being reborn as he transforms from a cynical mimic into a loving son and reclaims his heritage. He also keeps the spirit of masquerade, changing masks and creating hybrid identities as he does so. The resolution he reaches means that he no longer rejects his Indian selves, meaning that he now embodies the essence of the palimpsest. Whereas before he hid a void beneath his multiple masks because he abjured those Indian parts of his identity, he now has identity written over identity, the new selves overlaying the old and creating rich, new hybrid identities. This is the ideal of hybrid identity proposed by Rushdie.

Notes

1. In a similar vein, Diane Price Herndl writes, "Bakhtin's carnival, however much it exposed the arbitrariness of the social relations of power, remained an event allowed (if not sanctioned) by institutional authority, which served that institution by providing an outlet for the oppressed to prevent any *real* insurrection. It was an artificial subversion of hierarchies which prevented any organized question of them" (Herndl 19-20).
2. Rushdie observes the connection between the carnivalesque practice of masquerade and political revolution in *The Jaguar Smile* when he sees the masks covering the walls of the Nicaraguan Vice-President, the novelist Sergio Ramírez: "During the insurrection, Sandinista guerillas often went into action wearing masks of pink mesh with simple faces painted on them. These masks, too, originated in folk-dance. One night I went to see a ballet based on the country's popular dances, and saw

that one of the ballerinas was wearing a pink mask. The mask's associations with the revolution had grown so strong that it transformed her, in my eyes at least, into something wondrously strange: not a masked dancer, but a guerrilla in a tutu" (*JS* 25-6). The popular dance is another carnivalesque practice that combines with the mask to form an image of revolution in Rushdie's mind.

3. See, for example, John Solomos, *Race and Racism in Britain* and Paul Gilroy, *There Ain't no Black in the Union Jack*, on the policies of the Conservative government towards immigrants from the so-called "new commonwealth" (India, the Caribbean, Africa) and Pakistan.
4. Stuart Hall has made a similar point to the one that Rushdie is making here, noting that, "[...] the term 'black' was coined as a way of referencing the common experience of racism and marginalization in Britain and came to provide the organizing category of a new politics of resistance, amongst groups and communities with, in fact, very different histories, traditions and ethnic identities. In this moment, politically speaking, 'The Black experience,' as a singular and unifying framework based on the building up of identity across ethnic and cultural difference between the different communities, became 'hegemonic' over other ethnic/racial identities—though the latter did not, of course, disappear" (Hall 252).
5. In *The Jaguar Smile*, Rushdie observes that "[t]he true purpose of masks, as any actor will tell you, is not concealment, but transformation. A culture of masks is one that understands a good deal about the processes of metamorphosis" (*JS* 26). The transformation he writes of is the same as Bakhtin's notion of rebirth: the new subsuming the old.
6. Zeeny, Saladin's Indian lover, makes this racism explicit when she exclaims in exasperation at Saladin's blindspot: "They pay you to imitate them, as long as they don't have to look at you. Your voice becomes famous but they hide your face. Got any ideas why? Warts on your nose, cross-eyes, what? Anything come to mind, baby? You goddam lettuce brain, I swear" (*SV* 60).

Works Cited

Bakhtin, M.M. *Rabelais and his World*. Trans. Helene Iswolsky. Cambridge, Massachusetts: M.I.T. Press, 1968.

Bhabha, Homi. "Introduction: Locations of Culture." *The Location of Culture*. London: Routledge, 1994. 1-18.

____. "Representation and the Colonial Text: A Critical Exploration of Some Forms of Mimeticism." *The Theory of Reading*. Ed. Frank Gloversmith. Brighton: The Harvester Press, 1984. 93-122.

Gilroy, Paul. *There Ain't no Black in the Union Jack*. London: Hutchinson, 1987.

Hall, Stuart. "New Ethnicities." *'Race,' Culture & Difference.* Ed. James Donald and Ali Rattansi. London: SAGE, 1992. 252-59.

Harrison, James. *Salman Rushdie.* New York: Twayne, 1992.

Price Herndl, Diane. "The Dilemmas of a Feminine Dialogic." *Feminism, Bakhtin, and the Dialogic.* Ed. Dale M. Bauer and Susan Jaret McKinstry. New York: State U of New York P, 1991. 7-24.

Rushdie, Salman. *The Jaguar Smile: A Nicaraguan Journey.* London: Picador, 1987.

____. *The Satanic Verses.* London: Viking, 1988.

Russo, Mary. "Female Grotesques: Carnival and Theory." *Feminist Studies/ Critical Studies.* Ed. Teresa de Lauretis. Bloomington: Indiana UP, 1986. 213-29

Solomos, John. *Race and Racism in Britain.* 2nd ed. London: Macmillan, 1993.

Stallybrass, Peter and Allon White. *The Politics and Poetics of Transgression.* Ithaca, New York: Cornell UP, 1986.

Bibliography of Rushdie's Works

1. RUSHDIE'S WORKS

1.1. Books

1975. *Grimus.*
Published in February 1975.
Editions:
- London: Victor Gollancz, 1975. 319 pp.
- London: Alfred Knopf, 1975.
- London: Grafton/Panther Books, 1977. 271 pp.
- Woodstock, N.Y.: Overlook, 1979. 320 pp.
- London: Granada, 1981.
- Woodstock, N.Y.: Overlook, 1982. Paperback. 320 pp.
- London: Granada/Panther 1985
- London: Paladin, 1989. 253 pp.
- London: Viking/Penguin, 1991. 324 pp.
- New York: Penguin Books, 1991
- London: Vintage, 1996.

- Partly serialized in *Illustrated Weekly of India.* Part 1/2 *The Illustrated Weekly of India* Oct. 23 (1983): 52-59; part 2/2 *The Illustrated Weekly of India* Oct. 30 (1983): 60-7.

1981. *Midnight's Children.*
Published in February 1981.
Editions:
- London: Jonathan Cape, 1981. 442 pp.
- New York: Alfred A. Knopf, 1981. 448 pp.
- New York: Avon Books, 1981. 560 pp.
- London: Pan Books (Picador), 1982. 463 pp.
- New York: Avon Books, 1982. 560 pp.
- New York: Viking/Penguin, 1991. 448 pp.

- Booker 25th Anniversary edition. London: Jonathan Cape, 1993. New edition. 448 pp.
- New York: Alfred A. Knopf, 1995. New edition.

- Everyman's Library Classics edition. Introduction by Anita Desai.
- Everyman's Library Ltd., 1995. New edition. 512 pp.
- New York: Vintage, 1995. New edition. 448 pp.

1983. *Shame.*
Published in September 1983.
Editions:
- London: Jonathan Cape, 1983. 288 pp.
- New York: Alfred A. Knopf, 1983. 318 pp.
- Calcutta: Rupa, 1983.
- London: Picador, 1984. 288 pp.
- New Delhi: Rupa, 1985.
- New York: Vintage, 1995. New edition. 288 pp.
- Partly serialized in *The Times,* Aug. 29 (1983): 8, Aug. 30 (1983): 8, Aug. 31 (1983): 6.

1987. *The Jaguar Smile: A Nicaraguan Journey.*
Published in January 1987.
Editions:
- London: Pan Books, 1987. 176 pp.
- New York: Viking Penguin, 1987.
- New York: Viking Penguin 1988.
- London: Penguin Books 1988. 176 pp.
- ISIS Large Print Books, 1989. 146 pp.
- New York: Henry Holt, 1997.
- Excerpts in *Granta,* 20 (Wi 1986), pp.55-69 (from ch. 7., pp.73-90) and *The Guardian,* Jan. 17 (1987) p.19 (from ch. 13, pp.145-53).

1988. *The Satanic Verses.*
Published in September 1988.
Editions:
- London: Viking, 1988. 546 pp.
- New York: Viking Penguin, 1989. 496 pp.
- Consortium, 1992. Paperback. 546 pp.
- Excerpts in *Harper's Magazine* 277.1663 (Dec. 1988): 53-9; in *Colonial and Postcolonial Fiction in English: an Anthology.* Ed. Robert L. Ross. New York: Garland, 1999.

1990. *Haroun and the Sea of Stories.*
Published in September 1990.
Editions:
- London: Granta Books/Penguin, 1990. 224 pp.
- London: Granta Books/Penguin, 1991. New edition. 224 pp.
- Chivers North America, 1991. Large Type.
- Sound recording by Salman Rushdie. St. Paul: Penguin HighBridge Audio, 1991. 2 cassettes (180 min.)
- London: Granta Books/Penguin, 1993. New edition. 224 pp.
- London: Granta Books/Penguin, 1996. New edition. 224 pp.
- Excerpts in *The Sunday Times*, Books 23 Sep. (1990): 8-9; in *The Sunday Times*, Books 30 Sep. (1990): 6-7.
- *Salman Rushdie's 'Haroun and the Sea of Stories.'* Adapted by Tim Supple and David Tushingham. [A Play]. London: Faber & Faber, 1998.

1991. *Imaginary Homelands: Essays and Criticism 1981-1991.*
Published in March 1991.
Editions:
- London: Granta Books, 1991. 448 pp.
- New Delhi: Penguin, 1991.
- 2nd ed. London: Granta Books, 1992. 440 pp.

1992. *The Wizard of Oz.* Published in March 1992.
Editions:
- London: B.F.I. (British Film Institute) Publications, 1992. 72 pp.
- Indiana University Press, 1992.
- Partly in *The Independent on Sunday*, suppl May 3 (1992): 26-27.
- Partly in *Granta* 39 (Sp 1992): 245-54; in *East, West.* London: Jonathan Cape, 1994. 85-103.

1994. *East, West.*
Published in October 1994.
Editions:
- London: Jonathan Cape, 1994. 216 pp.

- New York: Pantheon Books, 1994.

Includes: "The Prophet's Hair" (1981), "The Free Radio" (1982), "Yorick" (1982), "Good Advice is Rarer than Rubies" (1987), "Christopher Columbus and Queen Isabella of Spain Consummate Their Relationship, Santa Fe, Jan. 1492" (1991), "At the Auction of the Ruby Slippers" (1992), "The Harmony of the Spheres" (1994), "Chekov and Zulu" (1994), "The Courter" (1994).

1995. *The Moor's Last Sigh*. Published in September 1995.
Editions:
- London: Jonathan Cape, 1995. 438 pp.
- New York: Pantheon Books, 1995.

1997. *The Vintage Book of Indian Writing, 1947-1997*. (UK edition) *Mirrorwork: Fifty Years of Indian Writing 1947-1997*. (US edition)

Ed. Salman Rushdie & Elizabeth West.
Published in March 1997.
Editions:
- London: Vintage. 1997.
- New York: Henry Holt, 1997.

1999. *The Ground Beneath Her Feet*. Published in April 1999.
Editions:
- London: Jonathan Cape 1999
- New York: Henry Holt, 1999.
- Pbk. London: Vintage, 2000.
- Partly in *The New Yorker* 75.6 (Apr. 5 1999): 68-79.
- Excerpt in *The Guardian*, Saturday Review Apr. 3 (1999).

1999. *The Screenplay of Midnight's Children*. Published in April 1999.
Editions:
- London: Vintage, 1999.
- Adapted from the Novel; introd. Salman Rushdie.

2001. *Fury*. Published in September 2001
Editions:
- New York: Random House, 2001.
- London: Jonathan Cape, 2001.

- *Woede*. Foreword Karina van Santen, Jan. Pieter van der Sterre & Martine Vosmaer. [Dutch] Amsterdam: Stichting Collectieve Propaganda, 2001. [March 2001]
- Excerpt *The Times* Aug. 15 (2001) at http://www.thetimes.co.uk/article/0,,2001170001-2001282192,00.html
- Partly in *The New Yorker* 16 Jul. (2001): 66-75.

1.2. SHORT STORIES AND PARTS OF BOOKS

"The Prophet's Hair."
- *The London Review of Books* 3.7 (Apr. 16 1981): 19-20.
- *The Atlantic Monthly* Sep. (1981): 61-66.
- In *The Penguin Book of Modern British Short Stories*. Ed. Malcolm Bradbury. London: Penguin, 1988 (1987) 389-99.
- *East, West*. London: Jonathan Cape, 1994. 33-58.
- In "Two Stories by Salman Rushdie." With five woodcuts and three linocuts by Bhuphen Khakhar. [s.l., s.n.] Sebastian Carter, 1989. 29-46.
- In Jerome Beaty & J. Paul Hunter, eds. *The Norton Introduction to Literature*. 7th ed. New York: Norton, 1999.

"The Free Radio."
- *The Atlantic Monthly* Jun. (1982): 75-77.
- In *Firebird 1: Writing Today*. Ed. T.J. Binding. Harmondsworth: Penguin, 1982. 225-33.
- *East, West*. London: Jonathan Cape, 1994. 17-32.
- In "Two Stories by Salman Rushdie." With five woodcuts and three linocuts by Bhuphen Khakhar. [s.l., s.n.] Sebastian Carter, 1989. 11-24.
- *The Penguin Book of the City*. Ed. Robert Drewe. Victoria: Penguin, 1997. London: Penguin, 1998. 79-91.

"Yorick."
- *Encounter* 59.3-4 (Sep./Oct. 1982): 3-8.
- *East, West*. London: Jonathan Cape, 1994. 61-83.
- *Shakespeare Stories*. Ed. Giles Gordon. Ill. Robin Jacques. London: Hamish Hamilton, 1982. 70-81.

"The Cord and the Noose." Excerpts from *Shame*.
- Part 1/3 of the partly serialized *Shame. The Times* Aug. 29 (1983): 8.

"A Great Man to Unmake Himself." Excerpts from *Shame.*
- Part 2/3 of the partly serialized *Shame. The Times* Aug. 30 (1983): 8.

"Such Is the Shape of Death." Excerpts from *Shame.*
- Part 3/3 of the partly serialized *Shame. The Times* Aug. 31 (1983): 6.

"Grimus." Excerpts from *Grimus.*
- Part 1/2 of the partly serialized *Grimus. The Illustrated Weekly of India* Oct. 23 (1983): 52-59.

"Grimus." Excerpts from *Grimus.*
- Part 2/2 of the partly serialized *Grimus. The Illustrated Weekly of India* Oct. 30 (1983): 60-67.

"The Golden Bough."
- *Granta* 7 (Best of Young British Novelists) (1983): 247-51.

"Good Advice is Rarer than Rubies."
- *The New Yorker* 63.18 (Jun. 22 1987): 26-28.
- *East, West.* London: Jonathan Cape, 1994. 3-16.

"Untime of the Imam." Excerpts from *The Satanic Verses.* 205-15.
- *Harper's Magazine,* 277.1663 (Dec. 1988): 53-59.

"The Angel Azraeel." Excerpt from *The Satanic Verses.*
- *Colonial and Postcolonial Fiction in English: an Anthology.* Ed. Robert L. Ross. New York: Garland, 1999.

"The Day the Ocean Dried Up." Excerpt from *Haroun and the Sea of Stories.* 13-27.
- *The Sunday Times,* Books 23 Sep. (1990): 8-9.

"Exclusive: *Haroun and the Sea of Stories* by Salman Rushdie." Excerpt from *Haroun and the Sea of Stories.* 61-75.
- *The Sunday Times* 30 Sep. (1990): 6-7.

"Christopher Columbus and Queen Isabella of Spain Consummate Their Relationship, Santa Fe, Jan. 1492."
- *The New Yorker* 67.17 (Jun. 17 1991): 32-35.
- *East, West.* London: Jonathan Cape, 1994. 105-19.
- *The Minerva Book of Short Stories,* 5. Eds. Giles Gordon & David Hughes. London: Minerva, 1993. 264-271

"At the Auction of the Ruby Slippers."
- In *The Wizard of Oz.* London: B.F.I. (British Film Institute) Publications, 1992. 58-65.

- *Granta* 39 (Sp 1992): 245-54.
- *East, West.* London: Jonathan Cape, 1994. 85-103.

"The Harmony of the Spheres."
- *East, West.* London: Jonathan Cape, 1994. 123-46.

"Chekov and Zulu."
- *East, West.* London: Jonathan Cape, 1994. 147-71.
- *New Yorker* 70.26 (Aug. 22 & 29 1994): 102-09.
- *The Longman Anthology of British Literature*, Volume 2C, The Twentieth Century. New York: Longman, 1999.

"The Courter."
-*East, West.* London: Jonathan Cape, 1994. 173-211.

"The Firebird's Nest."
- *The New Yorker* Jun. 23 & 30 (1997): 122-27.

"Vina Divina." Excerpt from *The Ground Beneath Her Feet.*
- "*The New Yorker* 75.6 (Apr. 5 1999): 68-79.

"The Keeper of Bees." Excerpt from *The Ground Beneath Her Feet.*
-januarymagazine.com Apr. (1999). http://www.januarymagazine.com/features/rushdie.html

"The Summer of Solanka." Excerpt from *Fury.*
- *The New Yorker* 16 Jul. (2001): 66-75.

"*Fury* by Salman Rushdie." Condensed plot of the Novel.
- *The Guardian* 8 Sep. (2001). http://www.guardian.co.uk/Archive/Article/0,4273,4252327,00.html

1.3. ESSAYS AND ARTICLES

"Works in Progress." Salman Rushdie & various other writers. *The New York Times Book Review* 87.23 (Jun. 6 1982): 11 & 48-49.

"The Empire Writes Back with a Vengeance." *The Times* 3 Jul. (1982): 8.

"Imaginary Homelands." *The London Review of Books* 4.18 (7 Oct. 1982): 18-19.
Debonair May (1983) 38-42. In *Imaginary Homelands.* 1991. 9-21. In *Creating Theory: Writers on Writing.* Ed. Jasbir Jain. Delhi: Pencraft, 2000. 213-24.

"Marquez the Magician." *The Sunday Times* 24 Oct. (1982): 41.

"The New Empire within Britain." *New Society* 62.1047 (9 Dec. 1982): 34-37. In *Imaginary Homelands.* 1991. 129-38.

"She Has Persuaded the Nation That Everything Which Goes Wrong Is an Act of God." *The Guardian* May 23 (1983): 9. As "A General Election," in *Imaginary Homelands.* 1991.159-62.

"*Midnight's Children* and *Shame.*" Lecture & interview at the University of Aarhus, Denmark Oct. 7 (1983). *Kunapipi* 7.1 (1985): 1-19.

"Last Chance." *Index on Censorship* 12.6 (Dec. 1983): 2. As "Casualties of Censorship," in *They Shoot Writers, Don't They?* Ed. George Theiner. New York: Faber & Faber, 1984. 84-87. As "Censorship," in *Imaginary Homelands.* 1991. 37-40.

"The Indian Writer in England." In *Eye of the Beholder: Indian Writing in English.* Ed. Maggie Butcher. London: Commonwealth Institute, 1983. 75-83. Pp.75-78 repr. as "Reclaiming a City and a History," in *Indian Express, Express Magazine* Mar. 11 (1984): 5. Pp.78-83 repr. as "Describing Reality is a Political Act," in *Indian Express, Express Magazine* Mar. 18 (1984): 5.

"Errata: Unreliable Narration in *Midnight's Children.*" Gothenburg Conference on Commonwealth Literature, Sep. 1983. Rev. ed. in *A Sense of Place: Essays in Postcolonial Literatures.* Congress of Commonwealth Language and Literature, September 1982. Gothenburg University Commonwealth Studies, 1. Eds. Britta Olinder & Inge Crosman. Göteborg: Gothenburg University, 1984. 98-100. In *Imaginary Homelands.* 1991. 22-25.

"'Commonwealth Literature' Does Not Exist." (1983). In *Imaginary Homelands.* 1991. 61-70.

"The Raj Revival." A shorter version of "Outside the Whale." *The Observer* Apr. 1 (1984): 19. As "Whitewashing the Raj" *Gentleman* May (1984) 61-66. In *The Black and White Media Book.* Ed. John Twitchin. Stoke-on-Trent: Trentham, 1988. 130-33.

"Outside the Whale." *Granta* 11 (Milan Kundera) (Apr. 1984): 123-41. *American Film* 10 (Jan./Feb. 1985): 16, 70, & 72-73. In *Imaginary Homelands*. 1991. 87-101. *The Longman Anthology of British Literature*, Volume 2C, The Twentieth Century. New York: Longman, 1999.

"Kundera and Kitsch." Letter. *The London Review of Books* 6.12 (5 Jul. 1984): 4.

"After Indira, an Awakening or the Whirlwind?" *The Times* 1 Nov. (1984): 16. As "Dynasty and Democracy: The Idea of India after the Death of Mrs. Gandhi." *The New Republic* 191.22 (26 Nov. 1984): 17-19. As "The Legacy of Indira Gandhi." *The Illustrated Weekly of India* 105.34 (30 Dec.1984): 50-51. As "The Assassination of Indira Gandhi." In *Imaginary Homelands*. 1991. 41-46.

"Shame about the Pirates." *The Times* 24 Nov. (1984): 8.

"The Council Housing That Kills." *The Guardian* 3 Dec. (1984): 12. As "An Unimportant Fire." In *Imaginary Homelands*. 1991. 139-42.

Introduction to *Home Front* by Derek Bishton and John Reardon. In Derek Bishton & John Reardon. *Home Front*. London: Jonathan Cape, 1984. 6-7. In *Imaginary Homelands*. 1991. 143-47.

"At the Adelaide Festival." (1984). In *Imaginary Homelands*. 1991. 226-31.

"Magnificent Obsession." *The Observer Magazine* May 26 (1985): 10-2. As "The Painter and the Pest." In *Imaginary Homelands*. 1991. 152-56.

Introduction to *The Nehrus & the Gandhis: An Indian Dynasty* by Tariq Ali. In Ali, Tariq. *The Nehrus & the Gandhis: An Indian Dynasty*. New York: Putnam, 1985. [no page no.s]. Repr. rev. as "The Myth of Indira's Dynasty." *The Guardian* Jan. 14 (1985): 7. As "Dynasty." In *Imaginary Homelands*. 1991. 47-52.

"'In God We Trust.'" (1985). In *Imaginary Homelands*. 1991. 376-92.

"Adventures and Epics." *The New York Times Magazine*, part 2, "The Sophisticated Traveler" Mar. 16 (1986): 26-27. As "On Adventure." In *Imaginary Homelands*. 1991. 222-25.

"Goodness: The American Neurosis." *The Nation* 242 (Mar. 22 1986): 344.

"Minority Literatures in a Multi-Cultural Society." Opening Speech, Conference at Kungliga Svenska Vitterhedsakademien, Stockholm, Oct. 1986. *The Dolphin* 15 (1987): 32-43. In *Displaced Persons*. Eds. Kirsten Holst Petersen & Anna Rutherford. Sidney, Australia: Dangaroo Press, 1988.

"Eating the Eggs of Love." Excerpt from *The Jaguar Smile*. 73-90. *Granta* 20 (In Trouble Again) (Wi 1986): 55-69.

"Yielding to the Force." *END* 25 (Dec.-Jan. 1986-87): 22-23.

"The War Widow Pressing for Peace." Edited excerpt from *The Jaguar Smile*. 145-53. *The Guardian* 17 Jan. (1987): 19.

"The Whole in the Centre." *The Guardian* 8 Jun. (1987): 19.

"After Midnight." *Vanity Fair* Sep. (1987): 88, 90 & 94. In Jonathan S. Weil "The United States and the Indian Constitution." Research Report. New Delhi: Indian Council for Cultural Relations, 20 Jan. 1988. As "Midnight's Real Children." *The Guardian* 25 Mar. (1988): 19.

"Speak and Be Damned." *The Observer* 17 Jul. (1988): 43.

"An End to the Nightmare." *The Independent* 19 Aug. (1988): 21. As "Zia Unmourned." *The Nation* 247.6 (19 Sep. 1988): 188-89. As "Zia ul-Haq, 17 Aug. 1988." In *Imaginary Homelands*. 1991. 53-55.

"An Open Letter to PM Rajiv Gandhi." 10 Oct. 1988. Broadcast in Indian Radio 10 Oct. 1988. In *The Rushdie File*. Eds. Lisa Appignanesi & Sara Maitland. London: 4th Estate, 1989. Syracuse: Syracuse University Press, 1990. 42-45. In *Sacrilege Versus Civility: Muslim Perspectives on The Satanic Verses Affair*. Eds. M. Manazir Ahsan & A.R. Kidwai. Leicester: The Islamic Foundation, 1991. Rev.ed. 1993. 62-64. Appeared in various papers:

* as "It's Between Us, Mr PM: Rushdie," in *The Times of India* 13 Oct. (1988): sec.1, 1 & 10;
* as "Personal view," in *The Sunday Times* 16 Oct. (1988): G4;
* as "India Bans a Book for Its Own Good," in *The New York Times* 19 Oct. (1988): A27;
* as "My Book Speaks for Itself," in *The New York Times* 17 Feb. (1989): A39.

"The Philistine Conspiracy." *The Illustrated Weekly of India* 30 Oct. (1988): 20-21. Repr. abr. as "In His Own Write," in *The Illustrated Weekly of India* 12 Mar. (1989): 19.

"Narrow Days." *Samizdat* 2 (Jan./Feb. 1989): 21. As "Why We Shouldn't Swallow Hogwash," in *The Guardian* 16 Jan. (1989): 16. As "Charter 88," in *Imaginary Homelands.* 1991. 163-65.

"Choice Between Light and Dark." *The Observer* 22 Jan. (1989): 11. As "A Clash of Faiths," in *Maclean's* 102.9 (27 Feb. 1989): 24. As "The Book Burning," in *The New York Review of Books* 36.3 (2 Mar. 1989): 26. Abr. in *The Rushdie File.* Eds. Lisa Appignanesi & Sara Maitland. London: 4th Estate, 1989. Syracuse: Syracuse University Press, 1990. 74-75. Abr. in *Contemporary Literary Criticism,* 55. Detroit, MI: Gale Research Inc., 1989. 222-23. Abr. in *The Observer* Jan. 28 (1990): 21. In *Critical Fictions: The Politics of Imaginative Writing.* Discussions in Contemporary Culture, DIA Center for the Arts, vol.7. Ed. Philomena Mariani. Seattle: Bay Press, 1991.

Statement on the fatwa. 18 Feb. 1989. In *The Observer* 19 Feb. (1989): 1.

"Arkady's Dreams in Alice Springs." *The Observer* 19 Nov. (1989): 45. As "Travelling with Chatwin." In *Imaginary Homelands.* 1991. 232-36.

"In Good Faith." *The Independent on Sunday* 4 Feb. (1990): 18-20. Published Separately: London: Granta, 1990. As "A Pen Against the Sword: In Good Faith," in *Newsweek* (US ed.) 95.7 (12 Feb. 1990): 52-57. Abr. in *Contemporary Literary Criticism,* 59. Detroit, MI: Gale Research Inc., 1990. 450-55. In *Imaginary Homelands.* 1991. 393-414. Abr. in *One World, Many Cultures.* Ed. Stuart Hirschberg. New York: Macmillan, 1992. 481-92.

"Yes." "Should the Paperback Be Published." *The Independent on Sunday* 4 Feb. (1990): 21.

"Is Nothing Sacred." The Herbert Read Memorial Lecture, 6 Feb. 1990 (read by Harold Pinter). Published Separately, Cambridge: Granta, 1990. In *Granta* 31 (Sp 1990): 99-111. Abr. in *The Guardian* 7 Feb. (1990): 4. In *The Guardian*

Weekly, 18 Feb. (1990): 4. In *Brick* 39 (Su 1990): 6-12. In *Imaginary Homelands*. 1991. 415-29.

"Rushdie Replies." Letter. *The Guardian* 15 Feb. (1990): 18.

"Any Country's Right to Choose Between Tanks and Mosques." *The Independent on Sunday* 6 May (1990): 18.

"Audiences for Satyajit Ray." *The London Review of Books* 12.9 (10 May 1990): 4.

Statement on the film *International Guerillas*. 17 Aug. 1990. In *The Guardian* 18 Aug. (1990): 19.

"Voices of Her People." Salman Rushdie and 24 other writers. *The Independent on Sunday, The Sunday Review* 25 Nov. (1990): 4-6.

"Books for Christmas." Salman Rushdie and other writers. *The Independent on Sunday, The Sunday Review* 2 Dec. (1990): 31-32.

Statement on islam. 24 Dec. 1990. As "The Writer's Statement," *The New York Times* 25 Dec. (1990) 26. In *Index on Censorship* 20.2 (Feb. 1991): 34.

"Why I Have Embraced Islam." *The Times* 28 Dec. (1990): 10. As "My Decision." *Index on Censorship* 20.2 (Feb. 1991): 34. In *Imaginary Homelands*. 1991. [only 1st ed.] 430-32.

Introduction to *Soldiers Three* and *In Black and White* by Rudyard Kipling. In *Imaginary Homelands*. 1991. 74-80. In Rudyard Kipling. *Soldiers Three and In Black and White*. London: Penguin, 1993. ix-xv.

"Salman Rushdie Speaks to English PEN." London, 16 Oct. 1991. In *PEN International* (ed. Tom Aitken) 42.1 (1992): 3-8.

"One Man in a Doomed Balloon." Speech at Columbia University, Dec. 1991. In *The Guardian* 13 Dec. (1991): 1 & 19. As "One Thousand Days in a Balloon," in *The Bookseller* 3 Jan. (1992): 14-19. In *Imaginary Homelands*. 1991. [2nd ed.] 430-39. As "What Is My Single Life Worth?" in *The Penguin Book of 20th Century Speeches*. Ed. Brian MacArthur. London: Penguin/Viking, 1993 (1992). 479-87. As "1,000 Days in a Balloon," in *The Rushdie Letters: Freedom to Speak, Freedom to Write*. Günter Grass et al. Ed. Steve MacDonogh. Lincoln: University of Nebraska Press, 1993. Dingle: Brandon Book Publishers Ltd, 1993. 13-24.

"A Personal Statement." *PEN International* 41.1 (1991): 3.

"I Must Not Be Forgotten." Speect at Stationers' Hall, London. 14 Feb. 1992. In *The Times* 15 Feb. (1992): 12.

"Angela Carter, 1940-92: A Very Good Wizard, a Very Dear Friend." *The New York Times Book Review* 8 Mar. (1992): 5.

"Out of Kansas." *New Yorker*68.12 11 May 1992): 93-103.

"Facing up to Harsh Realities in Sarajevo." Letter, with BoJan. Bujic et al. *The Guardian* 1 Jul. (1992): 18.

"20-20 Vision." *The Independent on Sunday*, Review 17 Jan. (1993): 24.

"Out of the Shadows." Cover title, "The Last Hostage." *The Sunday Times, Magazine* 7 Feb. (1993): 16-20.

"Give the Devil His Due." *The Nation* 257.6 (Feb. 1993): 194.

"Pawn in a Wider Game." *The Observer* 4 Jul. (1993): 23.

"Muslim World Needs Progressive Voices, Not a Culture Frozen in Time." Letter. *The Independent* 6 Jul. (1993): 21.

"Islamic Curses." *The Guardian* 13 Jul. (1993): 18.

"Rushdie on Cockburn." *New Statesman & Society* 6.263 (30 Jul. 1993): 26.

"A Reply." In *The Rushdie Letters: Freedom to Speak, Freedom to Write.* Günter Grass et al. Ed. Steve MacDonogh. Lincoln: University of Nebraska Press, 1993. Dingle: Brandon Book Publishers Ltd, 1993. 121-23.

"Declaration of Independence for Those Without Frontiers." Commemorating the inaugural presidency of the International Parliament of Writers, Feb. 1994. *The Independent* 14 Feb. (1994): 3.

"Nasreen's Heroism." Letter. *The Independent* 4 Mar. (1994): 17.

"The Next Step in Bosnia." An appeal, with Wolf Biermann et al. *New Statesman & Society* 7.294 (18 Mar. 1994): 43-44.

"Born in Bombay." Letter. *The London Review of Books* 16.7 (7 Apr. 1994): 4.

"Bosnia on My Mind." *Index on Censorship*, New Series 1/2 (156/7) (May/Jun. 1994): 16-20.

"Chère Taslima Nasreen." Open letter to Taslima Nasreen. In

French in *Libération* 13 Jul. (1994): 5. In English in Fishnet 2 Sep. (1994).

"Heavy, Man." *The Guardian, The Guardian Weekend* 28 Jan. (1995): 26-29.

"Currently Reading, 6: Salman Rushdie." *The Guardian, Friday Review* 9 Jun. (1995): 4.

Rushdie Competition. In "Diary." *The Sunday Times*, Books 3 Sep. (1995): 6.

Introduction to *Burning Your Boats: Stories* by Angela Carter. Carter, Angela. *Burning Your Boats: Stories.* Introduction by Salman Rushdie. London: Chatto & Windus, 1995. ix-xiv.

"Defeating the Fatwa." *The Nation* 262.10 11 Mar. 1996): 8.

"Keynote Address." ASNE (American Society for Newspaper Editors) Convention 1996, Keynote Breakfast 17 Apr. (1996). http://www.asne.org/kiosk/archive/convention/conv96/keynote.htm

"Commencement Address at Bard College." 25 May (1996). http://www.richmondreview.co.uk/library/rushdi01.html

"It Is by Defying the Gods That Human Beings Have Best Expressed Their Humanity."
Chronicle of Higher Education 42.39 (1996): B5.

"In Defense of the Novel, Yet Again." *The New Yorker* 72.17 (Special Fiction Issue) (24 Jun.-1 Jul. 1996): 48-50, 52, 55.

"How News Becomes Opinion, and Opinion Off-Limits." *The Nation* 24 Jun. (1996): 18-21.

"Why the Novel Is Not Dead." *The Sydney Morning Herald* 30 Aug. (1996).

"Reservoir Frogs (or, Places Called Mama's)." *The New Yorker* 72.28 (23 Sep. 1996): 104.

"On Leavened Bread." *The New Yorker* 72.40 (23-30 Dec. 1996): 72.

"From Salman Rushdie." *Index on Cencorship* 2 (1996).

"Notes on Writing and the Nation." *Index on Cencorship* 26.3 (1996): 34-38. In *Harper's Magazine* 1768 (Sep. 1997) 22-23.

"Foreword." William Nygaard. *The Price of Free Speech.* Oslo etc.: Scandinavian UP, 1996. 9-15.

"The Diplomatic Vices." *The Guardian* Feb. 14 (1997): 19.

"Europe's Shameful Trade in Silence." *The New York Times*146 (15 Feb. 1997): 23

"Writers and Nations." *The Guardian,* The Week 14 Jun. (1997): 3.

"India at Five-O." *Time* 150.6 (11 Aug. 1997): 14-16.

"A Fantasy Called India." *India Today* 18 Aug. (1997). http://www.india-today.com/itoday/18081997/rushdie.html

"A Land of Plenty." *Time* 150.6 (11 Aug. 1997): 20-21.

"Damme, This Is the Oriental Scene for You!" *New Yorker* 23-30 Jun. (1997): 50, 52, 54, 56-61.

"Introduction." *Vintage Book of Indian Writing 1947-1997.* Eds. Rushdie & West. 1997. xii-xx. As "India and World Literature." *Frontline* 14.16 (9 Aug. 1997): 101-05. http://www.flonnet.com/fl1416/14161010.htm

"Crash." *The New Yorker* 73.27 15 Sep. (1997): 68-69.

"Clash of Symbols." *The Sydney Morning Herald,* 2 May (1998).

Letters. *The Guardian* 18, 20 & 22 Nov. (1997). "John le Carré, Salman Rushdie and Christopher Hitchens Exchange Biting Letters."
http://www.rjgeib.com/thoughts/burning/le-carre-vs-rushdie.html

"The Pen Is Crueler Than the Sword." Correspondence between authors John le Carre and Salman Rushdie. Reprinted from *The Guardian,* 18-22 Nov. (1997). *Harper's Magazine* Feb. (1998).
http://www.findarticles.com/cf_dls/m1111/n1773_v296/20182341/p1/article.jhtml

"Mohandas Gandhi." *Time* 151.14 (13 Apr. 1998): 128-31.

http://www.time.com/time/time100/leaders/profile/gandhi.html

http://www.time.com/time/time100/leaders/profile/gandhi2.html

http://www.time.com/time/time100/leaders/profile/gandhi3.html

http://www.time.com/time/time100/leaders/profile/gandhi4.html

"Cancel the Debt: My Plan Would Make Millions Happier, Safer, and Better Off." *The Guardian* 6 Jan. (1999). http:/

/www.guardian.co.uk/Archive/Article/0,4273,3804466,00.html

"My Unfunny Valentine." *The New Yorker* 74.46 (15 Feb. 1999): 28-29.

"Ten Years After: My Unfunny Valentine: How the Fatwa and I Lived with Each Other." *India Today* 15 Feb. (1999). http://www.india-today.com/itoday/15021999/rushdie.html

"Debt Be Not Proud." *India Today* 18 Feb. (1999). http://www.india-today.com/itoday/18011999/rushdie.html

"Rethinking the War on American Culture." *The New York Times* 148 (5 Mar. 1999): A21.

"A Culture of Easy Criticism." *The Age* 10 Mar. (1999). http://www.theage.com.au/daily/990310/news/news27.html

"Sing of Freedom!" *The Age* 15 Apr. (1999). http://www.theage.com.au/daily/990415/news/news28.html

"For Services Rendered-to the Cause of Folly." *The Globe and Mail* 7 May (1999).

"Introduction." Rushdie. *The Screenplay of Midnight's Children.* 1999. 1-12.

"What Kosovo and Colorado Have in Common." http://nytsyn.com/syndicate/columnists/rushdie_eng.html

"Apologists for Terror." *The Age* 10 May (1999). http://www.theage.com.au/daily/990510/news/news28.html

"The People's Game: the Education of a Soccer Fan." *The New Yorker* 75.13 (31 May 1999): 56-65.

"Kashmir, the Imperiled Paradise." *The New York Times*, Op-Ed Jun. 3 (1999): A27.
http://www.mnet.fr/aiindex/Kargil/RushdieKashmir. html
http://www.gn.apc.org/cndyorks/news/articles/asia/kashmir.htm
http://groups.yahoo.com/group/act/message/91
http://167.216.192.98/indopaksummit/viewpointop10.shtml (An excerpt from *The New York Times*)

"A Plea for Paradise Lost." *The Age* 9 Jun. (1999).

http://www.theage.com.au/daily/990609/news/specials/news2.html

http://www.prop1.org/nucnews/9906nn/990604nn.106.htm

"Peace Can Wait: the Silence of the Guns Will Do for Now." *The Age* 9 Jul. (1999).

http://www.theage.com.au/daily/990709/news/specials/news3.html

"The Silence of the Guns Will Do-for Now." *The Sydney Morning Herald* 10 Jul. (1999).

"Kosovo's Cure: Realities." *The Washington Post* 4 Aug. (1999).

"Dreams and Reality in Kosovo." *The Boston Globe* 6 Aug. (1999).

"Giving up the Dream of a Tolerant Kosovo." *The Sydney Morning Herald* 12 Aug. (1999).

"Locking out That Disruptive Darwin Fellow." *The Globe and Mail* 2 Sep. (1999).

"And the Metaphor Was Made Flesh-in Kansas." *The Observer* 19 Sep. (1999). http://www.guardian.co.uk/Archive/Article/0,4273,3903406,00.html

"Welcome to the New Age of Unreason" *The Age* 30 Sep. (1999). http://www.theage.com.au/news/19990930/A31982-1999Sep29.html

http://www.theage.com.au/daily/990930/news/specials/news6.html

"Rushdie States His Case on UN Row: From Mr Salman Rushdie." *The Times* Letters To The Editor Oct. 15 (1999).

http://www.times-archive.co.uk/news/pages/tim/1999/10/15/timopnolt01004.html?999

"Taj Mahal." *National Geographic Traveler* 16.7 (Oct. 1999): 214-15.

"Murder, Treason, Vice: Who Can Save Pakistan?" *The Age* 12 Nov. (1999).

http://www.theage.com.au/news/19991112/A38725-1999Nov11.html

"Kansas and Evolution: In This Movie, Toto, We Can't Go Home again." *Church & State* 52.10 (Nov. 1999): 21.

"Silence Can't Bridge the Global Divide." *The Age* 14 Dec. (1999).

http://www.theage.com.au/news/19991214/A36141-1999Dec13.html

"Imagine There's No Heaven." *Letters to the Six Billionth World Citizen*. Eds. Toef Jaeger & Joke van Kampen. Amsterdam: Podium, 1999. 27-33.
http://www.freerepublic.com/forum/a380b67eb6a46. htm

"A New Battle Begins." *The Age* 27 Jan. (2000).
http://www.theage.com.au/news/20000127/A47638-2000Jan26.html

"Austria's Uglier Voice." *The New York Times* 2 Feb. (2000): A21.
http://groups.yahoo.com/group/act/message/414

"Nazism Stalks Europe Again." *The Age* 4 Feb. (2000).
http://www.theage.com.au/news/20000204/A63214-2000Feb3.html

"Wrong Can Help Support the Right." *The Sydney Morning Herald* 7 Feb. (2000).
http://www.smh.com.au/news/0002/07/features/features3.html

"Mistakes, in Black and White." *The Age* 11 Mar. (2000).
http://www.theage.com.au/news/20000311/A1954-2000Mar10.html

"No Excuses: This Was Simply Not New York's Finest Hour." *The New York Times* Mar. 14 (2000); *The Sydney Morning Herald* 14 Mar. (2000).
http://www.smh.com.au/news/0003/14/features/features5.html

"A Boy Exiled from Simple Humanity." *The Age* 10 Apr. (2000).
http://www.theage.com.au/news/20000410/A58581-2000Apr9.html

"Fiji's Bigotry of Domain." *The New York Times* 8 Jun. (2000): A27.
http://www.indianembassy.org/US_Media/2000/june/fiji_bigotry_june_8.htm
http://groups.yahoo.com/group/act/message/547

"In Idi Amin's Footsteps: Fiji's Racist Dilemma." *The Age* 10 Jun. (2000).
http://www.theage.com.au/news/20000610/A51066-2000Jun9.html

http://www.freerepublic.com/forum/a394174562e4c.htm http://www.lookinglassdesign.com/fijicoupmay2000/june2000/610-rushdie-theage.html

"Light on Coetzee." *The Sydney Morning Herald* 10 Jun. (2000). http://www.smh.com.au/news/0006/10/text/spectrum10.html

"Blood and Belonging in Fiji." *The Sydney Morning Herald* 12 Jun. (2000).
http://www.smh.com.au/news/0006/12/features/features06.html

"Back to the Land I Love." *The Times* Jun. 13 (2000).
http://www.times-archive.co.uk/news/pages/tim/2000/06/13/timfeafea02004.html

"Abba, I Have Reclaimed Our House." *The Times* 14 Jun. (2000). http://www.times-archive.co.uk/news/pages/tim/2000/06/14/timfeafea02005.html

"There Is Only Joy, Lots of Joy." *The Times* 15 Jun. (2000). http://www.times-archive.co.uk/news/pages/tim/2000/06/15/timfeafea02005.html

"A Dream of Glorious Return."*The New Yorker* 19-26 Jun. (2000): 94-112.

"Take It from a Meta-columnist: These Days Even Opinion Is a Metaphor." *The Independent* 6 Aug. (2000).
http://www.independent.co.uk/story.jsp?story=40640

"Crashes That Brought Us Back on Earth-Instantly." *The Sydney Morning Herald* Aug. 10 (2000).
http://www.smh.com.au/news/0008/10/features/features3.html

"Illusion, a Media Illness." *The Age* 10 Aug. (2000).
http://www.theage.com.au/news/20000810/A59605-2000Aug9.html

"The US Election Is an Act of Bad Faith." *The Age* 13 Sep. (2000). http://www.theage.com.au/news/20000913/A61586-2000Sep12.html

"Why I Left." *The Guardian* 27 Sep. (2000).
http://www.guardian.co.uk/Archive/Article/0,4273,4068603,00.html

"The Founding Fathers' Wisdom or Folly?" *The Age* 13 Nov. (2000).

http://www.theage.com.au/news/20001113/A45084-2000Nov12.html

"America-Let the Healing Begin." *The Guardian* 9 Dec. (2000). http://www.guardian.co.uk/Archive/Article/0,4273,4102567,00.html

"Winning Double: Why a Bush-Gore Alliance Gets My Vote." *The Age* 9 Dec. (2000). http://www.theage.com.au/news/2000/12/09/FFX40NCQGGC.html

"Sleaze's Slimy Inventiveness." *The Guardian* 7 Feb. (2001). http://www.guardian.co.uk/g2/story/0,3604,434453,00. html

"If the Cistern Cannot Be Fixed, It Must Be Destroyed." *The Age* 17 Feb. (2001). http://www.theage.com.au/news/2001/02/17/FFXTFZTQ8JC.html

"Can Hollywood See the Tiger?" *The New York Times* 9 Mar. (2001) A19. http://www.nytimes.com/2001/03/09/opinion/09RUSH.html

"Even by LA Standards the Cheering Was Astonishing." *The Guardian* 10 Mar. (2001). http://www.guardian.co.uk/Archive/Article/0,4273,4149220,00.html

"Enter the Dragon..." *The Age* 12 Mar. (2001). http://www.theage.com.au/entertainment/2001/03/12/FFXMB9ZL5KC.html

"Crouching Tigers Lie in Wait as LA Prepares to Strike." *The Sydney Morning Herald* 16 Mar. (2001). http://www.smh.com.au/news/0103/16/text/features6.html

"The Mantra of Our Age: Deny, Deny, Deny." *The Guardian* 9 Apr. (2001). http://www.guardian.co.uk/Archive/Article/0,4273,4167418,00.html

"The End of Shame." *The Age* 11 Apr. (2001). http://www.theage.com.au/news/2001/04/11/FFXX56BJCLC.html

"A World Where Black Is White and Night Is Day." *The Sydney Morning Herald* 17 Apr. (2001).

http://www.smh.com.au/news/0104/17/features/features4.html

"Women Beware Women." *The Guardian* 5 May (2001). http://www.guardian.co.uk/Archive/Article/0,4273,4181337,00.html

"Mother India Too Ready to Sacrifice her Daughters." *The Sydney Morning Herald* 7 May (2001). http://www.smh.com.au/news/0105/07/features/features5. html

"The Shame of a Land of Missing Sisters." *The Age* 10 May (2001). http://www.theage.com.au/cgi-bin print_article.pl?path =/news/2001/05/10/FFXEFEXYHMC.html http://www.lifeissues.net/briefs/2001/may/010504.html

"In Reality, It's Dangerous." *The Age* 7 Jun. (2001). http://www.theage.com.au/entertainment/2001/06/07/FFXFSCFZLNC.html

"Reality TV: A Dearth of Talent and the Death of Morality." *The Guardian*, Saturday Review 9 Jun. (2001). http://www.guardian.co.uk/Archive/Article/0,4273,4200982,00.html http://www.guardian.co.uk/saturday_review/story/0,3605,503921,00.html

"The Ground Beneath My Feet." *The Nation* 273.2 9 Jul. 2001): 42-44.

"Why Big Brother Will Soon Be After Your Blood." *The New York Times* 12 Jun. (2001). http://www.smh.com.au/news/0106/12/features/features3.html

"Reality TV: the Perils of Voyeurism." www.Sojo.net 12 Jun. 12 (2001). http://www.sojo.net/sojomail/index.cfm/action/sojomail/issue/061501.html

"Who Will Rehabilitate the British Tabloid Press?" *The Guardian* 7 Jul. (2001). http://www.guardian.co.uk/Archive/Article/0,4273,4217310,00.html

"Foolish Dam and a Writer's Freedom." *The New York Times*, Op-Ed 7 Aug. (2001): A19.

http://www.doccentre.org/TOD/foolishdam.htm & http://www.nytimes.com/2001/08/07/opinion/07RUSH.html

"Foolish Damning of Free Speech." *The Age* 9 Aug. (2001). http://www.theage.com.au/news/state/2001/08/09/FFXJ7EDH4QC.html

"India's Courts Flounder as Dam Pressure Builds." *The Guardian* 11 Aug. (2001). http://www.guardian.co.uk/Archive/Article/0,4273,4236878,00.html

"No Prizes for the Best Celebration of Cinema." *The Guardian,* Saturday Review 8 Sep. (2001). http://www.guardian.co.uk/Archive/Article/0,4273,4252519,00.html

"Fighting the Forces of Invisibility." *The Washington Post* 2 Oct. (2001): A25. http://www.washingtonpost.com/wp-dyn/articles/A55876-2001Oct1.html

"How to Defeat Terrorism." *The Age* 4 Oct. (2001). http://www.theage.com.au/news/state/2001/10/04/FFXCFGT0CSC.html http://groups.yahoo.com/group/trustthepeople-houston/message/1809

"Let's Get Back to Life." *The Guardian,* Saturday Review 6 Oct. (2001). http://www.guardian.co.uk/Archive/Article/0,4273,4271218,00.html http://www.guardian.co.uk/saturday_review/story/0,3605,563978,00.html http://www.his.com/~ckagy/weblog/ http://www.sulekha.com/chpost.asp?forum=books&oldurl=/12352.html/12352.html

"Winning the War by Not Allowing Fear to Rule." *The Sydney Morning Herald* 8 Oct. (2001). http://www.smh.com.au/news/0110/08/opinion/opinion2.html

"Yes, This Is About Islam." *The New York Times* 2 Nov. (2001).
http://college.nytimes.com/guests/articles/2001/11/02/877723.xml
http://www.nytimes.com/2001/11/02/opinion/02RUSH.html

"A War That Presents Us All with a Crisis of Faith." *The*

Guardian, Saturday Review 3 Nov. (2001). http://www.guardian.co.uk/Archive/Article/0,4273,4290897,00.html

1.4. REVIEWS

"Cuban Heels with Twisting Tongues: *Three Trapped Tigers* by Cabrera Infante." *The London Review of Books* 3.10 (4 Jun. 1981): 16.

"300 Years of Rubble: *The Meeting at Telgte* by Günter Grass." *New Statesman* 101.2623 (26 Jun. 1981): 21. Abr. in *Contemporary Literary Criticism*, 22. Detroit, MI: Gale Research Inc., 1982. 197. In *Imaginary Homelands*. 1991. 273-75.

"A Fable of Reclamation: *The Heritage* by Siegfrid Lenz." *The New York Times Book Review* 19 Jul. (1981): 6. Abr. in *Contemporary Literary Criticism*, 27. Detroit, MI: Gale Research Inc., 1982. 255. In *Imaginary Homelands*. 1991. 285-87.

"Exemplary Lives: *Crown Jewel* by Ralph de Boissière." *The Times Literary Supplement* 4088 (7 Aug. 1981): 910.

"Love and Immolation in Argentina: *On Heroes and Tombs* by Ernesto Sabato." *The Washington Post*, Book World 16 Aug. (1981): 5 & 12. Abr. in *Contemporary Literary Criticism*, 23. Detroit, MI: Gale Research Inc., 1982. 382.

"Calvino: *If on a Winter Night a Traveller, The Path to the Nest of Spiders, Our Ancestors, Cosmicomics, Invisible Cities* by Italo Calvino." *The London Review of Books* 3.17 (17 Sep. 1981): 16-17. In *Imaginary Homelands*. 1991. 254-61.

"Mullah's Tale: *Among the Believers* by V.S. Naipaul." *The Guardian* 1 Oct. (1981): 8. As "Naipaul Among the Believers," in *Imaginary Homelands*. 1991. 373-75.

"The Stuff of Marvels, *Gemini* by Michel Tournier." *The New York Times Book Review* 4 Oct. (1981): 12 & 31-32. Abr. in *Contemporary Literary Criticism*, 23. Detroit, MI: Gale Research Inc., 1982. 453-54. In *Imaginary Homelands*. 1991. 249-53.

"The Invisible Master: Elias Canetti." *The Sunday Times* 18 Oct. (1981): 39.

"The Worm of Learning Turns, Swallows Its Tail and Bites Itself in Half: *Auto da Fé* by Elias Canetti." *Listener* 106.2738 (3 Dec. 1981): 678-79. In *Essays in Honor of Elias Canetti.* Tr. Michael Hulse. New York: Farrar, Straus, & Giroux, 1987. Orig. *Hüter der verwandlung: Beiträge zum Werk von Elias Canetti.* Munich: C.Hanser, 1985. 81-87.

"*The Dean's December* by Saul Bellow." 1982. In *Imaginary Homelands.* 1991. 349-51.

"*The Safety Net* by Heinrich Böll." 1982. In *Imaginary Homelands.* 1991. 282-84.

"Men and Women Possessed: *The Royal Game and Other Stories* by Stefan Zweick." *The New York Times Book Review* 87.4 (24 Jan. 1982): 7.

"Mole: *Saki: A Life of Hector Hugo Munro* by A.J. Langguth." *The London Review of Books* 4.2 (4 Feb. 1982): 22.

"Angel Gabriel: *Chronicle of a Death Foretold* by Gabriel García Marquez." *The London Review of Books* 4.17 (16 Sep. 1982): 3-5. Abr. in *Contemporary Literary Criticism,* 27. Detroit, MI: Gale Research Inc., 1982. 150-51. In *Imaginary Homelands.* 1991. 299-305.

"Truth Retreats When the Saint Goes Marching In: *Gandhi* by Richard Attenborough." *The Times* 2 May (1983): 10. As "*Gandhi*: How and Why the British Are Continuing to Distort Our History," in *The Telegraph* (Calcutta) 15 Jun. (1983). As "Raggedy Gandhi," in *The Movies* Jul. (1983): 14. As "Attenborough's Gandhi," in *Imaginary Homelands.* 1991. 102-06.

"Tales of Two Berlins: *The Wall-Jumper* by Peter Schneider." *The New York Times Book Review* 22 Jan. (1984): 13. In *Imaginary Homelands.* 1991. 288-90.

"No One Is Ever Safe: *Something Out There* by Nadine Gordimer." *The New York Times Book Review* 89.31 (29 Jul. 1984): 7-8. In *Imaginary Homelands.* 1991. 187-92.

"Peruvian Master: *The War of the End of the World* by Mario Vargas Llosa." *The New Republic* 191.15 (8 Oct. 1984): 25-28. Abr. in *Contemporary Literary Criticism,* 31. Detroit, MI: Gale Research Inc., 1982. 448-49. In *Imaginary Homelands.* 1991. 308-13.

"Needs and Greeds: *The Needs of Strangers* by Michael Ignatieff." *The Guardian* 25 Oct. (1984): 20.

"*In Custody* by Anita Desai." 1984. In *Imaginary Homelands.* 1991. 71-73.

"The Location of *Brazil.*" *American Film* 10 (Jan./Feb. 1985): 50-53. In *Imaginary Homelands.* 1991. 118-25.

"Seeing Beyond the Bomb: *The Heavy Dancers* by E.P. Thompson." *The Guardian* 28 Mar. (1985): 12.

"On Günter Grass." *Granta* 15 (James Fenton) (Sep. 1985): 179-85. As Introduction to Günter Grass. *On Writing and Politics: 1967-1983.* Trans. Ralph Manheim. San Diego etc.: Harcourt Brace Jovanovich, 1986 (1985). ix-xv. In *Imaginary Homelands.* 1991. 276-81.

"The Great Work of Being Alive: *Later the Same Day* by Grace Paley." *The Guardian* 14 Nov. (1985): 20. In *Imaginary Homelands.* 1991. 362-63.

"*Hobson-Jobson* by Henry Yule and A.C. Burnell." 1985. In *Imaginary Homelands.* 1991. 81-83.

"New Maps for Old: *Maps* by Nuruddin Farah." *The Guardian* 24 Apr. (1986) 20. In *Imaginary Homelands.* 1991. 201-02.

"A Foaming Attack of Ideological Rabies: *Mad Dogs* by *END* Journal." *The Guardian* May 26 (1986) 7.

"If I Forget Thee...: *After the Last Sky* by Edward W. Said." *The Guardian* 19 Sep. (1986): 11.

"A Moderate Goes to Extremes: *The Real Life of Alejandro Mayta* by Mario Vargas Llosa." *The Guardian* 10 Oct. (1986): 18. In *The Guardian Weekly* 19 Oct. (1986). In *Imaginary Homelands.* 1991. 315-18.

"Escaping from One Nightmare into Another: *Cambodian Witness: The Autobiography of Someth May.*" *The Guardian* 7 Nov. (1986): 13. In *The Guardian Weekly* 14 Dec. (1986): 22.

"The Stars in Their Galaxies: *Debrett Goes to Hollywood* by Charles Kidd." *The Guardian* 28 Nov. (1986): 11.

"Pick of the Books of 1986." By J.G. Ballard, Ronald Blythe, Salman Rushdie et al. *The Guardian* 5 Dec. (1986): 14.

"Songs Doesn't Know the Score: *Handsworth Songs* by Black Audio Film Collective." *The Guardian* 17 Jan. (1987). In *Black Film: British Cinema.* ICA Documents, 7. London: Institute of Contemporary Arts, 1988. 16-17. As *"Handsworth Songs,"* in *Imaginary Homelands.* 1991. 115-17.

"Fog and the Foghorn: *Ways of Telling: the Work of John Berger* by Geoff Dyer." *The Guardian* 6 Feb. (1987): 11. As "John Berger," in *Imaginary Homelands.* 1991. 209-12.

"Reporting a Nightmare: *Another Day of Life* by Ryszard Kapuscinski." *The Guardian* 13 Feb. (1987): 15. In *The Guardian Weekly* Mar. 1 (1987) 21. In *Imaginary Homelands.* 1991. 203-06.

"A Sad Pastoral: *The Enigma of Arrival* by V.S. Naipaul." *The Guardian* 13 Mar. (1987): 12. In *Imaginary Homelands.* 1991. 148-51.

"Travels with a Golden Ass: *The Golden Ass* by Apuleius." *The Guardian* 17 Apr. (1987): 11. In *The Guardian Weekly* 3 May (1987): 19. In *Imaginary Homelands.* 1991. 364-67.

"Writers' Reading in 1987." By J.G. Ballard, Salman Rushdie et al. *The Guardian* 11 Dec. (1987): 13.

"Head Bangers: *A Brief History of Time* by Stephen Hawking." *The Observer* 10 Jul. (1988): 43. In *Imaginary Homelands.* 1991. 262-64. Abr. in *Contemporary Literary Criticism,* 63. Detroit, MI: Gale Research Inc., 1992. 151-52.

"Colour Guard: *Anti-Racism, A Mania Exposed* by Russell Lewis." *The Observer* 24 Jul. (1988): 42.

"Falling into South Africa: *The Essential Gesture* by Nadine Gordimer." *The Observer* 4 Sep. (1988): 41. In *Imaginary Homelands.* 1991. 192-95.

"Old Devil Rides Again: *The Captain and the Enemy* by Graham Greene." *The Observer* 11 Sep. (1988): 42. In *Imaginary Homelands.* 1991. 213-15.

"Satanic Reverses: *The Death of Methuselah* by Isaac Bashevis Singer." *The Observer* 16 Oct. (1988): 42. In *Imaginary Homelands.* 1991. 343-45.

"Princess of the People's Party: *Daughter of the East* by Benazir Bhutto." *The Observer* 23 Oct. (1988): 45. In *Imaginary Homelands.* 1991. 56-58.

"Let It Be: *McCartney: The Biography* by Cheth Flippo." *The Observer* 27 Oct. (1988): 42.

"Through the Forest With Her Guardian Angel: *Dear Mili* by Wilhelm Grimm." *The New York Times Book Review* 93.46 (13 Nov. 1988): 39. In *Imaginary Homelands.* 1991. 294-96.

"Knickers in a Twist: *The Standard Life of a Temporary Pantyhose Salesman* by Alberto Busi." *The Observer* 8 Jan. (1989): 46.

"Beginning of a Novelist's Thralldom: *The Facts* by Philip Roth." *The Observer* 26 Feb. (1989): 47.

"Before the Voice We Lost Fell Silent: *What Am I Doing Here* by Bruce Chatwin." *The Observer* 14 May (1989): 48. Abr. in *Contemporary Literary Criticism*, 59. Detroit, MI: Gale Research Inc., 1990. 276. In *Imaginary Homelands*. 1991. 237-40.

"What the Butler Didn't See: *The Remains of the Day* by Kazuo Ishiguro." *The Observer* 21 May (1989): 53. Abr. in *Contemporary Literary Criticism*, 59. Detroit, MI: Gale Research Inc., 1990. 160-61. In *Imaginary Homelands*. 1991. 244-46.

"New Wave Ark: *A History of the World in 102 Chapters* by Julian Barnes." *The Observer* 25 Jun. (1989): 45. In *Imaginary Homelands*. 1991. 241-43.

"From Russia without Love: *The Russia House* by John le Carré." *The Observer* 2 Jul. (1989): 45. In *Imaginary Homelands*. 1991. 219-21.

"A Tourist Guide to God: *The Divine Supermarket* by Malise Ruthven." *The Observer* 27 Aug. (1989): 39. In *Imaginary Homelands*. 1991. 368-70.

"Billy the Streetwise Kid: *Billy Bathgate* by E.L. Doctorow." *The Observer* 10 Sep. (1989): 51. In *Imaginary Homelands*. 1991. 330-02. Abr. in *Contemporary Literary Criticism*, 65. Detroit, MI: Gale Research Inc., 1990. 142-43.

"Where Memory Lives: *A New Path to the Waterfall* by Raymond Carver." *The Observer* 24 Sep. (1989): 46. In *Imaginary Homelands*. 1991. 340-42.

"A Donkey's Tail for Pinochet: *Clandestine in Chile* by Gabriel García Marquez." *The Times Literary Supplement* 4514 (6 Oct. 1989): 1088. In *Imaginary Homelands*. 1991. 305-57.

"Cabbalistic Babble and Gobbledygook: *Foucault's Pendulum* by Umberto Eco." *The Observer* 15 Oct. (1989): 49. Abr. in *Contemporary Literary Criticism*, 59. Detroit, MI: Gale Research Inc., 1990. 115. In *Imaginary Homelands*. 1991. 269-72.

"Greene and His Gruntlement: *Yours Etc.: Letters to the Press 1945-89* by Graham Greene." *The Observer* 29 Oct. (1989): 49. In *Imaginary Homelands.* 1991. 216-18.

"Still Crazy After All These Years: *Vineland* by Thomas Pynchon." *The New York Times Book Review* 14 Jan. (1990): 1 & 36-37. In *Imaginary Homelands.* 1991. 352-57.

"Homage to Satyajit Ray: *Satyajit Ray: The Inner Eye,* by Andrew Robinson." *The London Review of Books* 12:5 (8 Mar. 1990): 9. In *Imaginary Homelands.* 1991. 107-14.

"Black Sheep of the White Tribe: *My Traitor's Heart* by Rian Malan." *The Independent on Sunday,* The Sunday Review 29 Apr. (1990): 15. In *Imaginary Homelands.* 1991. 196-200.

"Artist Crushed by the Myths of a Tyrant: *Last World* by Christoph Ransmayr." *The Independent on Sunday,* The Sunday Review 13 May (1990): 17. In *Imaginary Homelands.* 1991. 291-93.

"Tianmen: Words to Fit the Pictures: *Moving the Mountain* by Li Lu." *The Independent on Sunday,* The Sunday Review 3 Jun. (1990): 15.

"Sakharov. The Courage of His Convictions: *Memoirs I.*" *The Washington Post,* Book World 20:25 (24 Jun. 1990): 1-2. As "Sakharov's *Memoirs I,*" in *Imaginary Homelands.* 1991. 265-68.

"Small Hearts on Fire in Nowheresville: *Wildlife* by Richard Ford." *The Independent on Sunday, The Sunday Review* 5 Aug. (1990): 28. In *Imaginary Homelands.* 1991. 337-39.

"The Nam That Can Never Go Away: *Hocus Pocus* by Kurt Vonnegut." *The Independent on Sunday, The Sunday Review* 21 Oct. (1990): 31. In *Imaginary Homelands.* 1991. 358-61.

"The World from Colonel Baxter's Bathchair: *The Billiard Table Murders* by Glen Baxter." *The Independent on Sunday, The Sunday Review* 4 Nov. (1990): 35.

"The Language of the Pack: *Big Deal: One Year as a Professional Poker-Player* by A. Holder and *The Oxford Guide to Card Games* by D. Parlett." *The Times Literary Supplement* 4572 (16 Nov. 1990): 1239. In *Imaginary Homelands.* 1991. 321-25.

"The Boy, the Butcher and the Wizard of Gaz: *All Played Out* by Pete Davies, and *Gazza! A Biography* by Robin McGibbon." *The Independent on Sunday*, The Sunday Review 18 Nov. (1990): 34.

"In Defence of Brodkey: *The Runaway Soul* by Harold Brodkey." *The Independent on Sunday*, The Sunday Review 24 Nov. (1991): 38.

"Where the Art Is: *The Wizard of Oz* by Victor Fleming." *Independent on Sunday*, suppl 3 May (1992): 26-27. Edited extract of ch.1, "A Short Story about Magic," in Rushdie. *The Wizard of Oz*. London: B.F.I. (British Film Institute) Publications, 1992. 5-19, & 55-57.

"Between New Love and Old Home: *Beirut Blues* by Hanan al-Shaykh." *The Independent on Sunday*, Review 26 Mar. (1993): 40.

"No Mere Digestive Tract: *Millroy the Magician* by Paul Theroux." *The Independent on Sunday*, Review 10 Oct. (1993): 46.

"The Best Fears of Our Lives: *The Robber Bride* by Margaret Atwood." *The Independent on Sunday*, Review 17 Oct. (1993): 47.

"Armies of Pleasure: The Rolling Stones." *The Observer*, Review 16 Jul. (1995): 2-3.

1.5. INTERVIEWS & DISCUSSIONS

1.5.1. Rushdie Interview Anthologies

- Chauhan, Pradyumna S., ed. *Salman Rushdie Interviews: a Sourcebook of His Ideas*. Westport: Greenwood P, 2001.
- Reder, Michael R., ed. *Conversations with Salman Rushdie*. Jackson: U Mississippi P, 2000.

1.5.2. Interviews

"A Big City Novel." Interview with Bonny Mukherjee. *India Today* 16 May (1981): 126-27.

"Round Midnight: *Midnight's Children*." Interview with Dave Leppard. *The Guardian* 23 Oct. (1981): 10.

"A Novelist in the Country of the Mind." Interview with Victoria Glendinning. *The Sunday Times* 25 Oct. (1981): 38. Chauhan,

Pradyumna S., ed. *Salman Rushdie Interviews: a Sourcebook of His Ideas.* Westport: Greenwood P, 2001. 3-6.

"*CA* Interview." With Jean W. Ross. Interview by phone Jun. 1 (1982). *Contemporary Authors: A Current Bio-Bibliographical Guide to Current Writers in Fiction, General Nonfiction, Poetry, Journalism, Drama, Motion Pictures, Television, and Other Fields,*111. Ed. Hal May. Detroit, MI: Gale Research Co., 1984. 414-17. Reder, Michael R., ed. *Conversations with Salman Rushdie.* Jackson: U Mississippi P, 2000. 1-7

"Interview: Salman Rushdie" With Rani Dube. *Debonair* Feb. (1982): 10-13 & 54-56. Chauhan, Pradyumna S., ed. *Salman Rushdie Interviews: a Sourcebook of His Ideas.* Westport: Greenwood P, 2001. 7-20.

"Interview with Salman Rushdie." With Jéan-Pierre Durix, Kirsten Holst Petersen, Jacqueline Bardolph, Anna Rutherford, Carole Durix. Gothenburg, Sweden, 5 Sep. (1982). *Kunapipi* 4.2 (1982): 17-26. Reder, Michael R., ed. *Conversations with Salman Rushdie.* Jackson: U Mississippi P, 2000. 8-16.

Chaudhuri, Una. "Imaginative Maps." London, 1983. *Turnstile* 2.1 (1990): 36-47. Chauhan, Pradyumna S., ed. *Salman Rushdie Interviews: a Sourcebook of His Ideas.* Westport: Greenwood P, 2001. 21-32.

"Dialogue with History: Interview with Salman Rushdie." With Chinweizu. *South* Jan. (1983): 24-25.

"`You Fight to Like Where You Live.'" Interview with Malavika Rajbans Sanghvi. *Indian Express, Express Magazine* 20 Mar. (1983): 1. Chauhan, Pradyumna S., ed. *Salman Rushdie Interviews: a Sourcebook of His Ideas.* Westport: Greenwood P, 2001. 39-45.

"An Interview with Salman Rushdie." By M.L. Pandit. All India Radio, Srinagar. March 1983. Pandit. *New Commonwealth Writing: A Critical Response.* New Delhi: Prestige, 1996. 41-44.

"The Other Side of *Midnight's Children*: Salman Rushdie in Conversation with Binoy Thomas." *Society* Apr. (1983): 18-23.

"The Last-and the Best- Salman Rushdie Interview in India!" With Salil Tripathi. *Celebrity* May (1983): 29-34. Reder, Michael R., ed. *Conversations with Salman Rushdie.* Jackson: U Mississippi P, 2000. 20-29.

"Interview with Salman Rushdie." With John Haffenden. *The Literary Review* Sep. (1983): 26-31. As "Salman Rushdie." In *Novelists in Interview: Martin Amis, Ray Bradbury, Anita Brookner, Angela Carter, William Golding, Russell Hoban, David Lodge, Ian McEwan, Iris Murdoch, V.S. Pritchett, Salman Rushdie, David Storey, Emma Tennant, Fay Weldon.* Ed. John Haffenden. London: Methuen, 1985. 231-61. Reder, Michael R., ed. *Conversations with Salman Rushdie.* Jackson: U Mississippi P, 2000. 30-56.

"History into Myth." Interview with Ronald Hayman. *Books and Bookmen* 336 (Sep. 1983): 19-20.

"*PW* Interviews: Salman Rushdie." With Amanda Smith. *Publishers Weekly* 11 Nov. (1983): 49-50.

"Author from Three Countries." Interview with Michael T. Kaufman. *The New York Times Book Review* 88.46 (13 Nov. 1983): 22-23. Abr. *Contemporary Literary Criticism,* 31. Detroit, MI: Gale Research Inc., 1984. 356-57.

"I Borrowed My Expressions from the East." Interview with Anwar Iqbal. *The Muslim* 18 Nov. (1983): 1.

"Interview with Salman Rushdie." With Rani Dharker. *New Quest* 42 (Nov.-Dec. 1983): 351-60. Chauhan, Pradyumna S., ed. *Salman Rushdie Interviews: a Sourcebook of His Ideas.* Westport: Greenwood P, 2001. 47-62.

"Interview with Salman Rushdie." With Chandrabhanu Pattanayak. *The Literary Criterion* 18.3 (1983): 19-22. Reder, Michael R., ed. *Conversations with Salman Rushdie.* Jackson: U Mississippi P, 2000. 17-19.

"A Quiet Anger: Gentleman of the Year." Interview with Gordon Wise. *Gentleman* Feb. (1984): 55-59 & 102-03.

"Interview with Salman Rushdie." With David Brooks. Adelaide, 6 Mar., 1984. *Helix* 19&20 (1984-5): 55-69. Reder, Michael R., ed. *Conversations with Salman Rushdie.* Jackson: U Mississippi P, 2000. 57-71.

"Without Shame." Interview with Malavika Sanghvi. *The Illustrated Weekly of India* 25 Mar. (1984): 20-22.

"Interview with Salman Rushdie." With Kumkum Sangari. *The Book Review* 8.5 (Mar.-Apr. 1984): 247-53. Chauhan, Pradyumna S., ed. *Salman Rushdie Interviews: a Sourcebook of His Ideas.* Westport: Greenwood P, 2001. 63-74.

"Rushdie and Mirza." Interview with Saeed Mirza. *Gentleman* Apr. (1984): 6 & 66-70.

"A Dangerous Art Form." Interview with *Third World Book Review. Third World Book Review* 1 (1984) 3-5.

"On Reality, Fantasy, and Fiction: a Conversation with Salman Rushdie." With J.F. Galván Reula. 8th Conference of AEDEAN (Spanish Association for Anglo-American Studies) Málaga, Spain 20 Dec. (1984). *Atlantis* 6.1-2 (Jun.-Nov. 1984): 93-101.

"Interview with Salman Rushdie." With *Justice. Justice* 1 (May 1985): 15.

"Fictions Are Lies that Tell the Truth: Salman Rushdie and Günter Grass in Conversation." Channel 4, "Voices." 26 Jun. (1985) at 11 pm. *Listener* 113 (27 Jun., 1985): 14-15. In *Voices: Writers and Politics.* From the Channel 4 Television Series. Eds. Bill Bourne, Udi Eichler, and David Herman. Nottingham: Spokesman, & Atlantic Highlands, NJ: Hobo Press, 1987. Reder, Michael R., ed. *Conversations with Salman Rushdie.* Jackson: U Mississippi P, 2000. 72-78.

"Interview with Salman Rushdie." By Peter Craven, Michael Heyward, and Penny Hueston. *Scripsi* 3.2-3 (Aug. 1985): 107-26.

"The Press -International Viewpoints: Hope, Vargas Llosa, Rushdie, Zinik." Interview with *The Times Literary Supplement. The Times Literary Supplement* 4325 (21 Feb. 1986): 190.

"Edward W. Said with Salman Rushdie." Interview with Salman Rushdie. Writers Talk, No.28. London: ICA Video & Northbrook, IL: The Roland Collection, 1986. As "On Palestinian Identity: a Conversation with Edward Said." With Salman Rushdie. *New Left Review* 160 (Nov.-Dec. 1986): 63-81. In Edward W. Said *After the Last Sky: Palestinian Lives.* Photographs by Jean Mohr. New York: Pantheon & London: Faber, 1986. 166-84. In *Imaginary Homelands.*

1991. 166-84. In Edward W. Said. *The Politics of Dispossession: The Struggle for Palestinian Self-Determination 1969-1994.* London: Chatto & Windus, 1994. London: Vintage, 1995. 107-29.

"Central American Time: Salman Rushdie." Interview with Bianca Jagger. *Interview* Mar. (1987): 85-86.

"A Conversation with Salman Rushdie." Sedge Thomson. San Francisco: American Poetry Archive, 1987. Videorecording. Chauhan, Pradyumna S., ed. *Salman Rushdie Interviews: a Sourcebook of His Ideas.* Westport: Greenwood P, 2001. 75-88.

"Angels and Devils Are Becoming Confused Ideas." By Salil Tripathi & Dina Vakil. *Indian Post* 13 Sep. (1987). Reder, Michael R., ed. *Conversations with Salman Rushdie.* Jackson: U Mississippi P, 2000. 79-86.

"Salman Rushdie." Interview with Charlotte Cornwell. Writers in Conversation, 81. London: ICA Video, in conjunction with Trilion, 1987. "SALMAN RUSHDIE: interview with the author addresses writing and politics in Latin America." Video from the Roland Collection. http://www.scils.rutgers.edu/~kvander/salmanrushdie.html

"Salman Rushdie Interview." By Sorabjee. *Illustrated Weekly of India.* 12 Mar. (1988): 12-17.

"Discussion Between Five Chinese and British Writers." Graham C. Greene, Margaret Drabble, Barry Hines, Salman Rushdie, Wang Meng, Lin Suola." London, June 21, 1988. Trans. Huang Youyi & Christopher Smith. *Chinese Literature* (Su 1989): 174-87.

"My Theme Is Fanaticism: An Interview." With Madhu Jain. *India Today* 15 Sep. (1988): 98-99. Abr. in *The Rushdie File.* Eds. Lisa Appignanesi & Sara Maitland. London: 4th Estate, 1989. Syracuse: Syracuse University Press, 1990. 38-40. Abr. in *Contemporary Literary Criticism,* 55. Detroit, MI: Gale Research Inc., 1989. 216. Abr. in *Sacrilege Versus Civility: Muslim Perspectives on The Satanic Verses Affair.* Eds. M. Manazir Ahsan & A.R. Kidwai. Leicester: The Islamic Foundation, 1991. Rev.ed. 1993. 61-62.

"Of Satan, Archangels, and Prophets: An Interview." With

Sharabani Basu. *Sunday* 18-24 Sep. (1988). Abr. in *The Rushdie File*. Eds. Lisa Appignanesi & Sara Maitland. London: 4th Estate, 1989. Syracuse: Syracuse University Press, 1990. 40-41.

"Sean French Talks to Salman Rushdie." *The Observer* 25 Sep. (1988): 43. Abr. in *The Rushdie File*. Eds. Lisa Appignanesi & Sara Maitland. London: 4th Estate, 1989. Syracuse: Syracuse University Press, 1990. 8-10. Chauhan, Pradyumna S., ed. *Salman Rushdie Interviews: a Sourcebook of His Ideas*. Westport: Greenwood P, 2001. 89-92.

"Between God and Devil." Interview with John Mitchinson. *Waterstone's Selection Catalogue*, Sep. 1988. Abr. in *The Bookseller* 31 Mar. (1989): 1151-56. Chauhan, Pradyumna S., ed. *Salman Rushdie Interviews: a Sourcebook of His Ideas*. Westport: Greenwood P, 2001. 93-97.

"Salman Rushdie." Interview with W.L. Webb. Guardian Conversations, Writers, 89. ICA Video, in conjunction with Trilion. Dir. Fenella Greenfield. Reder, Michael R., ed. *Conversations with Salman Rushdie*. Jackson: U Mississippi P, 2000. 87-100. "SALMAN RUSHDIE: interview with the author addresses the background of 'The Satanic Verses." Video from the Roland Collection. 47:04 mins. http://www.scils.rutgers.edu/~kvander/salmanrushdie.html

"Salman Rushdie Talks to Nisha Puri." *The Indian Post* 9 Oct. (1988): 7.

"'My Book Being Put in Jail': Rushdie." Interview with N. Ram. *The Hindu* 10 Oct. (1988): 1.

"An Interview with Salman Rushdie." By John Clement Ball. CHLN-FM Title-Waves. Toronto, Oct. 1988. *The Toronto South Asian Review* 10.1 (Sum 1991): 30-7. Reder, Michael R., ed. *Conversations with Salman Rushdie*. Jackson: U Mississippi P, 2000. 101-19.

"Yippee, We're All Gonna Die: *Dispatches* by Michael Herr: An Interview with Salman Rushdie." *The Observer* 15 Jan. (1989): 49. In *Imaginary Homelands*. 1991. 333-36.

"Portrait of the Author as a Martyr with His Ironies Firmly in the Fire." Interview with Valerie Grove. *The Sunday Times* 22 Jan. (1989): B5.

"Fictions Embattled Infidel." Interview with Gerald Marzorati. *The New York Times Magazine* 29 Jan. (1989): 24-27, 47-49 & 100.

"Salman Rushdie." Interview with Ameena Meer. *BOMB* 27 (Sp 1989): 35-37. "The Truths That Mustn't Be Told." *Mail on Sunday,* Extra 18 Jun. (1989): 1-3. *Bomb Interviews.* Ed. Betsy Sussler. San Francisco: City Lights, 1992. 61-74. Reder, Michael R., ed. *Conversations with Salman Rushdie.* Jackson: U Mississippi P. 2000. 110-22.

"Bonfire of the Certainties." Interview with Bandung File. Recorded 27 Jan. (1989) by Bandung File. Channel 4, Bandung File 14 Feb. (1989) at 9 pm. *The Guardian* 15 Feb. (1989): 23. Abr. *The Illustrated Weekly of India* Mar. 12 (1989) 12-19. Abr. *The Rushdie File.* Eds. Lisa Appignanesi & Sara Maitland. London: 4th Estate, 1989. Syracuse: Syracuse UP, 1990. 27-31.

"Fact, Faith, and Fiction: Interview with Salman Rushdie." *Far Eastern Economic Review* 143.9 2 Mar. (1989): 11-12. Chauhan, Pradyumna S., ed. *Salman Rushdie Interviews: a Sourcebook of His Ideas.* Westport: Greenwood P, 2001. 99-102.

"The Weekly Interview." With *The Illustrated Weekly of India. The Illustrated Weekly of India,* Mar. 1989.

"Salman Rushdie." Interview with Roger Buford Mason. *PN Review* 15.4 (66) (1989): 15-9.

"Salman Rushdie: An Interview." By Catherine Bush. *Conjunctions* 14 (1989): 7-20.

"Sentenced to the Prison of the World." Interview with John Cunningham. *The Guardian* 15 Jan. (1990): 17. *The Guardian Weekly* 28 Jan. (1990): 26.

"Interview with Salman Rushdie." With Blake Morrison. 4 Feb. (1990). Abr. as "Rushdie Breaks His Silence." *The Independent on Sunday* 4 Feb. (1990): 1 *Granta* 31 (Sp 1990): 113-25. Reder, Michael R., ed. *Conversations with Salman Rushdie.* Jackson: U Mississippi P, 2000. 132-41.

"An Exclusive Talk with Salman Rushdie." Interview with Sarah Crichton & Laura Shapiro. *Newsweek* 115.7 (12 Feb. 1990): 40-44. Abr. as "My Not-So-Funny Valentine." *The Observer* 11 Feb. (1990): 21. Reder, Michael R., ed. *Conversations with Salman Rushdie.* Jackson: U Mississippi P, 2000. 123-31.

"Rushdie interview." BBC Radio 4, *Today.* 27 Apr. (1990) at 6.30 am.

"Stories of Childhood." An Interview with Melvyn Bragg. London Weekend Television, *The South Bank Show.* 30 Sep. (1990) at 10.35 pm. As "Histoires d'enfance." Trans. Evelyne Pisier. *Esprit* 8/9 (Août-Sep. 1993). 5-23.

"Rushdie in Hiding: an Interview." With Gerald Marzorati. *The New York Times Magazine* 90 (4 Nov. 1990): 30-33, 68, 78 & 84.

"Start the Week." Interview with Melvyn Bragg. BBC Radio 4. 10 Dec. (1990) at 9 am.

"Cant and Recant." Interview with Sebastian Faulks. *The Independent on Sunday* (30 Dec. 1990): 17.

"Rendezvous with Rushdie." Interview with Martin Amis. *Vanity Fair* 53.12 (Dec. 1990): 160-63.

"Salman Rushdie: a New Chapter." Interview with Akbar S. Ahmed. *The Guardian* 17 Jan. (1991): 19 & 21. Reder, Michael R., ed. *Conversations with Salman Rushdie.* Jackson: U Mississippi P, 2000. 142-51.

"Keeping Up with Salman Rushdie: Salman Rushdie's *Haroun and the Sea of Stories,* and an Interview." With James Fenton. *The New York Review of Books* 38.6 (28 Mar. 1991): 24-32; interview, 26-32.

"Stranger than History." Interview with James Wood. *The Guardian* 21 Sep. (1991): 1 & 23.

"Free Speech Is Life Itself." By Karsten Prager. *Time* 138.25 (23 Dec. 1991): 50-51.

"Things Fall Apart, the Centre Holds." Interview with Sara Rance. *The Observer* 3 May (1992): 54. Chauhan, Pradyumna S., ed. *Salman Rushdie Interviews: a Sourcebook of His Ideas.* Westport: Greenwood P, 2001. 105-08.

"A World Apart." Interview with John Mortimer. *The Sunday Times* 16 Feb. (1992): sec 7, 1-2.

"An Interview with Toni Morrison." With Salman Rushdie. BBC 2, *The Late Show.* 3 Jun. (1992) at 15 pm. *Brick* 44 (1992): 33-39.

"The Real Life of Salman Rushdie." Interview with Hunter Davies. *The Independent* 11 Feb. (1993): 12.

"Interview with Salman Rushdie." With John Barville. *The New York Review of Books* 40.5 (4 Mar. 1993): 34-36. Reder, Michael R., ed. *Conversations with Salman Rushdie.* Jackson: U Mississippi P, 2000. 152-61.

"Homeless Is Where the Art Is." *The Bookseller* 15 Jul. (1994) Reder, Michael R., ed. *Conversations with Salman Rushdie.* Jackson: U Mississippi P, 2000. 162-66.

"Rushdie's Oceans." By Michael Davie. *The Age* 30 Sep. (1994).

"The Years of Living Dangerously." Interview with Tom Shone. Photograph by Sally Soames.*The Sunday Times,* Culture, 2 Oct. (1994): 6-7.

"Salman Rushdie Talks to Alastair Niven." Queen Mary & Westfileld College, Sep. 1994. *Wasafiri* 26 (1997): 52-57. Chauhan, Pradyumna S., ed. *Salman Rushdie Interviews: a Sourcebook of His Ideas.* Westport: Greenwood P, 2001. 231-42.

A talk with Salman." Interview by Sybil Steinberg. *Publishers Weekly* 242.5 (30 Jan. 1995): 80-82.

"Underground but Unbowed." Interview with Sarah Crichton. *Newsweek* 125.6 (6 Feb. 1995): 53-54

"I Get Around!" Copenhagen, 8 May (1995). Niels Fried-Nielsen, ed. *Freedom of Expression: the Acid Test.* Stockholm: Nordic Council, 1995. 81-88.

"Goodfellas." Interview with David Cronenberg. *Shift* 3.4 (Jul./ Aug. 1995): 20-27. http://www.cronenberg.freeserve.co.uk/cr_rushd.htm. Chauhan, Pradyumna S., ed. *Salman Rushdie Interviews: a Sourcebook of His Ideas.* Westport: Greenwood P, 2001. 167-78.

"Kaleidoscope Feature." Interview with Hermione Lee. BBC Radio 4. 2 Sep. (1995) at 7.20 pm.

"The Last Laugh." Interview with Maya Jaggi. *New Statesman & Society* 8.369 (8 Sep. 1995): 20-21.

"I Am Pessimistic abou the Changes Occurring in India." By Amrit Dhillon. *India Today* 30 Sep. (1995): 136-39. Reder, Michael R., ed. *Conversations with Salman Rushdie.* Jackson: U Mississippi P, 2000. 167-74.

"Salman Says." By Louise Carbines. *The Age* 16 Dec. (1995).

"The SALON Interview: Salman Rushdie; When Life Becomes a Bad Novel." *Salon* 27 Jan. (1996). http://www.salon.com/06/features/interview.html & http://www.salon.com/06/features/interview2.html. Chauhan, Pradyumna S., ed. *Salman Rushdie Interviews: a Sourcebook of His Ideas.* Westport: Greenwood P, 2001. 193-98.

"Laughing Well Is the Best Revenge." Interview with Francine Prose. *Elle* (Jan. 1996): 84. Chauhan, Pradyumna S., ed. *Salman Rushdie Interviews: a Sourcebook of His Ideas.* Westport: Greenwood P, 2001. 187-88.

Interview by Sharon Basco. *Christian Science Monitor* 88.50 7 Feb. 1996): 13.

"Playboy Interview: Salman Rushdie." With David Sheff. *Playboy* (Apr. 1996): 49-62 & 165. Reder, Michael R., ed. *Conversations with Salman Rushdie.* Jackson: U Mississippi P, 2000. 175-98.

"The Last Sigh of Diversity." Interview by Alvaro Vargas Llosa. *NPQ: New Perspectives Quarterly* 13.2 (Spr 1996): 47-49.

"Interview: Salman Rushdie Talks to the London Consortium about *The Satanic Verses.*" With Colin MacCabe, Laura Mulvey et al. *Critical Quarterly* 38.2 (1996): 51-70. Chauhan, Pradyumna S., ed. *Salman Rushdie Interviews: a Sourcebook of His Ideas.* Westport: Greenwood P, 2001. 213-30.

"The Moor's Last Sigh." By Charlie Rose. The Charlie Rose Show. 18 Jan. (1996). Transcript. Reder, Michael R., ed. *Conversations with Salman Rushdie.* Jackson: U Mississippi P, 2000. 199-215.

"CNN Interview: Author Salman Rushdie Talks about 'Living Day to Day.'" 14 Feb. (1997). http://www.cnn.com/WORLD/9702/14/rushdie/

"Almost Home." By Edward Pilkington. *The Guardian*, The Week 14 Jun. (1997): 3.

"Salman Rushdie." Interview by Christopher Hitchens *Progressive* 61.10 (Oct. 1997): 34-37.

"Sitting with Salman." 1999. Interview by Brian Stewart. Parts 1-8. Video total 16:41 mins.
http://www.infoculture.cbc.ca/archives/special_coverage/rushdie/special_coverage_ rushdie_a.html
http://www.infoculture.cbc.ca/archives/special_ coverage/rushdie/special_coverage_ rushdie_b.html
http://www.infoculture.cbc.ca/archives/special_ coverage/rushdie/special_coverage_rushdie_ c.html
http://www.infoculture.cbc.ca/archives/special_ coverage/rushdie/special_coverage_rushdie_d.html
http://www.infoculture.cbc.ca/archives/special_ coverage/rushdie/special_coverage_rushdie_e.html
http://www.infoculture.cbc.ca/archives/special_ coverage/rushdie/special_coverage_rushdie_f.html
http://www.infoculture.cbc.ca/archives/special_ coverage/rushdie/special_coverage_rushdie_g.html
http://www.infoculture.cbc.ca/archives/special_ coverage/rushdie/special_coverage_rushdie_h.html. Chauhan, Pradyumna S., ed. *Salman Rushdie Interviews: a Sourcebook of His Ideas*. Westport: Greenwood P, 2001. 291-98.

"Bombay Mix." Interview by Sam Wollaston. *Guardian Unlimited* 2 Apr. (1999).
http://www.guardian.co.uk/Archive/Article/0,4273,3847229,00.html

"Salman Speaks." Interview by Peter Kadzis. *Boston Phoenix* 7 May (1999): 28-31.
http://www.bostonphoenix.com/archive/books/99/05/06/SALMAN_RUSHDIE.html. Reder, Michael R., ed. *Conversations with Salman Rushdie*. Jackson: U Mississippi P, 2000. 216-28.

"Q&A." Interview by David Fricke. *Rolling Stone* 812 (13 May 1999): 28.

"Salman Rushdie Banned, on the Run." Interview by Lakshmi Chaudhry. *Mother Jones* 24.4 (Jul./Aug. 1999): 78-79.

"Salman Rushdie's Rock 'n' roll." Interview by Deborah Treisman. Interview May (1999). http://www.findarticles.com/m1285/5_29/54546012/p1/article.jhtml

"Marvels of the World Unveiled: Salman Rushdie on Bombay, Rock'n'roll, and the *Satanic Verses*." Interview by Vijaya Nagarajan. *Whole Earth* 98 (Aut. 1999): 4-10. http://www.wholeearthmag.com/ArticleBin/267.html

"Sons and Writers." Interview by Geraldine Brennan. *Times Educational Supplement* 4353 (3 Dec. 1999): 6-7.

"A Touch of Vulgarity." Interview by Laura Miller. Salon.com (1999). http://www.salon.com/books/int/1999/04/16/rushdie/index.html

"A Memorable Homecoming." Interview by Swapan Dasgupta & Ashok Malik. *India Today* 22 Apr. (2000). http://www.india-today.com/webexclusive/interviews/20000422rushdie.html

"The Rediff Interview: Salman Rushdie." 'If somebody is trying to shut you up, then you should try and talk louder.'" Rediff.com (2000). http://www.rediff.com/news/2000/apr/17inter.htm & http://www.rediff.com/news/2000/apr/17inter1.htm & http://www.rediff.com/news/2000/apr/18inter.htm

"In Conversation: Salman Rushdie with Harish Trivedi." *The Book Review* (May 2000): 12-13.

"The Concrete Beneath His Feet." Interview by D.T. Max. *The New York Times Magazine* 17 Sep. (2000).

"Manhattan Transfer." Interview with D.T. Max *Observer* 24 Sep. (2000). http://www.guardian.co.uk/Archive/Article/0,4273,4067223,00.htm

"The Crucial Book of Salman Rushdie." Interview by Margot Dijkgraaf. Trans. K. Gwan Go. Mar. 2001. http://www.wsu.edu/~brians/anglophone/satanic_verses/joyce.html

Sujan, Dheera. "I Love Salman." Radio Netherlands Wereldomroep (RNW) 10 May (2001). http://www.rnw.nl/culture/html/rushdie010316.html

"*PW* Talks with Salman Rushdie." Interview by Sybil Steinberg. *Publishers Weekly* 248.29 (16 Jul. 2001): 165.

1.6. POEMS

"6 March 1989." *Granta* 28 (Birthday Special) (Aut 1989): 28-29.

"Crusoe." *Granta* 31 (The General) (Sp 1990): 128; Vijay Mishra. "Postcolonial Differend: Diasporic Narratives of Salman Rushdie." *Ariel* 26.3 (Jul. 1995): 43, note 3.

"Those Salman Rushdie Lyrics in Full..." From Rushdie. *The Ground Beneath Her Feet.* 1999. 475. *Guardian Unlimited* 22 Jan. (1999). http://www.guardian.co.uk/Archive/Article/0,4273, 3811250,00.html

"How the Grinch Stole America." (A verse for the inauguration, with apologies to Dr Seuss). *Guardian* Jan. 4 (2001). http://www.guardian.co.uk/Archive/Article/0,4273, 4112192,00.html http://www.guardian.co.uk/bush/story/ 0,7369,417914,00.html

1.7. TV, RADIO, VIDEO

"The Worm of Learning Turns, Swallows Its Tail and Bites Itself in Half: Elias Canetti, *Auto da Fé.*" BBC Radio 3, "What Books I Please." 1 Dec. (1981) at 8.40 pm. *Listener* 106.2738, 3 Dec. (1981): 678-79. In *Essays in Honor of Elias Canetti.* Tr. Michael Hulse. New York: Farrar, Straus, & Giroux, 1987. Orig. *Hüter der verwandlung: Beiträge zum Werk von Elias Canetti.* Munich: C.Hanser, 1985. 81-87.

"The New Empire within Britain." Channel 4, "Opinions" 6 Dec. (1982) at 9 pm; *New Society* 62.1047 (9 Dec.1982): 34-37. Available at http://www.pinn.net/~calvino/wc/essays/rushdie.html.

"A Tall Story." Arena Series. UK: BBC, 1982. Videorecording. 45 min.

"The Painter and the Pest." Channel 4. 2 Jun. (1985) at 9.15 pm. As "Magnificent Obsession." *The Observer Magazine* (26 May 1985): 10-12.

"Fictions Are Lies that Tell the Truth: Salman Rushdie and Günter Grass in Conversation." Channel 4, "Voices." 26

Jun. (1985) at 11 pm. *Listener* 113, 27 Jun. (1985): 14-15. In *Voices: Writers and Politics*. From the Channel 4 Television Series. Eds. Bill Bourne, Udi Eichler, and David Herman. Nottingham: Spokesman, & Atlantic Highlands, NJ: Hobo Press, 1987.

"Edward W. Said with Salman Rushdie." Interview with Salman Rushdie. Writers Talk, No.28. London: ICA Video & Northbrook, IL: The Roland Collection, 1986. "On Palestinian Identity: a Conversation with Edward Said." With Salman Rushdie. *New Left Review* 160 (Nov.-Dec. 1986): 63-81. In Edward W. Said. *After the Last Sky: Palestinian Lives*. Photographs by Jean Mohr. New York: Pantheon & London: Faber, 1986. 166-84; Rushdie. *Imaginary Homelands*. 1991. 166-84.

"A Conversation with Salman Rushdie." Sedge Thomson. San Francisco: American Poetry Archive, 1987. Videorecording.

"Salman Rushdie." Interview with Charlotte Cornwell. Writers in Conversation, No.81. London: ICA Video, in conjunction with Trilion, 1987.

"The Riddle of Midnight: India, August 1987." Channel 4. 27 Mar. (1988) at 8.45 pm. A 90-minute tv-documentary; "After Midnight." *Vanity Fair* (Sep. 1987): 88, 90 & 94. In Jonathan S. Weil "The United States and the Indian Constitution." Research Report. New Delhi: Indian Council for Cultural Relations 20 Jan. (1988). As "Midnight's Real Children." *The Guardian* 25 Mar. (1988): 19.

"Desert Island Discs: Novelist Salman Rushdie." BBC Radio 4. 8 Sep. (1988) at 12.15 pm.

"Salman Rushdie." Interview with W.L. Webb. Guardian Conversations, Writers. ICA Video, 89. Dir. Fenella Greenfield. London: ICA Video, in conjunction with Trilion. Northbrook, IL: ICA Video, 1989.

"Books by My Bedside." ITV. 8 Feb. (1989) at 1.30 am.

"Bonfire of the Certainties." Interview with Bandung File. Recorded 27 Jan. (1989) by Bandung File. Channel 4, Bandung File 14 Feb. (1989) at 9 pm. *The Guardian* 15 Feb. (1989): 23. Abr. *The Illustrated Weekly of India* 12 Mar. (1989): 12-19. Abr. *The Rushdie File*. Eds. Lisa

Appignanesi & Sara Maitland. London: 4th Estate, 1989. Syracuse: Syracuse University Press, 1990. 27-31.

"Rushdie interview." BBC Radio 4, *Today*. 27 Apr. (1990) at 6.30 am.

"Is Nothing Sacred." BBC 2, *The Late Show*. 6 Feb. (1990) at 11.15 pm. The Herbert Read Memorial Lecture, 6 Feb. (1990) (read by Harold Pinter). Cambridge: Granta, 1990. *Granta* 31 (1990): 99-111. Abr. *The Guardian* 7 Feb. (1990): 4. *Brick* 39 (1990): 6-12. In *Imaginary Homelands*. 1991. 415-29.

"Stories of Childhood." An Interview with Melvyn Bragg. London Weekend Television, *The South Bank Show*. 30 Sep. (1990) at 10.35 pm. "Histoires d'enfance." Trans. Evelyne Pisier. *Esprit* 8/9 (Août-Sep. 1993): 5-23.

"Start the Week." Interview with Melvyn Bragg. BBC Radio 4. 10 Dec. (1990) at 9 am.

"An Interview with Toni Morrison." With Salman Rushdie. BBC 2, *The Late Show*. 3 Jun. (1992) at 15 pm. *Brick* 44 (1992): 33-39.

"Salman Rushdie: In the Shadow of the Fatwa." Ed. Keith Lucas, prod. Udi Eichler, dir. Gred Lanning. A Brook Production for Channel 4. Channel 4 Television, 1993. 37 min. Channel 4. 7 Feb. (1993) at 8 pm.

"Have I Got News for You." BBC 2. 10 Jun. (1994) at 10 pm.

"Kaleidoscope Feature." Interview with Hermione Lee. BBC Radio 4. 2 Sep. (1995) at 7.20 pm.

"Salman Rushdie and The Lost Portrait." Dir. Chris Granlund, ed. Michael Poole. Readings by Ben Kingsley. BBC/RM Arts co-production, 1995. 45 min. BBC 2. 11 Sep. (1995) at 11.15 pm.

1.8. LIFE AND WORKS

C., J. "Rushdie, (Ahmed) Salman." *The Encyclopedia of Science Fiction*. Ed. Peter Nicholls. London etc.: Granada, 1979. 510. Rev. ed., eds. John Chute & Peter Nicholls. London: Orbit, 1993. 1035.

"(Ahmed) Salman Rushdie." *Contemporary Authors: A Current Bio-Bibliographical Guide to Current Writers in Fiction, General Nonfiction, Poetry, Journalism, Drama, Motion*

Pictures, Television, and Other Fields, 108. Ed. Hal May. Detroit, MI: Gale Research Co., 1983. 364-69.

"Rushdie, (Ahmed) Salman." *Contemporary Literary Criticism*, 23. Detroit, MI: Gale Research Inc., 1982.

Sims, Lilian S. "Rushdie, (Ahmed) Salman." *Contemporary Authors: A Current Bio-Bibliographical Guide to Current Writers in Fiction, General Nonfiction, Poetry, Journalism, Drama, Motion Pictures, Television, and Other Fields*, 111. Ed. Hal May. Detroit, MI: Gale Research Co., 1984. 412-14.

"(Ahmed) Salman Rushdie." *Contemporary Literary Criticism*, 31. Detroit, MI: Gale Research Inc., 1982. 353-60.

"Rushdie, (Ahmed) Salman." *World Authors 1975-1980: A Volume in the Wilson Authors Series*. Ed. Vineta Colby. New York: W.H. Wilson Co., 1985. 643-45.

Marshall, Tom. "Salman Rushdie." *Postmodern Fiction: a Bio-bibliographical Guide*. Ed. Larry McCaffery. New York: Greenwood Press, 1986. 498-501.

Chew, Shirley. "Salman Rushdie." *Contemporary Novelists*. 4th ed. Ed. D.L. Kirkpatrick. New York: St. Martins Press, 1986. 727-29.

"Rushdie, (Ahmed) Salman." *Benét's Reader's Encyclopedia*. New York etc.: Harper & Row, 1987. 852-53.

"(Ahmed) Salman Rushdie: *The Satanic Verses*." *Contemporary Literary Criticism*, 55. Detroit, MI: Gale Research Inc., 1989. 214-63.

"Salman Rushdie: Author of *The Satanic Verses*." *Bestsellers: Books & Authors in the News*. Ed. Donna Olendorf. Detroit etc.: Gale Research Inc., 1989. 61-65.

"Rushdie, Salman." *Bloomsbury Guide to English Literature: The New Authority on English Literature*. Ed. Marion Wynne-Davies. London: Bloomsbury, 1989. 867 & 874.

"*The Satanic Verses* Controversy, Part II." *Contemporary Literary Criticism*, 59. Detroit, MI: Gale Research Inc., 1990. 404-56.

Weller, Paul. "Literature Update on the Salman Rushdie Affair." *Discernment* 4.2 (1990): 35-41.

Fletcher, M.D. "Salman Rushdie: An Annotated Bibliography of Articles about His Fiction." *Journal of Indian Writing in English* 19.1 (1991): 15-23; *Reading Rushdie: Perspectives on the Fiction of Salman Rushdie*. Ed. M.D. Fletcher. Cross/Cultures: Readings in the Post/Colonial Literatures in English, 16. Amsterdam & Atlanta, GA: Rodopi, 1994. 361-96.

Goonetilleke, D.C.R.A. "Rushdie, Salman." *Contemporary Novelists*. 5th ed. Ed. Lesley Hendersson. Chicago & London: St. James Press, 1991. 789-91.

Punter, David. "Rushdie, (Ahmed) Salman." *Reference Guide to English Literature*, 2. 2nd ed. Ed. D.L. Kirkpatrick. Chicago & London: St. James Press, 1991. 1167-68.

"Rushdie, (Ahmed) Salman." *Major Twentieth-Century Writers*. Ed. Bryan Ryan. Detroit, MI: Gale Research Co., 1991.

"Rushdie, (Ahmed) Salman." *Contemporary Authors: A Bio-Bibliographical Guide to Current Writers in Fiction, General Non-Fiction, Poetry, Journalism, Drama, Motion Pictures, Television & Other Fields*. New Revision Series, 33. Detroit, MI: Gale Research Inc., 1991. 380-84.

"Rushdie, Salman." *A Dictionary of 20th Century World Biography*. Ed. Asa Briggs. London etc.: BCA, 1992.

Fletcher, M.D. "An Annotated Bibliography of Articles about Salman Rushdie's Fiction." *Journal of Indian Writing in English* 20.1-2 (1992): 6-23. In *Reading Rushdie: Perspectives on the Fiction of Salman Rushdie*. Ed. M.D. Fletcher. Cross/Cultures: Readings in the Post/Colonial Literatures in English, 16. Amsterdam & Atlanta, GA: Rodopi, 1994. 361-68.

"Rushdie, (Ahmed) Salman." *The International Authors & Writers Who's Who*. 13th ed. Consultant ed. M.J. Shields. Cambridge, UK: International Biographical Centre, 1993. 751.

Fletcher, M.D. "Appendix." *Reading Rushdie: Perspectives on the Fiction of Salman Rushdie*. Ed. M.D. Fletcher. Cross/Cultures: Readings in the Post/Colonial Literatures in English, 16. Amsterdam & Atlanta, GA: Rodopi, 1994. 353-59.

Fletcher, M.D. "Salman Rushdie: An Annotated Bibliography of English Language Articles about His Fiction." With index. *Reading Rushdie: Perspectives on the Fiction of Salman Rushdie*. Ed. M.D. Fletcher. Cross/Cultures: Readings in the Post/Colonial Literatures in English, 16. Amsterdam & Atlanta, GA: Rodopi, 1994. 361-68.

"Rushdie, (Ahmed) Salman." *The New Encyclopaedia Britannica, Micropaedia*, vol. 10. 15th ed. Chicago etc.: Encyclopaedia Britannica Inc., 1994 (1974). 247.

Parameswaran, Uma. "Rushdie, Salman." *The Encyclopedia of Postcolonial Literatures in English*. Vol. 2. Ed. Eugene Benson & I.W. Conolly. London & New York: Routledge, 1994. 1390-92.

"Rushdie, Salman." *Larousse Dictionary of Literary Characters*. Ed. Rosemary Goring. Edinburgh: Larousse plc., 1994. 133, 251-52, 329, 611, & 663.

Hamilton, Ian. "Biography: The First Life of Salman Rushdie." *New Yorker* 71.42 (25 Dec. 1995): 90-113.

"Salman Rushdie." *DISCover Authors: Modules and Major Twentieth-Century Writers*. Detroit, MI: Gale Research Co., 1995.

"Rushdie, (Ahmed) Salman." *St.James Guide to Fantasy Writers*. Ed. David Pringle. New York: St.James Press, 1996.

Kuortti, Joel. The *Salman Rushdie Bibliography: A Bibliography of Salman Rushdie's Work and Rushdie Criticism*. Frankfurt aM etc.: Peter Lang, 1997.

Ho, Cynthia. "Salman Rushdie (19 June 1947-)." *Dictionary of Literary Biography*, 194: British Novelists since 1960, 2nd ser. Ed. Merritt Moseley. Detroit, Washington & London: Gale Research, 1998. 249-61.

1.9. Miscellaneous

"Two Stories by Salman Rushdie." With five woodcuts and three linocuts by Bhuphen Khakhar. [s.l., s.n.] Sebastian Carter, 1989, 46 pp. Limited edition, 60 copies bound in cloth, numbered 1-60, signed by Salman Rushdie; 12 copies bound in full leather, with an extra set of signed prints by Bhuphen Khakhar, numbered I-XII. Designed and printed privately by Sebastian Carter. Set in Monotype Joanna. The blocks printed from the wood/lino. Paper: Arches Vélin. Bound by Romilly S. Smith. Includes: 1. "The Free Radio," pp.11-24, with four pictures by Khakhar: on p.9 a title picture, on p.13 "So they all poured into the rickshaw," on p.17 "Truly you have the looks of the Lord Krishna himself," on p.20 "I sat under the banyan tree"; 2. "The Prophets Hair," pp.29-46, with four pictures by Khakhar: on p.26 a picture of a mosque, on p.27 a title picture, on p.33 "And you, sir, will be the thief I have been requesting?," on p.43 "The shrine of Hazratbal."

"Salman Rushdie: The Moor." Portrait by Bhuphen Khakhar (b.1934), no.6352, National Portrait Gallery, London, England. Oil on linen, signed in Gujarati, dated 25 Jul. 1995. Portrays the author Salman Rushdie with characters and episodes from his Novel *The Moor's Last Sigh* (1995) around the perimeter of the canvas.

"Salman Rushdie." Photographic Portrait. Sally Soames. *Writers: Photographs by Sally Soames.* Preface by Norman Mailer.London: André Deutsch; San Francisco: Chronicle Books, 1995. 84-85. Quotation from *The Satanic Verses* (1988): 84. Photograph repr. in "The Years of Living Dangerously." Interview with Tom Shone. *The Sunday Times* "The Culture," 2 Oct. (1994): 10-11.

"Salman Rushdie." Portrait by Tom Phillips. Oil on canvas, 50 x 60 cm, 1992.
http://www.tomphillips.co.uk/portrait/srus/

"Salman Rushdie as D.I.Y. Zola." Portrait by Tom Phillips. Lithograph, 15 x 11 cm, 1993.
http://www.tomphillips.co.uk/portrait/srus/

CONTRIBUTORS

Ball, John C. : Department of English, University of New Brunswick, P.O. Box 4400, Fredericton, NB E3B 5A3 Canada.

Bassi, Shaul : Dipartimento di studi linguistici, e letterari europei e postcoloniali, Università degli Studi di Venezia-Ca' Foscari, Zattere - Dorsoduro 1405, 30125 Venezia, Italy.

Kuortti, Joel : Department of English, FIN-33014 University of Tampere, Finland.

Mahoney, Blair : Department of English and Cultural Studies, University of Melbourne, Parkville, Vic 3052 Australia.

Mujeebuddin, Syed : Department of English, University of Hyderabad, Gachibowli, Hyderabad 506 046 AP India.

Petersson, Margareta : Comparative Literature Department of the Humanities, Växjö University, S-351 95 Växjö, Sweden.

Piciucco, Pier Paolo : Corso Salvemini 45, 10137 Torino, Italy.

Silva, Neluka : Department of English, University of Colombo, Sri Lanka.